Cycling North

by

Steven Herrick

Cover photograph by Steven Herrick
Also published as a paperback by CreateSpace 2015.
ISBN - 13: 978-1517547639
ISBN - 10: 1517547639

Eurovelo Series Book One: *'baguettes and bicycles'* published by Amazon and CreateSpace in 2012.
Eurovelo Series Book Two: *'bordeaux and bicycles'* published by Amazon and CreateSpace in 2013.
Eurovelo Series Book Three: *'bratwurst and bicycles'* published by Amazon and CreateSpace in 2014.
Eurovelo Series Book Four: *'cycling to Bohemia'* published by Amazon and CreateSpace in 2015

Table of contents:

About the Author

Steven Herrick is the author of twenty-two books for children and young adults. In Australia, his books have won the New South Wales Premier's Literary Award in 2000 and 2005 and the Western Australia Premier's Literary Award in 2013. His books have also been shortlisted for the prestigious Children's Book Council of Australia Book of the Year Awards on eight occasions. He is published in the USA by Simon and Schuster and Boyds Mill Press. He has also been published in the UK and The Netherlands.

Steven has written travel articles, features and restaurant reviews for newspapers and magazines and regularly travels the world performing his poetry and conducting author talks in schools. He lives in the Blue Mountains in Australia with his wife Cathie, a belly dance teacher. They have two adult sons, Jack and Joe.

This is his fifth travel book, following on from the successful *'baguettes and bicycles' 'bordeaux and bicycles' 'bratwurst and bicycles'* and *'cycling to Bohemia.'*

www.stevenherrick.com.au

dothebikething.blogspot.com.au

Introduction:

As a teenager, I would spread a map of Australia across the kitchen table. I'd run my fingers along the thin red line leading up the east coast from Melbourne in one long arc to Brisbane, where I lived, continuing all the way north to Cairns alongside the majestic Great Barrier Reef. With a ruler and scale I'd calculate the distance, a cool three thousand kilometres, following the rim of the continent beside the blue Pacific Ocean.

I decided when I bought a car, I'd drive to all of those towns to learn about my country. I was a sucker for the romance of Indigenous place names - Caboolture, Mallacoota and Ulladulla. I'd rather spend the summer beside the beach at Ulladulla, watching the whales swimming north than stuck in a suburban home in Brisbane wondering what to do with my working-class life. With little education, a future of factory or fruit-picking beckoned. I chose the outdoors. From the age of eighteen to twenty, I wandered aimlessly, getting work where I could and always returning home to my Mum with a car full of dirty clothes and exaggerated stories.

After rambling around my teenage years, I was lucky enough to be offered a place at University and settled down to a career as an author of books for children and young adults. But I never lost my wanderlust or the sense that a map spread across a table was a tableau of endless possibilities - so many roads, so many adventures.

In middle-age, I've swapped my car for a bicycle. I survey my travel options on a computer screen, checking for bicycle lanes and the likelihood of mountain ranges on my selected path.

This morning in my study with the sun rising over Sydney on the distant plains, I plot a route with Google.

But I don't start at Caboolture or Mallacoota in the heat and dust of Australia. I leap oceans and continents in the single click of a mouse and land on the edge of the Mediterranean Sea in the French port of Marseille. My wife, Cathie sits beside me. She smiles and waits.

East, West or North?

In 2014, we cycled east from St Malo in Brittany all the way to Prague in the Czech Republic. To cycle west from Marseille would only take us a few hundred kilometres to Spain and Portugal.

'North?' she suggests.

Our eyes stray to Google and the possibility of Norway.

'Do you think we could make it to the fjords?' I ask.

'I'll need lots of fuel,' she smiles.

Food. The joy of travel.

I continue our virtual journey north, following the back roads of France to the Swiss border at Geneva.

'My friend told me of a good restaurant in Geneva,' Cathie says. 'Cheap, even for Switzerland.'

From Geneva, I trace a route across the Champagne region of France into Belgium and on to The Netherlands, a flatland of cycling nirvana. Cathie suggests we follow the coast route and hope for tailwinds and on-time ferries. Last year, we loved cycling through Zeeland and Nord-Brabant with its multitude of bicycle paths and friendly locals. The Netherlands deserved further exploration. I mention an International school in Groningen is interested in hosting a visit in my other capacity as a children's author.

'You could mix work with pleasure,' Cathie says.

'Pleasure with pleasure,' I respond. Visiting schools hardly seems like work.

North from Groningen, Uncle Google offers a simple itinerary across Germany before entering Denmark where we choose the lesser-travelled path to Aalborg before a quick ferry across the channel to Kristiansand in Norway.

'When will we arrive in Norway?' Cathie asks.

'Early June,' I venture.

'It'll still be cold,' she says. We both remember being caught in a snow storm in Sweden a few years ago. And coming across a frozen lake, which for we residents of the hottest continent on earth was quite an experience. I spent an hour tossing large rocks onto the white sheet covering the water. Not once did the ice break.

'We'll pedal to keep warm,' I suggest.

I plot a route on the computer up the coast to Stavanger, the oil capital of Norway. I look at Cathie. She knows what I'm thinking. How much further?

'From the Mediterranean to the fjords,' she says.

I trace a line along the coast of Norway, the famed North Sea cycle route all the way to Bergen, capital of fjordland.

'How far is that?' Cathie asks.

'Four thousand kilometres,' I say.

'Spring in Marseille,' Cathie says.

'Can you overtake a season on a bicycle?' I ask.

Cathie smiles. 'Not if we ride slowly.'

'And eat regularly,' I add.

'Frequently,' she responds.

So, it's decided. North, from the azure coastline of France to the fjord wonderland of Norway. We've even bought new bicycles to attempt the trip. Craig and Jenny, the beloved but creaky bikes of our previous European adventures have been retired to the gentle confines of a barn in the Loire Valley where the owner takes them on easy jaunts to the nearby boulangerie.

In their place are two steel-framed touring bicycles we've dubbed Bruce and Aiwa. My steed is given the name of a dinky-di Aussie bloke, one you can rely on to help with odd-jobs around the house or when it comes time to renovate. A man named Bruce can hammer a nail and mow a lawn, all before lunch. I wonder if he can fix his own punctures?

Aiwa, Cathie's choice, is an Arabic word meaning 'yes.' As the bike model is a Specialized Awol, Cathie thought Aiwa was close enough.

Bruce and Aiwa. Each carrying a set of rear panniers, hopefully with enough warm clothes for two months on the bike.

I close the computer screen and look at the bikes resting in the corner of my study.

'What's the national dish of Norway?' Cathie asks.

Our trip is set. Beside every back road, we hope for a quiet restaurant or a green field for a picnic.

Fuel. Because cycling is just an interlude between meals.

Chapter One: France

Marseille is a teeming metropolis of fishermen and football fanatics, a young tough with a cigarette hanging from surly lips, a cluster of fishing boats in the harbour and dark alleys full of cats and cunning. The rough second-cousin to elegant Paris, it stares across the Mediterranean to Africa. As a port it has always welcomed immigrants. Greeks and Italians began arriving at the end of the 19th century, soon followed by Russians fleeing the Revolution, Spanish escaping the Civil War and Algerians after 1962. A third of all Marseille residents can claim Italian heritage in the distant past. More recent arrivals come across the sea from north Africa - Algeria, Tunisia and Morocco - and lodge themselves on the slopes leading up from the port and give the city its frenetic cosmopolitan atmosphere.

The town crackles with this immigrant energy. Is it any wonder that the dish of Marseille is Bouillabaisse - a stew mixing a raffish variety of fish plucked from the Mediterranean along with sea urchins, mussels and spider crabs - thrown together in a pot with saffron, garlic and other herbs and spices. In food as in life, the dish simmers in the open and is usually served to numerous guests. Bouillabaisse is for the whole street to enjoy.

We spend a morning wandering the alleys and streets down on the port. The weather is warm with a breeze blowing off the water past the stalls of fresh fish on sale at Quai des Belges, where a stout woman in overalls and gumboots offers red mullet and bream. Old ladies discuss the day's catch and count out the exact money when it's time to pay.

A few blocks east of the market is café DeBout, a rare French café that roasts its own coffee. The French can do everything well, except brew coffee. They use Robusta beans instead of the better quality Arabica. DeBout is down a narrow street of cream-coloured three-storey buildings. The lady behind the counter has a shock of blonde hair and looks like she's stepped off a movie set from the 1970s - flowing dress, large jewellery and an orange scarf. She makes us an acceptable coffee as we sit at the red metal chairs on the pavement and watch the city wake up. Motor scooters whine down the street and a boy of North African descent walks along carrying a football. I think of the summer of 1998 when Marseille's most celebrated citizen gave France reason to party. Zinedine Zidane, son of Algerian immigrants, scored twice in the World Cup Final in Paris. While not the captain, Zidane was unmistakably the leader, the energy that gave France its only Copa Mondial. Zidane was of Berber descent - a local from the tough northern part of Marseille - a place of high-rise housing complexes and dirt football fields.

In the afternoon, we take a train to La Ciotat, a beach side village where our bicycles, Bruce and Aiwa wait patiently for tomorrow's exertions. La Ciotat is bounded by a arc of white sand and palm trees stretching east to a promenade of cafés, restaurants and French holidaymakers strolling in the weak light. Trees dot the seaside expanse. Shade and colour are as important to any bather as a liberal dose of sunscreen, soft sand and a gelato. Beyond the palm trees is a line of low-rise apartments and hotels proudly sporting holiday names - Le Marina, Horizon Bleu, Rio Brasilia - perhaps some overstate their importance. La Ciotat is not Copacobana but on this warming Thursday, it's a pleasant seaside idyll. We debate the merits of a glass of beer at Le Marina or a sweet crepe from the stall on the sand. Or perhaps both?

I'm pleased to see more space is given to walkers and cyclists on the corniche than cars. Seafood restaurants and oyster bars outnumber the boats in the harbour. The port is home to wizened old men and people down on their luck. The cafés are full of locals, children laugh in a playground of plastic sailboats and climbing frames. Narrow alleys lead up from the water to faded beige buildings with washing hanging from lines strung outside. If I reach up, I can help myself to a clean white bed sheet. Two Algerian men call up to an apartment for a friend, their van idles nearby. Behind the church is an Italian-styled piazza of gelato shops and apartment blocks - an old lady looks down at the children playing below. We indulge in affogato and bite size cakes.

In the evening, we eat at Restaurant Le Golfe. I order magret de canard and sweet potatoes. The waitress brings me steak and frites. I point out the error and she laughs heartily, taking the errant dish and returning with a small bowl of frites to keep me amused while I wait for my duck. Cathie has an delicious goat's cheese salad. One day into our trip and we have already reverted to our default dishes, goat's cheese and duck. For twenty euro, La Golfe offers an excellent three-course meal. They even make their own punch, although we stick to pichet de rosé. Later, I walk down to the water's edge and stare across the blue expanse. Tomorrow, we head north away from the sea, inland across France. In two months, I hope to sit on a bench seat, not unlike this green painted one I sit on now and look across a fjord in Norway. From sea to fjord, by bicycle.

I wake, pull back the curtains and am greeted by clouds, a lone palm tree on the promenade and the morning whine of a motor scooter labouring up the hill. Which is what Cathie and I will be doing in a few minutes, after the obligatory croissant and coffee for breakfast. In the car park, Bruce and Aiwa have camped under an awning and are now loaded with twin panniers at the back. Our preference is for full stomachs and light panniers.

The sun wins its battle with the clouds as we head up the first hill of many leading away from the sea. Today is all mountains. Yellow and purple wildflowers bloom beside the D559. Thankfully most of the cars turn onto the motorway while we wind slowly uphill. Bruce and Aiwa are designed for touring and the 5% gradient doesn't trouble them as much as it does their riders.

But what goes up, comes down into the ancient village of Aubagne, now popular as a wealthy satellite suburb of Marseille. At café Noailles, an immaculately dressed woman in slacks and yellow blouse serves us coffee and biscuits outdoors, in the sun. I sigh, contentedly.

'What's up?' Cathie asks.

'Only three thousand, nine hundred and eighty kilometres to go,' I say.

Cathie smiles, 'All the more reason for another biscuit.'

On the outskirts of Aubagne, we stop on the footpath. Cathie consults the map on her phone.

'I go left,' she says.

Cathie and I will now separate for a few hours. My wise partner will cycle the direct route north to the next village of Auriol. I'll veer to the east and confront the sun-drenched realities of the Col de l'Espigoulier, a category one Tour de France climb that winds pleasantly through the forest north of Gemenos.

Call me stupid, but there's nothing I enjoy more than the quiet relaxation of a French mountain climb. Cycling up mountains has nothing to do with excess testosterone on my part but a simple desire to slowly pedal my way through the rolling landscape. The roads in the mountains are always quiet and atmospheric. I'm following in the tyre tracks of the Tour de France cyclists, albeit at a vastly reduced pace.

While I prefer to relax and take in the views, the Tour riders dance on the pedals and consider an attack just before the summit. The only attack I consider is one of the heart.

Cathie and I kiss and she tells me to have fun. I watch her pedal away and count my blessings I have a wife who allows me such indulgences. When her pink jersey is a dot in the pale green landscape, I hop on Bruce and cycle downhill (ha!) into Gemenos where I buy a trio of chocolate donuts. I stash them in my panniers for later, when I'm desperate.

The climb begins steadily, crossing a stream where I admire a beekeeper tending his hive. A few hundred metres above is a long wire mesh fence designed to stop boulders from rolling downhill and squashing the honey gatherer. The donkey trails begin across the harsh pale scree foothills. I'm reminded of the classic French movie, *Jean de Florette*. The story of a brave yet naive office worker who believes he can make a living as a farmer in this sun-blasted landscape. Every morning he leads his donkey to gather water from the well down the mountain in a vain attempt to survive here with his wife and daughter. It's Gerard Depardieu's finest role.

After a few kilometres, I pass two cyclists. One is rugged up in long trousers and a jacket, even though the temperature is rising much quicker than we are. The other forges ahead. Both of the men are my age, perhaps older. I cycle beside the leader and we discuss our favourite mountain climbs - he enjoys Mont Ventoux, mine is Croix de Fer in the French Alps. The road winds skywards and offers us views all the way to Marseille. Poppies bloom beside the road as we enter the switchbacks. A motorbike roars past us and my friend curses to have his peace interrupted.

The Tour de France has climbed this mountain three times and I'm reminded of a lovely story of the first man to the top in 1957. Jean Stablinski was a Frenchman of Polish descent. His father had been killed in the war, fighting for the Resistance. Fearing for his mother, young Jean advertised for a husband for the widow. A man with a daughter answered the advert. The mother married the man, and Jean later married the daughter. Jean said it was the best franc he'd ever spent for that advertisement.

My cycling buddy stops and tells me he'll wait for his partner, still puffing along two switchbacks below. I wave and push Bruce forward. I'm surprised how well Bruce is coping with this mountain. He has three cogs at the front and a long wheelbase, so although he's not fast, he offers a relaxed riding dynamic. Although up this incline, *dynamic* is perhaps not the word.

The truth is I'm thrilled beyond words to be climbing, to be in the sunshine with nothing to do but rotate the pedals, admire the view and think about lunch. Finally, among the stunted pine trees I reach the summit. I celebrate with one donut. I'll save the rest for Cathie. I look up at the pale blue sky, the brittle cliffs towering above and shrug on my jacket. A lone bird soars above the cliff. I imagine the descent will be colder than the ascent. I join the D2 and give up on pedalling for eleven kilometres as Bruce and I cruise into Auriol. Sitting on a bench seat in a park beside a stream is my beautiful wife. She has already chosen a restaurant for lunch. She asks me if I had a pleasant morning and smiles indulgently at my blathering.

We sit at a table under the plane trees and both order the lunch special - three courses for thirteen euros. The highlight is a main course of moules and frites, the mussels cooked in a wine, cream and parsley sauce. I can't resist dipping my bread. After all, I've climbed a mountain! Dessert is tiramisu and I tip my coffee on top to increase the flavour. Or to mask the flavour of the coffee? The waitress wears black biker boots and sports an impressive array of tattoos. She flirts with the table of workmen sitting near the entrance. I glance to the street where their old Renault van is parked. The best way to choose a restaurant in France - go where the work vans are parked. The nearest restaurant will offer the best meal for the lowest price.

The afternoon unwinds with a long slow ride through vineyards and open fields to our accommodation for the evening just outside of Rousset. The Aux Terres Rouges is a 19th century farmhouse of pale stone and creeping vines with a vineyard at the rear and a swimming pool in the garden. After Henriette, the owner shows us our room, we change into swimmers and run to the pool. Cathie falls asleep in the afternoon sun and I dive into the cold water. It's late April and too early for such indulgences but I can't resist. After our first day, we're pleased to be in such luxurious surrounds. We're even more pleased the tariff is less than the cost of an overnight stay in a dowdy country motel in Australia.

Henriette tells us to avoid the restaurants in town for two reasons. Firstly, they're located up a steep hill and secondly, the pizza truck parked opposite the horse-riding school just down the road offers better food. We're sceptical, but cycle Bruce and Aiwa to the truck in the cool of the evening. The owner is a Corsican man who knows how to cook pizza. His speciality is a giant wheel of light and crispy crust topped with merguez sausage, artichokes and olives. It's superb. We sit on the grass and eat it, washed down with Corsican beer. The locals who stop for take-away are all highly amused at our picnic habit. The pizza is so good I order another. And two more beers. We toast a perfect first day of cycling.

The best sleeping pill that can be prescribed is seventy-two kilometres of cycling. We went to bed at the farmer's hour and slept all night. Madame indulges us by waking early on a Saturday to serve copious amounts of brioche, bread and tasty marmalade. The weather is cloudy and cool as we wheel Bruce and Aiwa out of the barn. As is my habit, I check the tyres. My previous bicycle, the temperamental Craig had a nasty habit of deflating in the evening as if exhausted from his travails during the day. Bruce shows a much hardier attitude.

The morning is spent cycling in the shadow of the imposing Montagne Sainte-Victoire, an eighteen kilometre limestone ridge, craggy and dark in the early light. A haunt of artists, Victoire is featured in paintings by Paul Cezanne who could see it from his studio in Aix-en-Provence. Pablo Picasso bought a château in the foothills around here in 1959. He was proud to own property so close to Sainte-Victoire, although he never included the mountain in his paintings. His body is buried in the grounds next to his wife, a sculpture of *Woman with a vase* on the grave.

Along the D17 back road, the stone houses are rendered in shades of ochre and earth. Two winnebagos are parked on a vacant lot, the owners still asleep. Their respective dogs sniff each other's territory. They appear hesitant, unsure whether they can claim such temporary lodgings as their own. In Le Tholonet, a bust of Cezanne graces a fountain near the old Moulin. He used to dine in the local restaurant, which now bears his name. It's a quiet village of beige stone houses with white shutters. Opposite the Relais Cezanne is a park with white chairs and stately trees.

We cycle around Aix, overwhelmed by the morning traffic and narrow one-way streets. It's a relief to speed downhill to Meyrargues and a pleasant flat road for twenty-five kilometres beside a canal. Is there anything better than a bike lane and a tailwind? We arrive in Cadenet, situated on a hill overlooking the valley of Durance in time for lunch. The boulangerie offers a special of jambon fromage baguette, poire tart and a drink for the princely sum of five euro. We're served by a young man with a smiling demeanour and happy clientele. The baguette is so large, I consider saving my tart for later. But it's so tasty I end up scoffing the lot.

We climb a narrow road beside a rock wall to the village of Loumarin where a wedding is taking place. The car park is full of BMW and Mercedes, the footpaths awash with suits and party frocks. As we pass, I notice the guests are speaking in English.

This sunburnt corner of Provence is the tableau of legend. From the hard-scrabble existence of the downtrodden illiterate farmers of Pagnol's novels to the pastel-coloured indulgence of ex-pats sunning themselves beside a pool and a newly-renovated stone house in Peter Mayle's *A Year in Provence*.

While it's hard to believe that the austerity of Pagnol's characters would have attracted anyone to buy property in this region, Mayle's story of renovating a stone house amid the vineyards and orchards led to an explosion of English retiring here, all with pen poised or canvas stretched, eager to live the life of an artist. Perhaps the ancestors of Pagnol's books grew rich selling their farm sheds to wealthy foreigners who didn't need a ready water source to survive, having a secure pension pumped into their foreign bank accounts.

France is now littered with these ex-pats. Many run web-sites on *living in France*, a few write books and even more open up their spare bedrooms as bed and breakfast accommodation. A patch of England dwells in these French towns. Many are so charmed by their new homeland, they settle easily into the life of the community, becoming respected citizens who through their wealth and contacts bring an economic lifeline to previously-dying villages.

It's a curious trend. While English towns are populated by immigrants from Africa and Europe, a native English population have decamped to the quiet splendour of the French countryside. Both are economic refugees - one is fleeing poverty, war or government neglect while the other is escaping modernity, searching for a bucolic rural existence they remember from their 'green and pleasant land' childhood. Peter Mayle, who now lives in Loumarin, has a lot to answer for.

It's a quiet and pleasant climb over the Col du Pointu, so easy in fact that when I tell Cathie she has climbed a French mountain pass, she looks at me incredulously, as if I'm making a joke.

'But we ...' she begins.

'Hardly raised a sweat,' I say.

From Pointu, we follow the bike signs past lavender farms and closed stalls advertising honey for sale. If Julius Caesar named a town, I suggest it's worth visiting. So we cycle into Apt in the late afternoon and find our lodging near Place Carnot. We've rented a lovely front room in a two-storey building from a kindly old gentleman who wears pleated trousers, a waistcoat and a charming expression. He opens the window to reveal a view of the Church of Saint Anne, where construction began in the 11th century, but wasn't fully completed until the 12th century. Imagine that occurring today?

'Sure, we're starting work on the Town Hall - expected completion date? 2125.'

Although it could be argued that the majesty of Saint Anne will outlast anything we build today, such is our desire for speed and the transient and temporary. While the Church of Saint Anne will last another millennium, today's Town Hall may well be turned into a shopping mall within the decade.

After changing out of our lycra we wander the pedestrian alleys and end up at the Central Soul bar. We sit at a table on the footpath and wait to be served. And wait. I glance inside but can't see any activity. A few people are sitting at the other tables. I notice none of them have a drink. They are just sitting, one old man is rolling a cigarette. I get up and walk to the door. It's locked. The café is closed. At 5pm on a Saturday afternoon. We move precisely three metres next door to a bar that is most certainly open. The surly waitress takes our order and returns with two beers and a bill. She waits for me to pay, before I've even had a sip of my Kronenbourg. Merde!

Dinner is at the Restaurant Mona Lisa, a narrow space filled by two overworked but friendly waitresses and a crowd of locals. I begin with an excellent chèvre salad and finish with a magret de canard. I never tire of eating French duck. Or drinking French wine. We return to our lovely room where I fling open the window and gaze at the gold statue of Madonna on top of Saint Anne. She opens her arms, in blessing. In the square, a man gingerly hops on his old bicycle and clatters across the cobblestones. He is singing, gloriously out of tune.

On our third day, we have planned a very short cycle from Apt to Sault, a village dwarfed by the giant that is Mont Ventoux. We are keenly aware that the following day will test our climbing abilities to the limit. But that is tomorrow. This morning, we cycle from Apt with a full stomach under a heavy cloud. It threatens rain but offers only a meek wind and a mild shower.

Saint-Saturnin-les-Apt is a village of beige-coloured houses looking over a valley of vineyards. The château ruins command the high ground. The church is relegated to a hill in the village. I try to decipher the Latin numerals above the front entrance - MDCCCLXII - 1862? It's a superbly proportioned building with a curious statue of a stone horse and a little stone man, like a leprechaun, sitting opposite gazing up at the clock on the steeple. I do like a church that keeps accurate time. Ten o'clock on a Sunday morning.

The climb up the col is across a series of dry gullies turning into parched canyons as we gain altitude. It's a splendid road winding through brittle countryside, the verge blooming with poppies and irises. We haven't seen a car in the past hour. We cycle over pale stone arched bridges and look down at the fifty-metre drop to a creek bed of shale and boulders. This region was home to resistance fighters in the Second World War. The brave and resourceful farmers of the area hid among the winding canyons and remote caves, their presence an irritation to the invading Germans. The fighters were supported by locals who would offer them potatoes, vegetables and wine to help in the struggle. Over the next ridge, on a winter's morning in 1943 a band of resistance fighters was discovered by a platoon of German soldiers. A few escaped but some were taken prisoner, to end up in concentration camps further east. A plaque opposite a lonely farmhouse tells the story of one fighter who was caught in 1944 and subsequently died in Buchenvald, a thousand miles and heartbeats away from his homeland.

As we climb, I notice the cliffs are stained with pale blue streaks like an exotic French cheese. With a long view down the canyon, we sit on a rock and eat a café éclair and coco framboise tart. At midday, we reach the Château de Javon, a multi-turreted pile of stone approached through a field of yellow flowers. It sits lonely on top of the hill. The nearest neighbour is a handsome young goat herder who tends his flock as we cycle past. Cathie can't resist waving. He smiles and touches his cap in response. His goats bleat and scale the rocks. The land opens up to pig scrub and we detour via a back road to Monieux. Although up here everything is a back road. It's a cyclist's dream - wide smooth surfaces with few cars and long easy climbs.

We plunge downhill to the medieval fortress that is Monieux. Tucked into a cliff, it was the site of a pogrom against the Jews in the 11th century. Many were killed, a few survived and fled, making their way further south. Today it's a quiet village with an elegant restaurant offering views down the valley. We make do with a fougasse from the boulangerie and eat it looking up at the church, a rather drab building dating from the 12th century. It looks much less grand and impressive than its age suggests. At first glance, I thought it was made of besser blocks. Unusually, it was built outside the town walls. Perhaps the villagers thought it was rather plain and should be excommunicated? We count the number of gleaming C5 Citroens parked outside the restaurant while we eat. Nice place for a family lunch.

We finish the day riding along the valley floor trying to spot Mont Ventoux. It stays hidden behind the nearest ridge. Our lodging tonight is a wooden gypsy caravan with blue trim and iron wheels. It's parked in the garden of a bed and breakfast. The owner isn't home when we arrive but we let ourselves into the caravan. It has a double bed, a small table and chairs and a tiny balcony. It's impossibly cute with heart-shaped windows and a curved metal roof. And because the bathroom and toilet are located in the laundry area of the main house, it's ridiculously cheap for an overnight stay. Cathie notices we have a metal pan under the bed.

'It's a little cold ... and small,' I say.

'Après vous,' Cathie smiles.

I sit on the petit balcony and look up at the rocky hills and scudding clouds. If this weather doesn't improve, the view from Ventoux tomorrow may be limited. If we make it to the top at all. A man walks his boxer dog along the road beside the caravan. He has a looping scar on his chin which makes him look like an extra from a French noir film. The dog eyes me suspiciously. Why am I wearing shorts in this weather? And sitting in a caravan painted baby blue? Is that lycra hanging from the railing and do I wear it in public? They lumber up the hill and I go back to dreaming of Mont Ventoux.

The owner is a middle-aged woman who talks excitedly about the feng shui attributes of the Gypsy caravan. She bustles around looking for her mobile phone to book us a table at the restaurant in Sault. She's a little distracted and I end up asking her three times what the weather holds for tomorrow. She finds her phone and rings her boyfriend in Sault. She assures us he knows everything, including the forecast. Monsieur Encyclopedia phones back with the bad news of rain and - as it's Sunday - the choice of only one restaurant in Sault. Madame kindly offers to drive us in at the appointed hour. She tells us to speak to the waitress about a lift home. That'll be interesting.

Madame spends more time on the phone during our drive, getting another update on the weather forecast. It appears to be getting worse by the hour. As she drops us at La Provencal restaurant, she tells us she's staying at her boyfriend's house but will be back to prepare breakfast, rain or shine.

We're greeted with an empty restaurant and a lovely waitress. The menu offers a special cyclist's choice of lasagna, salad and dessert but we both opt for the more traditional entree of in-season asparagus, followed by duck leg with broad beans, potato gratin and a delicious olive sauce. The next course is four thimble-size varieties of cheese drizzled in olive oil. I keep reasoning that we're climbing a big mountain tomorrow so all this food is necessary. Which helps explain why we accept dessert of pistachio ice-cream and an espresso. Four courses, all prepared expertly for the basement price of seventeen euro.

When it's time to depart, I ask the waitress if she'd phone us a taxi. She shakes her head, ruefully, explaining the taxi is not working on Sunday evening. Cathie and I look at each other. A four kilometre walk home in the late evening? The waitress smiles in a charming gap-toothed way and says she'll phone her boyfriend. He'll take us home. I say, 'no, no,' but mean 'yes, please.' She waves me away and rings Mr Heroic.

He arrives within ten minutes and happily drives us home. He's particularly impressed when we tell him we'll attempt Ventoux tomorrow although he winces and says two words, 'the weather.' I offer him money as he drops us at the caravan but he refuses to take it. I insist and he finally accepts. He wishes us 'bonne chance pour la montagne' as he races away. Great food, lovely town, wonderful people. Please don't tell me the French are aloof and snobby. It is a lie.

Early in the morning, I draw back the curtains already aware that it's raining by the sound on the metal roof. I sigh. Madame returns from the omnipotent boyfriend and brings us bowls of coffee, bread, confiture and croissants. We eat in the lovely caravan, wondering what true gypsies would do on a day like today. Stay indoors, if they're wise. Rain this early bodes poorly for the conditions on Ventoux which is renowned for wind and sleet and, on occasions, snow. It's cold enough down here on the plain.

There is nothing to be done but shrug into our rain jackets and leggings. We trundle the four kilometres back into Sault and are soaked and cold by the time we reach the centre-ville. I don't fancy putting

Cathie through the rigours of Ventoux in this weather. At a café in town, I approach the waitress and ask if she knows of anyone going to Vaison. There are no takers in the bar so she phones the taxi company - working this morning - and we negotiate a suitable price for one bicycle and a very drenched woman.

I am a stupid man. I plan to at least attempt the climb from Sault. Cathie blows me a kiss from the café window.

I climbed Ventoux twice a few years ago. Once from Sault and once from the much more difficult Bedoin side. I don't need to do this but I can't think of an acceptable route around the mountain to our accommodation in Vaison-la-Romaine. It's cycle or a taxi. As I start the climb, the rain relents and dissolves into a fine mist cloaking the lavender fields. The land is hushed and still. A few kilometres into the climb, the first ROUTE FERME sign appears. Oh dear. If the road is closed on the summit, I won't be able to continue to Malaucene and will have to detour via Bedoin, which demands another climb over the Col de Madeleine. Am I capable of two mountains in these conditions? There is no barrier, just a simple sign so I keep cycling. I don't really have a choice. Long worms wriggle slowly across the bitumen and I do my best to avoid squashing them. I hardly have to worry about traffic on this lonely road. Sheep and chickens shelter under a tin roof barn.

Mont Ventoux is one of the three legendary climbs of the Tour de France, along with Alpe de Huez and Col du Tourmalet. It's forever etched in legend because of the tragic death of British cyclist Tom Simpson in the 1967 race. On a day of hellish temperature, Simpson fell from his bike with exhaustion a kilometre from the summit. Despite the protests of his team, he demanded to be helped back onto the bicycle. He staggered another few metres before collapsing again, never to recover. His death is marked by a Memorial near the spot where he fell. Every year, thousands of cyclists stop at the stone tablet to leave a tribute brought from the plain - a cap, an old jersey, an empty bidon. I have numerous chocolate bars. Too many to eat.

The ascent from Sault is an steady gradient of 4.5% through farmland and a forest of pine trees. The mist and I settle into an accord of muted silence. Despite my wet feet and soaked gloves, I'm enjoying this time alone on the mountain. It's a beautiful climb. The authorities have repaired the road since my last visit three years ago and Bruce seems to enjoy the extra workload. Two kilometres from Chalet Reynard, the road flattens and I power to the chalet where the Sault and Bedoin roads meet. Normally the car park is filled with cyclists and tourist buses. Today, it's not even open. I'm shocked. I really am alone up here. As I begin the final five kilometre climb through the treeless moonscape of rock and scree, I dodge another FERME sign. It's obvious the road over the summit is closed and if I make it to the top, I'll have to return here and take the Bedoin detour.

The rain returns accompanied by wind blowing harshly into my face. A single car trundles slowly from the summit. I wave him down. Did he drive up from Malaucene? He shakes his head. Bedoin. The road is closed for vehicles.

'Perhaps a velo?' he says sceptically.

But I know I can't risk it. If I get half-way down the Malaucene side and the road is blocked, it means a torturous climb back up. No thanks. I decide to labour ahead to the summit and return via Bedoin. The motorist wishes me 'bonne chance' and putters away. The rain is now accompanied by falling ice. It's not hail, just tiny specks of ice-drops pinging off my helmet. A stream of water flows down the road. Bruce manfully pushes on, his wide tyres holding firm. I pass the first snow drift, unusual for this time of year. I remind myself I'm still in Provence. The gods of Ventoux don't agree. They send more ice and water and wind. I've climbed the mountain before in perfect sunshine. There's a lovely view all the way to the French Alps from the summit. But not today. The gradient ramps up and I round the last bend and the final steep pitch before rolling into an utterly deserted summit. Even the Mont Ventoux sign is missing. The wind howls across the vacant car park. I rest Bruce against a wall and take a hurried picture. I shelter under the stairs of the radio communication tower and peer out into the gloom while eating a chocolate bar. A celebration, of sorts.

Before jumping back on Bruce, I cast a longing glance down the Malaucene side. The road appears to be open, but I know I can't risk it. I sigh and head towards Bedoin. The surface could be devilishly icy. I clamp on the brakes as best I can in the cold. At Simpson's Memorial, I leave a chocolate bar among the empty bottles. The Memorial includes two plaques from his daughters, one in 1997 on the 30th anniversary of his death and another in 2007. Never forgotten.

I'm shaking with cold and soaked to the skin and no matter how hard I apply the brakes on this steep descent, the speed and cold are a menacing combination. In the forest section above Bedoin, where the gradient is a fierce 9%, my arms shake uncontrollably. This is much harder than going uphill where my exertions kept me warm. Despite this, the forest is lovely with new shoots on the trees and yellow flowers carpeting the undergrowth. A deer scurries across the road a few metres ahead. She turns to look at me as if wondering why the hell I'm out here in these conditions. I can't blame her.

Suddenly I'm in Bedoin. And starving. I look at my watch. It's early afternoon. A market is packing up in the main street. I'm chilled to the core as I enter a galette restaurant and sit at a table near the counter. The waitress brings me a menu and three tables of diners stare at me. I can't stop shaking. A man at the opposite table smiles and starts patting himself robustly as if to tell me that's the best way to warm up. I do as he suggests and it helps a bit. I'm embarrassed to realise everyone is concerned for my well-being. The chef comes out from his kitchen and offers me a dry t-shirt. I go to the bathroom and change into this precious gift. Like a magic coat, it works immediately. I return to the restaurant. Everyone looks up, expectantly. I smile and do a pirouette to show I am no longer the crazed cold madman of a few minutes ago. The chef calls 'bravo' and despite being the last person to enter the restaurant, my meal arrives first. I am very grateful. Every tasty bite returns me to the world of the sane. The world where stupid men don't cycle to the top of mountains in freezing conditions. I love Mont Ventoux. Today I learned to respect it.

After returning the t-shirt to its generous owner and finishing a second cup of coffee, I return to Bruce refreshed and ready for the next mountain. I'd like to recommend the restaurant to anyone visiting Bedoin but in my addled state I did not notice the name. It's opposite a few bike shops and offers an excellent ham, cheese and egg galette. And free clothing!

The rain has stopped. I can even see patches of blue sky. Col de Madeliene is a lovely gentle climb. A goat herder walks his flock among the stunted pines. I look over the edge to vineyards and stone houses in the valley. Smoke wafts from a single chimney.

It's twenty-four kilometres, mostly downhill to Vaison-la-Romaine. I find the guesthouse easily and am welcomed by my concerned wife and the owner Brigitte, a kindly woman who offers me a change of clothes, a dressing gown and a warm room. I stand under the hot shower for a long time. Cathie tells me the taxi driver knew a detour on relatively flat roads and she arrived here at the ridiculously early hour of eleven in the morning. Brigitte offered her lunch and a glass of wine.

'She kept shaking her head and wondering why you'd climb Ventoux in these conditions,' Cathie says.

'Because I am an idiot,' I say.

Brigitte knocks on the door and brings me biscuits, orange cake and a thermos of coffee. Both women smile indulgently at the fool stuffing his face. When we tell Brigitte we intend to cycle to Norway, she laughs heartily and says, in fractured English, 'After Ventoux, easy!' We hope so.

Vaison is a medieval town of narrow alleyways, stone arches and the fast-flowing river Ouveze. It's a curious place where the Roman ruins are clustered around the hillside yet most of the activity centres on the main town across the river. We wander the streets on both sides, take an obligatory tourist photo on the historic bridge before retreating to the Restaurant Le Comtoir des Voconces. Beer for me, Picon for Cathie and a shared sucre citron crepe. We sit at a table near the entrance watching the light fade and the town grow quiet. We've been here so long, reliving every moment of my frenzied day, when a waitress approaches with the dinner menu. It's dark outside and time for dinner. Why not? Two courses starting with zucchini soup and moving onto roast veal and potatoes. Simple hardy fare for eleven euro.

Do I need to tell you I slept well?

Brigitte serves us a breakfast so large I imagine she fears we won't have another meal until Norway. This is the first time we've booked a place through AirBnB. I sure hope it's indicative of the standard. The weather is cool and cloudy with a stiff breeze. Brigitte shakes her head and utters a single word, 'Mistral.' It's no surprise to learn the name comes from the Occitan dialect meaning 'masterly.' The mistral blows from the north-west and is one of the main reasons farmhouses face the South, turning their back on its cold and bullying presence. Today we feel its fury. What's worse - an icy mountain or buffeting wind?

We cycle past vineyards and olive groves all the way to Nyons where we cross the Roman pont and seek shelter in the sunny main street. I enter a boulangerie where an old man is buying a baguette. As he turns from the counter, he mockingly advises me to shop elsewhere, casting a mischievous grin towards the young female owner. She smiles indulgently while I order a nut slice and café éclair. I take them across the street where Cathie is sitting in the sun at a café. I like a town with a medieval church. The steeple is open to the elements, just a frame of metal holding the bells. I wonder if it's to let the mistral blow through?

We leave Nyons and turn north-west to get thumped by the wind, struggling through numerous villages with romantic three-tiered names - Rousset-les-Vignes, Montbrison-sur-Lez and Roche-Saint-Secret. All are boarded up against the might of the mistral. A lonely white Renault van trundles past us. The lavender fields are still a few months away from blooming. From the 19th century, the flowering herb has covered the fields of Provence and Drome. As demand increased, the village of Grasse on the Cote d'Azur became the perfume capital of the world. Lavender is still widely cultivated in the region, but with cheap labour and intensive farming in China and Eastern Europe, the French trade now focuses on 'lifestyle lavender' - the countless markets and shops selling lavender soap, pot-pourri, body oil and scented candles. Is there no end to our desire to decorate our homes and bodies with this purple flower?

Near Montjoux we descend into a narrow valley where a stream is surrounded by barren farms and forests. No matter which way the road turns, we seem to have a headwind. We've been cycling for over three hours and have ridden only forty kilometres. Snail's pace. At Bartols, we labour up a hill and seek shelter in Le Relais Du Serre, a restaurant with a sign at the entrance announcing their love of cyclists. How can we resist. The waitress quickly establishes their credentials by bringing a litre of cold red wine. There is no menu, just the three-course workers' lunch. We forget the mistral in a second and pour a glass of chilled wine. Spinach omelette, duck and peas cooked with a salty ham, and a sweet baked apple for dessert. The walls are lime green, brass pots hang from rails and the waitress asks if we'd like a coffee. I hold up my glass of wine in reply. When we reluctantly leave, the two owners are sitting down to a well-earned lunch. It is the same menu we have enjoyed, of course.

Noticeably heavier than an hour ago, Bruce and Aiwa struggle up Col de Ventebrun, a lovely winding path of dense forest where someone has strung up an adventure land playground of ropes and walkways between the trees. I'm tempted to try my luck but the afternoon is closing in with heavy cloud. A castle of two imposing towers looks down from on high as we battle the switchbacks. On the summit, I'm sorely tempted to take the back road to Le Poet Celard. Firstly, because of the romance of such a name, but it also offers a potential shortcut. Who cares about romance when we can slice ten kilometres from the Mistral! We stand at the crossroads for a long time.

'Would you trust a poet?' Cathie asks.

'Ha!'

We stick to the main route. It's a rollicking descent to Bordeaux which proudly boasts a medieval ruin on a ridge. Across a stream and along a valley floor, we come upon the connecting road to Le Poet Celard. I look back up the mountain path. Undulating is perhaps an understatement. Cathie smiles, knowingly.

The D538 is a magnificent route alongside jagged mountains and bare cliffs all the way to Saou, before we climb one more mountain pass and steam into Crest, home of the highest medieval tower in France. The tower was once part of a castle that guarded the mountain pass. The river Drome surges through town. We cross the bridge and celebrate our arrival with cake and coffee from one of the many chocolatier shops in the cobblestoned main street. We buy a variety of chocolates as a present for the people we're staying with tonight.

Marie-Aude and Regis are a vibrant couple in their early thirties who are avid bushwalkers and cyclists. Consequently, they occasionally offer weary travellers a free meal and accommodation through the cycling web-site Warm Showers - a wonderful resource that encourages reciprocity. While Cathie and I will benefit from a meal and room tonight, in the future we'll open our home in Australia to fellow cyclists. A world of generosity and assistance, not built on the power of the dollar but on mutual support and shared values. I could live in that world.

Marie-Aude welcomes us to their fourth floor apartment and excitedly shows the views from each side of the flat.

'To the west, the Massif,' she says, before walking down the hallway and opening the curtains on the east side, 'And here, the Vercors.'

'Endless paths for us to walk,' adds Regis.

We spend a lovely evening eating cous cous and local cheese, drinking four varieties of beer from the region and each talking of our travels. They are generous, optimistic and dedicated to the ideal of creating a better world through living within their means and eating only sustainable local foods where possible.

Whenever the news of the day - the tabloid horror of murder, wars and terrorism - weighs heavily on my soul, I think of people such as these. If there's hope for the world, it's with young people. The sooner those in power listen to the views of the next generation, the better.

Marie-Aude tells us of an organisation she works for who seek donations from wealthy citizens. With this money, the collective buys small farms and through an extensive selection process sign these farms over to people in need of housing and employment. The only requirement is that the land be farmed organically. Support is given to the new farmers through education in organic techniques and advice on how to run a small business. So far, the success rate has been remarkably high.

How do we save the world? One person at a time.

For breakfast, I eat as much lavender honey as is humanly possible. Sweet, fragrant and produced just a few kilometres away. Marie-Aude smiles indulgently. Not content with providing us with food and shelter and stimulating conversation, Regis is going to lead us out of town on his bicycle before he starts work at the local high school as a Maths teacher. Kisses and handshakes all round before we hit the road and cycle in sunshine between fields of wheat, garlic and rape.

Today we are shadowing the Vercors - a series of limestone mountains and plateaus covering over 300,000 acres. The brittle rocks are peppered with caves and proved to be a perfect hiding area for the French Resistance during the Second World War. So successful was this resistance that a Free Republic of Vercors was established for a brief period during the final years of the war. Its flag was marked with a prominent V for Vercors and Victory. And so it would prove, although the numerous memorials in the park speak of the harsh price paid in loss of life among the fighters.

At Montelier, we turn towards the mountains and slowly climb a potted farm road. The Vercors look like a line of camels heading east, round-humped and ponderous. With their shadow looming ever larger, we take the D125 all the way to lunch at Hostun, a village of flowering trees and a wide main street. We have the choice of two restaurants. A pizza bar or a workers' café. Easy. How much duck can one cyclist eat? When it's tasty and accompanied by an entree of terrine and followed by café glacé, quite a lot! La Tacot café is crowded with men in fluorescent vests and work boots. They look at my lycra with amusement and wish me bon appetit. The waitress is a classic example of a young French woman - tousled hair, pout and tight jeans. The matronly woman at the bar barks orders for her to clean the table the moment the workers leave. We all envy the young.

We follow the Isere river alongside a grove of walnut trees with the Vercors stretching along the right bank. In the distance are the snow-capped French Alps. It's a pleasant afternoon, the pea-green water rolling slowly into La Sone, a haven of stone buildings and a faded tabac opposite the green-painted suspension bridge. Did they paint the bridge to reflect the colour of the river? Along this picturesque road, I don't want the day to end. Just let me glide beside the river, the mountains framing the background, the birds serenading the afternoon.

The town of Saint Marcellin arrives too soon. For years, Cathie and I have chosen the round soft cow's milk cheese bearing the name of this town whenever we've entered a supermarket. Usually sold in small sizes, it's a perfect partner for a crusty baguette at lunch. We're very excited to be entering the town of its origin. Alas, Saint Marcellin the town does not live up to the reputation of its primary product. Too many cars clogging the main square, too little thought given to the amenity of its citizens. Yes, you might be able to park across the road from your favourite bar, but that very choice means when you sit at an outdoor table in the afternoon sun, you breathe fumes and listen to honking horns. We retreat to our accommodation for the evening.

The auberge is down a narrow lane and the front door is opened by Madame, a woman in her mid-forties rather distracted by the photographer who is snapping pictures for a real estate window. Madame is selling up. We're shown to our large room on the first floor, with a bathroom down the hallway. Soon after arriving, I step into the hallway wearing a towel only to be accidentally snapped by the photographer. Will the house ever sell with pictures of a semi-naked Australian?

We spend the evening looking for a restaurant. There are five - count them - five pizza joints and two grill restaurants that look to have seen better days. A town without French restaurants is a town with no soul. Signs throughout the village tell of a long and distinguished history - 'here was a town hall, here a convent.'

There is a tacky café with a foul-mouthed waiter and across the road is a fire hydrant, its shell cracked and fallen onto the footpath, the insides exposed. I wonder if it still works? I wonder if there's anything worth saving in such a town? Near the train station are two more restaurants. Both pizza bars.

Sigh. How can a town so boring produce such a delicious and inspiring cheese?

Eventually we choose one of the grill restaurants. It's empty and the owner seems genuinely pleased to have customers. He quickly ushers us into a booth near the window. We have a view of a nondescript alley. He's a lovely man who offers the menu with a flourish and seems to approve of our choice - 350g steak for me, Saint Marcellin cheese in filo pastry with salad for Cathie. He asks how I'd like to the steak cooked and I reply, 'a point' - medium-rare, with an emphasis on rare. The owners smiles and says in English, 'medium.'

Fair enough.

He then asks me what size beer I'd like. I respond, 'a point' and he laughs heartily.

The food is cheap and hearty and I wish there were more customers for our generous host, but on a Wednesday night in late April the town has fallen asleep. And soon enough, in our large bedroom with the ornate red lounge chairs and the wide windows, Cathie and I do the same.

At breakfast, Madame remains distracted, talking about a possible sale and lecturing us on whether we should have milk in our coffee. Apparently it's bad for digestion. As she only offers us a few slices of stale bread, I doubt we'll have to worry too much. It's a lovely house of high ceilings and stately furniture. Someone should buy it.

The letter V figures prominently on today's route. Continuing alongside the Vercors range, we cycle through Vinay, the walnut capital of the world and the small village of Vourey all the way to Voiron where Bruce inexplicably loses his panniers in a car park. Someone didn't mount them properly this morning and thirty kilometres of shaking leads to an embarrassing moment in the centre of town. We park the bicycles against a wall and retire to a chocolate shop for cake and coffee. I study the map to find the home of our favourite liqueur, here in this small French town.

Chartreuse, the only liqueur which lends its name to a colour, has been distilled by Carthusian monks since 1737 from a recipe given to them one hundred years earlier. I'm not quite sure why it took them a century to create this masterpiece, but I'm very glad they did. A mixture of one hundred and thirty herbs in alcohol, it is the nectar of Gods and cyclists. After coffee, we hurry around the corner to the factory. It's in a rather drab building housing a shop and museum of ancient Chartreuse bottles and historical photos.

The exact recipe of both the original green chartreuse and the more recent yellow version are known only by two monks who are responsible for the correct blending of the herbs. I doubt these two overworked gentlemen get a lot of time to pray. I assume the recipe is locked in a safe deposit box of a Swiss bank or else we're only two heart attacks away from an end to production.

The liqueur and the religious order responsible for its production has endured a long history of persecution and exile. Created as an 'elixir of life' and a medicine, chartreuse became extremely popular in the late 18th century before the Cathusian monks were driven from France. They were allowed to return a few decades later and promptly created the milder yellow version. They were expelled again at the turn of the century and sought refuge in Spain. It was not until after World War Two that the French government reinstated citizenship to the monks and production began once again.

The selection, crushing and mixing of the herbs is still done in the monastery in the hills outside of Voiron before the mixture is returned here to the factory to be blended with wine alcohol and distilled. It's then aged in huge oak barrels in the world's longest cellar, right under my feet. We tread carefully around the museum and can't resist buying a small bottle of the milder yellow chartreuse. I pack the elixir of life in my panniers, wreathed in clothes to protect such valuable cargo.

Of all the liqueurs, chartreuse is my favourite. It has a haunting scent and a satisfyingly long after-taste. It's like drinking an exotic perfume. The distillery notes describe it as 'an iron fist in a velvet glove.' I prefer the quote from Brideshead Revisited where one character, after drinking green chartreuse, claims it's like 'swallowing a spectrum.' Such is the power of its alluring colour and taste. I'm not religious, but I hope the Cathusians have a long and prosperous existence.

After scaling the road out of Voiron, we head into a narrow valley flanked by snow capped mountains and - dare I say it - chartreuse coloured fields. The only restaurant in Saint-Joseph-de-Riviere features black tiled floors, photos of bears on the white walls and the obligatory beautiful waitress who serves us a tasty three-course menu for a pittance, which to my great delight has chartreuse ice-cream for dessert. It's intoxicating. Cathie and I savour every bite.

'We could buy vanilla ice-cream and tip our yellow chartreuse over it for dessert tonight,' I suggest.

'Or just eat the ice-cream and drink the alcohol. One mouthful, one sip.' Cathie replies.

'Or just order another bowl right now!' I say.

We restrain ourselves from such indulgence and it proves a wise move as the afternoon brings a mountain climb over the Col du Couz which includes a rather scary tunnel. Cars, trucks and bicycles in confined spaces don't mix well. After five hundred metres on a bicycle in a tunnel, I need a stiff drink!

And so to Chambery, the capital of the Savoie region, an alluring town of narrow laneways and pastel coloured buildings. In one cobblestone lane, four children stare up at the first floor window where a cat sits on the ledge. One boy holds up his hands as if willing the feline to leap. The cat wisely remains aloof. The children return to their game of football.

We check into our hotel in the centre of town and wander the streets. Curiously, there are numerous shops selling lingerie. Glossy photos of semi-naked women decorate the many windows. We retreat to a bar on the town square and sit in the afternoon sunshine, admiring the pink and white Hotel de Ville surrounded by ornate and historic buildings on three sides and the horror show of a modern five storey apartment block to the north. Who on earth thought that was an appropriate construction for this historic centre? We face our chairs away from the monstrosity and order another Kronenbourg.

After fifty-six years on this planet I decide to try fondue, a regional speciality. The Brasserie du Theatre is a casual restaurant of black tables and chairs, yellow walls adorned with modernist prints and a menu offering the melted cheese dish and a plate of local charcuterie for eighteen euro. The waitress brings a saucepan which she places on a stand over a spirit lamp. Simmering gently inside the pot is a concoction of three cheeses - comte, emmental and beaufort. We are each given a long-stemmed fork and a large basket of bread chunks. Cathie and I take a deep breath and dig, or should I say, *dip* in.

Bread and melted cheese. What's not to like?

We spend an inordinate amount of time dragging the bread along the bottom of the pan to remove the crusty layer. We eat melted cheese for nearly an hour. I sit back and wonder at how one man can get melted cheese over the table, a salad bowl, a serving pot and his jacket. I have never been an elegant diner, but this is embarrassing. I use the cloth napkin to remove the cheese tendrils. The waitress pretends not to notice. Cathie orders another pichet de rosé and we enter a time warp back to the 1970s where moustaches, smoking jackets and fondue parties were all the rage.

Back at the hotel, the bed creaks under the increased weight. I hope they don't offer me cheese for breakfast.

I'm no fan of chain hotels, but I do admire their breakfast array. Businessmen and women demand choice and the hotel meets this with lashings of pastries, juices, cold cuts, eggs - everything is in the plural. We oblige by stealing multiple chocolate croissants for morning tea. Outside, it's raining and the temperature is struggling to reach double figures. Today is the first of May. The traditional May Day holiday. We'll celebrate by labouring in the elements.

As we cycle through town, old ladies are out in force selling lilies of the valley, a traditional offering of friendship on this day. We follow a path beside a wildly rushing stream, dodging the snails and overhanging branches. Within five kilometres, we are soaked through.

'The trees smell savoury, in the damp,' says Cathie.

I suppress a laugh.

'We've just eaten breakfast,' I say.

'What's your point?'

'Nothing,' I say, 'We'll stop at the next boulangerie.'

Aix-les-Bains is a French resort town steeped in the Belle Epoque era. A faded jewel of yachts, castles and elegant hotels. Located on Lac de Bouget, the largest glacial lake in France, the town owes its existence to the desires of rich people to pamper themselves. Is there anything more decadent than sitting in a mineral bath for an hour?

We cycle along the lake. Windsurfers ride the white horses, ducks ignore the rain and the orange two-metre bullrushes are starkly beautiful along the bank.

We spot a boulangerie and park Bruce and Aiwa under a flapping umbrella. Everyone is indoors out of the rain. We slosh to the counter and order an excellent almond croissant and a moist cannelle. A large table of middle-aged women exclaim at our drenched state. The French are quite effusive in their praise of outdoor activity, particularly if it's someone else doing it while they scoff pastries. Wise people. I go to the bathroom and dry my bandanna under the hot air blower. I'm tempted to strip naked and dry all my clothes but it would take forever.

Once free of traffic jams caused by too many BMW and Mercedes trying to get a park close to their destination, we cycle on the D49 alongside meadows of lush grass fed by gushing streams. Pint-sized donkeys watch us steam past. Even though we're soaked beyond flood, away from the swish of car tyres it's immediately relaxing and I contemplate the cute barns stacked with firewood and the swallows swooping from the rafters. From this high road, I spy the busy highway and wonder what every French family is doing to celebrate the holiday. A family lunch, the encore of their usual Sunday ritual? Or do they swish onward to Annecy for a stroll along the lake shore, umbrellas aloft, holding hands and contemplating a chocolate chaud?

We enter a tapas bar at Alby-sur-Cheran. Well, at least that's what the sign outside proclaims. I see no hint of the Spanish. A rather harried owner tells us the only meal on offer is steak and frites. Perfect. A boisterous crowd of locals stand at the bar. We choose a cosy booth and I remove my shoes under the table, hoping no-one will notice. The beer is cold and the steak extremely rare. I can't help but smile. No Australian chef in a country pub would dare serve his customer a piece of meat cooked so lightly. Our food culture is based on the barbecue. Consequently, we overcook everything, from seafood to steak. Nowhere in rural Australia could I hope for a meal like this. A rare steak, a garnish of mustard and perfectly prepared frites. We scoff the lot.

After a short downhill, we arrive at Annecy where the receptionist at the hotel is aghast when she sees our dripping bicycles. She fusses around in the back room and tells us to park them on the stretch of cardboard she has arranged near the wall. Bruce and Aiwa don't mind her manner. They're just pleased to be out of the deluge. Our room on the first floor has a large heater turned up high as we clean the mud from our lycra. The romance of long-distance cycling.

Dressed in street clothes, armed with two hotel umbrellas and a map we set off to explore Annecy. Every town in Europe with a stream flowing through its centre is dubbed 'Little Venice.' Annecy is no exception. We stroll across numerous arched bridges, alongside promenades of flowers and cafés and past gelato-coloured buildings erected on canals. It's a lovely old town dating from Roman times built where the river Thiou flows into the lake past rows of stately plane trees.

Despite the weather, the French tourists resolutely flock to the ice-cream stalls. A family of four stand under an awning out of the rain focused only on their treats. The husband has a double scoop, the wife and children each a single. The boy says something and everyone laughs. Ice-cream makes everything better. And so does French beer.

La Pichet restaurant has a friendly waitress who encourages us to stay for dinner, so we do. Cathie orders the three-course special featuring a whole trout as main course and a sorbet flavoured with genepi for dessert.

'Almost as good as your chartreuse ice-cream yesterday,' she says.

We have a half bottle of the 'elixir of life' back in our hotel room. We refuse the offer of coffee and skip lightly through the town puddles. We have a date with a enchantingly coloured liqueur.

The next day brings the hint of sunshine peeking over the mountains. We cycle along the lake even though it's in the opposite direction to our destination. In the early morning, joggers dance around the puddles and skip between commuters on bicycles. It's a lovely view down the lake with glistening water and green mountains. A swan swims close to me as I pose for the obligatory photo. Is she expecting an exotic French treat or posing because she has a long neck and brown eyes?

We regretfully turn away from the lake and cycle through the suburbs on a rather convoluted route designed to avoid the motorways. Each night, I map out a choice of routes between towns, but on the flat screen of a computer, I have little understanding of the contours of the land or the likely traffic conditions. Uncle Google gives us some elevation advice, but so far it's proven to have dramatically understated the amount of climbing each day. Today is no exception. It's up and down along atmospheric back roads with mountains on our right and steep meadows to our left. It's pleasant to feel the sun on our backs. We pass numerous farms with signs offering cheese for sale although most appear to be closed. We detour up to Evires hoping for a boulangerie but find only an impressive church with a dome-shaped steeple and another closed cheese shop. Fromage blank, indeed!

At lunchtime, we consult the map again and try to locate a town on our route. They all look too small to have restaurants. On my app, I can see an impressively large settlement off to the right. Cathie nods in agreement. As if my magic, after we cross the Col de Evires, the road loops ferociously downhill and like a crazy man on a luge, I barrel into La -Roche-sur-Foron.

Is it a cliché to say a medieval town has seen better days? La Roche hides its charms behind a staggering number of seedy bars and glum restaurants. We pick our way through the traffic jams and lean Bruce and Aiwa against a street sign while I go off in search of a welcoming place to eat. It takes much longer than usual in a French town of this size. Everyone seems to be drinking, not eating. Eventually, I stumble upon La Cabanon, a corner restaurant featuring the Haute Savoie speciality of tartiflette. The waiter with a hipster beard and a silver earring brings us a cast-iron skillet sizzling with melted reblochon cheese, diced potatoes, onion and bacon. A meal designed for farmers coming in after a long day in the winter paddocks. I can't decide whether it's a rich man's fondue, or a poor man's stew? We have ordered too much. Yet again.

I can barely throw my leg over Bruce before we struggle back to the D2 and a downhill ride into Annemasse past flooded fields. The river in town is a muddy torrent surging towards Lake Geneva.

We have chosen this border town as our overnight stop so we can visit Geneva tomorrow on our rest day. It offers much cheaper accommodation than across the Swiss border. We walk past the entrance to our apartment three times before realising our accommodation is above a shopping mall. A sleek structure of glass and metal, with wood detail painted to emphasize the horizontal lines, it's among a hash of modern French apartment blocks, housing the commuter belt workers for Geneva.

Unfortunately, the *modern* doesn't particularly like us checking in early, but eventually I convince the young lady that as we're staying here two days perhaps she could make an exception. I don't bother asking if there is a garage for Bruce and Aiwa. They join us in the lift to the sixth floor and rest their weary gears against a wall in the roomy apartment.

'Look, I can see into the apartment across the alley!'

Annemasse profits from its location, with shops such as those underneath our apartment reliant on Swiss customers, loaded with francs, making weekly excursions to fill the larder or the wardrobe. Of course, the trade works the other way as well. Annemasse provides Switzerland with a stable, cheap workforce. Capitalism respects no boundaries. It knows the price of everything and the value of nothing.

My beautiful wife has a nose for a good restaurant. We wander among the sushi bars and kebab shops of Annemasse wondering where France has gone. Cathie leads me down a side street to what at first appears to be an Algerian tea-room. We stroll inside to the blindingly white furnishings and a long counter stacked with honey-dipped pastries and Middle-Eastern morsels. The smell of brewed tea comes from the kitchen.

The small menu lists lots of dessert and drink options, yet down the bottom also offers cous cous. We order two bowls, one with chicken, the other with spicy meatballs. A cake shop with dinner as an afterthought?

The owner is a French woman of Algerian descent who is run off her feet serving regular customers and numerous people coming in for take-aways. Finally, her daughter arrives to assist. We're in no hurry, content to languidly debate which cakes we'll choose for dessert. Our meals arrive on a long tray and include an extra bowl of spicy sauce to spoon over the cous cous and vegetables. The chicken is so tender, it falls off the bone and the spicy meat balls are ... spicy! Both dishes are huge, easily large enough to feed a family of four. So that's why there are so many people coming in for take-away.

We eat what we can muster. Oh, who am I kidding. We scoff the lot, except a small amount of cous cous in a rather pathetic attempt to show we're not gluttons. We promise the woman we'll return to eat here again tomorrow. Geneva may be a global financial and tourist centre, but we're certain it doesn't have a restaurant to rival La Cerise sur la Chameau - the cherry on the camel.

We retire to a bar around the corner. Le Jet Lag is adorned with a superhero mural on the wall, subdued lighting and several low-slung lounges with braided cushions. It's not really our scene but we wanted to celebrate our good fortune with a beer. The bartender wears a tight black t-shirt and jeans. A blonde woman in a puffy jacket and a green skirt sits opposite, telling us she likes to speak English. She promptly turns to her friend, a woman wearing a blue leather jacket, black tights and high heels and starts a long conversation in their native French.

Five pretty young women walk in and our two friends get up and follow them to the bar. Everyone starts flirting with the handsome bartender. It's Saturday night in Annemasse. We finish our drinks and wander the streets. A crescendo of horns announce a wedding party is heading home after an evening of drunken revelry. Hip hop blasts from open windows as two weary cyclists make their way to a shopping mall apartment hotel.

Whatever happened to hilltop medieval towns and one-star hotels with crooked floors and floral wallpaper?

Chapter Two - Switzerland

I spent a few hours last night trying to list famous living Swiss people. I'm embarrassed to admit the only two that immediately sprang to mind were tennis ace Roger Federer and FIFA boss Sepp Blatter. I wondered if either of these men were representative of how we view the Swiss.

Federer is well-spoken, popular, dependable but perhaps a little bland. Sepp Blatter may be respected in a few African and Asian countries, but less kind souls would view him as ruthless, manipulative and shrewd. An operator who has used his neutrality to profit only himself. Deft or deceitful?

Can you see where I'm heading with this?

Do we really like the Swiss?

We may admire their apparent neutrality; covet their substantial wealth and high standard of living; envy their breathtaking landscape while devouring their excellent chocolate, but when it comes to describing the citizens of this landlocked country, we end up listing what they do rather than their character. They are bankers, watchmakers, administrators. They ski in winter and host international conferences in summer.

The Swiss army knife or the Swiss bank vault? Hardy, dependable Roger or shrewd conniving Sepp. Cow bells and chocolate or FIFA and Insurance bonds.

The Swiss have historically profited from their location in central Europe and their uncanny ability to remain aloof and at arm's length from the world's problems. But given the recent financial crisis, perhaps our view of bankers has turned from dependable and helpful to crooked and unscrupulous.

I realise the everyday Swiss worker is none of these things, but I fear the country may be characterised by its prominent citizens and institutions rather than the common man or woman.

This morning, we catch a bus into the heart of Geneva. Our first stop is a bank. I need to withdraw Swiss francs from a machine. It greets me in six languages and charges me a small fee for the pleasure of withdrawing the precious francs. Despite being early on Sunday the streets are crowded with runners in bibs and shorts and a large crowd cheering them through the rain. A fun run! Cashed up, we join the throng and walk down to the curve of Lake Geneva. The water is teal green and necklaced with fishing boats and elegant steam cruisers. We walk along the promenade and look back at the town - a ring of solid five-storey historic buildings rising to green hills swathed in cloud. Out on the pier, four hardy souls are dressed in swimmers. They climb over the rocks and dive into the water. Marathon runners and ice-cold bathers. They're a hardy lot.

A jazz samba band plays loudly to spur the runners onto the final kilometre and as each competitor crosses the finish line, a woman in traditional dress rings a cow bell. A nice touch. In Jardin Anglais, tents are crowded with sweaty competitors and their proud families as they each receive a medal and line up to buy a world of food from bratwurst to sushi.

Ranked in the Top Ten of global financial cities, the location of numerous United Nations institutions including the UNHCR, home of the Red Cross and regarded as one of the top five most expensive cities in the world, Geneva is also surprisingly beautiful and accessible. The lack of high-rise buildings lends a human scale and as the city rises gently up the hill, views extend to green hills and water. On a clear day, you can see Mont Blanc.

I admire any city with trams. The clatter, the peaked cap of the driver, the slow pace speaks of history with a human focus. I like Geneva very much. Even if it's also home to bling manufacturers, Rolex and Raymond Weil. I guess Geneva can't be responsible for who buys its watches.

Instead of window shopping at all the silver and gold baubles on Rue de Rhone, we pay homage to the most popular tree in Geneva along the Promenade de la Treille. This hoary old chestnut is designated as the official harbinger of spring. Each year since 1818, town officials have recorded the date of the first buds and formally announced the arrival of Spring. In truth, there have been three trees used since the 19th century. This latest one, planted in 1929 is so bent over it has to be propped up with a pole. Not surprisingly, each year it buds earlier. The scientists would have something to say about that.

We stroll up hill to the 14th century Cathedral Saint Pierre. It's a plain yet imposing building with views across the old town. Despite the number of people here for the marathon, many restaurants are closed and we seek shelter from the rain in Chez Ma Cousine, a humble restaurant recommended by a friend who spent a few years in Geneva. The roast chicken is succulent and comes with Provencal potatoes and salad for sixteen francs. In this town, an absolute bargain.

When we take the bus back to Annemasse in France, I note that the fare is double that of what it was this morning. It's cheaper to arrive than to depart. The cruel and heartless would say the Swiss want more of your money than the French.

We can't resist returning to La Cerise sur la Chameau for dinner and even more of the delectable cous cous. In the evening, I browse lists of prominent Swiss people and note that the roll-call of the deceased is much more exciting than the living. Carl Jung, Herman Hesse, Le Corbusier, Robert Frank and Paul Klee just to name a few from the past century. Among the living, we dress in white shorts and sports socks to welcome dear Roger accompanied by Martina Hingis and Stan Wawrinka. From literature, art, philosophy and architecture to hitting a ball over a net is perhaps not so much the fault of the Swiss education system or its cultural values as a loud and clear signal that what the modern world treasures is a crisp forehand and a neat headband before difficult theories on the collective unconscious and modernist architecture.

The rain continues to fall the next morning. We shrug into our jackets and reload Bruce and Aiwa, fresh after their first rest day of the tour. We cycle into Monday morning peak hour where Swiss cyclists ignore red lights and traffic etiquette. We're forced to the footpath on more than one occasion because we don't have nerves of steel or the dexterity of a Tour de France racer. It's a relief to stop for breakfast in a café not far from Rue December 31st. It's nice of Geneva to name a street after my birthday. The waitress is friendly and doesn't seem to mind when we hang our wet jackets over the vacant chairs. The coffee is better in Switzerland and is accompanied by a small square of chocolate. Lovely.

The lake is covered in an ethereal mist as we cycle through splendid parks dotted with small châteaus and gardens in full bloom. The UNHCR building is looking rather more regal than the camps where its employees do their valuable work. We follow the back roads hugging the lake wherever possible past elegant homes ringed by leafy trees and colourful hedges. At Nyon, I compare the modernist glass edifice that is the home of UEFA to the pale multi-turreted château and wonder which one will exist in one hundred years time.

The mist is slowly rising, revealing a glorious expanse of lake ringed by snow-capped mountains on the far shore. It's like cycling through a postcard. Sunshine, snowy mountains, glistening water, grassy meadows. Time to sit on a wooden pier and take endless photos of Bruce and Aiwa for the folks back home. And what better location than the beautiful village of Saint Prez. Justly awarded the Wakker Prize for preservation of its cultural and architectural heritage, the town is on a peninsula jutting into the lake. In summer, the ferry stops at the pier. But today, we have it all to ourselves. A sign, 'Bain des Dames' points towards the small beach. It's perhaps too early in the season for ladies to be swimming in the chill waters, but I envy a place where you can stroll a few hundred metres from a medieval town centre to swim in clear water while gazing at snow-capped mountains. I read last night that Switzerland was awarded 'the world's happiest country' in a recent survey. I've no doubt the judges visited Saint Prez.

We finally hop back on our bicycles and cycle through vineyards on the east side of town. On the outskirts of Lausanne, we turn towards the foothills of rape fields and wheat. It's a long slow climb to our accommodation for the evening in the town of Cossonay. The bed and breakfast is located next to a modern funicular that ferries commuters to the railway station at Penthalaz. We're greeted at reception by a man who looks like an extra from a bad British comedy show. He has round glasses, is slightly balding and paunchy, has nervous eyes but is marvellously friendly and welcoming. He proudly leads us to our upper floor room and steps inside pointing towards the wide window near the desk. A vista of mountains and lake.

'It is the best room in the house,' he says.

'Are we deserving?' I ask.

'You have come all the way from Australia,' he answers, as if that is reason enough.

He goes into great detail describing each of the restaurants in Cossonay, apologises ahead of time for the limited abilities of their respective chefs and warns us they are expensive. Before leaving, he smiles and says,

'But our breakfast is substantial. And free.'

What a lovely man.

Cathie has a shower. I sit at the desk and wonder what it would be like to write a novel from this chair, with this view. Would I get any work done or just stare in wonder? At this very moment, my phone beeps with a message from my Australian publisher. My latest novel has been shortlisted for a prestigious award. Maybe I *could* afford to stay here and write? After all, the breakfast is free. I knock gently on the bathroom door to tell Cathie the good news. She's standing under the shower staring out at the same wonderful view.

'This must be the world's best bathroom,' she says. 'Oh yeah, congratulations as well!'

One of the abiding joys of eating in a Swiss restaurant is saying under your breath, 'You want to charge me how much for roast beef!' The lovely black-haired waitress with excellent English perhaps mistakes my eye-watering as sentimentality for roast beef rather than me considering whether I should take out a mortgage to pay for dessert. Instead I order another Feldschlosschen Amber ale which is very good and relatively cheap. Can I get enough energy for cycling from drinking beer rather than eating? Perhaps not. I give in and order the roast beef and decide my children don't really need an inheritance. Cathie orders fish and chips because it's the cheapest item on the menu at thirty-three francs. The food is acceptable. For dessert we have another glass of beer. We walk home in the full moon light. Bruce and Aiwa are safely locked in a wooden barn near the funicular and the forecast for the next few days promises fine weather. Tomorrow, we return to France.

The owner greets us with a rueful smile this morning. It's raining.
'You promised me ...' I begin.
'It is El Nino,' he says, 'Rain and ...' he searches for the word in English, his lips curling in distaste, 'Humidity.'
'We sweat on the bike no matter what the weather,' I smile.
He looks at the computer screen. 'Tomorrow is better and after that sunshine for a week.'
'We'll be in Belgium in a week,' I say.
'Beer and frites,' he says, as if that will encourage us to pedal faster to reach the flatlands.
He leads us into the breakfast room and a table near the window. We eat eggs and cheese and bread and he keeps a close watch on our coffee cups, offering a refill regularly. It's as if he's trying to prolong our stay, perhaps until the rain stops. We watch the workers walking to the funicular, dressed in overcoats and carrying umbrellas. I can't help but notice how young they are. While the youth of Switzerland go off to their respective occupations, we old people prepare to spend the day cycling. It doesn't seem fair.

The owner's delaying tactics have succeeded. By the time we load our bicycles, the rain has stopped and we cycle away into a cool cloudy day continuing a long slow climb beside a train track among fields of wheat and rape. There are few cars as the fields give way to forests of fir and beech. At La Sarraz, I take a wrong turn and follow a dirt track alongside the railway line. A truck approaches and the driver indicates a dead-end ahead. I'm too lazy to turn around and go back the way we've come, so suggest to Cathie I'll carry the bikes across the train tracks. She rolls her eyes.

'It's only a few kilometres back,' she says.

'Bruce and Aiwa don't weigh much and besides, there would only be one train a day on this track.'

Yes. I've just finished taking Aiwa across the tracks when a roaring express train thunders past. My beautiful wife doesn't say a word. She doesn't have to. Back on Route 9, it's a long drop over the edge of the road. We're riding alongside the top of the trees. We trace a line down their trunks to the green undergrowth fifty metres below.

Vallorbe is the last Swiss town before the border and farewells us with a lovely river running through the village flowing over a weir and in between pink and apricot painted stone houses. A village famous for its caves in the nearby mountains and now surviving on tourists and logging. As we cross the border into France, I look back to the Swiss side. High on a hill is a farm with a huge red and white Swiss cross, painted on the side of a barn for the whole valley to see.

The road narrows and becomes busy with trucks who patiently wait for an opportunity to pass us. We enter the Doubs region of France, the forest is thick and dark with fir trees, occasionally opening out to ski fields. Snow ploughs and chair lifts are idle, the ski-hire shops closed. At Jougne, there is a lovely statue of a woman holding the flame of liberty, beside her is a soldier dressed in a heavy overcoat, in his hands a staff. Looking up at them is a statue of a small boy, standing to attention. Flowers bloom around the base of the memorial. These figures turn their back on a long view down a narrow green valley.

We continue on to Le Hopitaux-Vieux for lunch: a fromage and jambon crepe and a beer. I look twice at the prices on the menu. It's so cheap. Welcome back to France.

As we roll over the 1000 metres high elevation, the road relents and decides to let gravity take its course. For fifteen whooping kilometres we surge downhill, not bothering to pedal, our hands ready over the brakes. I'm not sure if my grin is from elation or because I'm gritting my teeth with the cold.

As we turn to cut through the Cluses de Pontarlier, a narrow gap in the mountains, I look up to see the majestic Fort de Joux. High walls, an imposing tower, fluttering flags and gun turrets, it's every child's dream of a castle on a hill. The fort has been dominating this narrow passage for centuries, captured and recaptured by invading armies, used as an outpost, a château and a prison. Occupying the high ground on the main road between France and Switzerland, it has hosted a list of regal owners - Charles the Bald, Mary of Burgundy, Maximilian the first and Margaret of Austria.

However, I prefer the roll call of prisoners to owners. The Black Napoleon, Toussaint Louverture the liberator of Haiti, died in his cell here in 1802. The French revolutionary Mirabeau and the German Romantic poet and novelist, Heinrich von Kleist both spent periods of incarceration behind the stone walls. Mirabeau became a national hero and was honoured with internment in the Pantheon in Paris. Kleist, a misguided and torn figure, fell in love with a terminally ill woman and killed her and himself in a lover's pact.

Like so many national monuments, this lonely outpost is now a tourist attraction, housing a military museum of rare weapons to be perused by day-trippers on their way to the ski-fields or Germans in RVs circling Europe. Or cyclists hoping for a café?

For that, we must wait until we reach Pontarlier. I have an immediate affection for a town made famous by alcohol. In this case, it's the dreaded absinthe, the green fiery liquid wrongly accused of sending people insane while under its hallucinogenic powers. None of it was true of course, but the fact that a drunk Swiss farmer killed his family and himself after drinking absinthe in 1805 didn't help matters. Absinthe struggled through various bans and prohibition eras with the economy of Pontarlier rising or falling on the reputation of the drink. It's back in favour again now and Pontarlier looks all the rosier for it.

It's too early for alcohol, so we enter a tea room with coffee bean tiles on the floor and a roasting machine in the corner. Despite the sunny yellow decor and the roaster, the coffee is dull and bitter. The owners are friendly and we can't resist an excellent fraise vanilla slice. When the heavy-set woman brings our cake she asks us where we began our adventure. When I answer, 'Marseille,' she looks at Cathie and says, 'Madame, voiture, velo, voiture.' Cathie smiles and answers, 'velo, velo, velo.' The woman shakes her head, exclaiming 'ooh la la.' When we leave, she stands and opens the door for us as if any extra effort on our part should be avoided. She smiles at Cathie and says, 'bonne courage.'

Our accommodation is on a D road just outside of town. It's a budget hotel requiring a code to enter the foyer where a machine takes my credit details and spits out another code. This allows us entry into our first floor capsule-like room which has a triple bed and a shower cubicle built for slim people only. I squeeze inside and turn on the taps. The shower streams a fine spray of water and pulsates with red, green, yellow and orange disco lights. Why on earth do I need this light show to wash myself? If the cubicle was bigger, Cathie could turn on some music and I could dance the night away. It's beguilingly stupid and unnecessary and I stay much too long in the shower grinning inanely at the flashing lights. Forgive me.

The rain begins to tumble down outside and I look up at the clouds, wondering if the heavens could emulate our shower cubicle. No. It's just grey and forboding. We shrug into our jackets and head next door to the more upmarket hotel. By upmarket, I mean it has a human at reception not a machine. The lovely blonde-haired woman in a crisp blue uniform doubles as the waitress and receptionist. The restaurant is crowded with businessmen and women, all eating alone, gazing distractedly into their smart phones.

I'm tremendously excited to be back in France where for nine euros fifty we can order two courses each. First course is the ubiquitous terrine campagne followed by a salmon fillet and potatoes. It's simple and tasty fare that would require a bank loan if we were dining sixty kilometres east in Switzerland. We order a carafe of rosé to celebrate. I'm tempted to order a thimble of absinthe but worry I'd return to the hotel room, turn on the technicolour shower and lose my mind.

Chapter Three - Northern France

I jump out of bed the next morning, eager to stand under the disco shower. In the breakfast room, there's an amusing sight of a long line of businessmen and women waiting patiently for the stupid Australian to work out how to operate the coffee machine. Eventually a man shows me how it's done. Remove the cup from under the spout, push the button and then quickly replace it before coffee gushes all over the floor. C'est logical! Non.

The rain has blown east to torment the Swiss and left a morning of sunshine and dew glistening in the fields. A fox scampers across the road and runs through the meadows to the safety of the forest. I'm very excited by the prospect of ninety-five kilometres with the overwhelming majority being downhill. Predictably, within five minutes of leaving the hotel we are labouring up a hill. Oh well.

Soon enough we are indeed scooting down a long looping hill. When I was a child, the joy of cycling was the wind in my hair and a determination to break the speed of sound on the downward rush. I'd climb hills in our suburb just to turn around at the top and whoop down the incline, a grin of childish abandon etched on my face. Danger was as foreign as lycra and panniers. I imagined I was going one hundred miles per hour. If the video camera had been invented then surely it should be filming the ten year old rocket blasting past!

Now I'm an old man aware of potholes and trucks and loose gravel. Despite myself, I still get a thrill when the Garmin nudges fifty kph even though my hands are hovering over the brakes rather than contemplating a 'no hands, look at me Mum' moment. As a youngster, I would never stop half-way down - halfway down! - to take a wide angle photo of the green hills and meadows of yellow flowers cradling a perfectly wide tarmac. Cathie zooms past to remind me of my childhood self. But then she is three years younger.

In the village of Livier, a tiny chapel prays beside a large red barn. The names engraved in stone above the door are of three brothers from the Mercier family who gave their lives for France in the First World War. A red peony blooms near the front door, the colour of blood and sacrifice. The history of Livier is tormented. In 1636, the town was destroyed by fire and pestilence only to be sacked by the Swedes just three years later. In 1718 Livier was aflame with eighty houses lost. A generation later, the fires returned to destroy the village in 1749. Today, the majority of the houses are made of stone. A cat sleeps on a window ledge, five chickens peck in a large compost heap beside the barn and we search in vain for a boulangerie. A golden retriever stretches itself in the sun on a doorstep as we cycle out of town.

In the next village of Villeneuvre d'Amont, all the houses are large yet perversely squat, half-barn, half-residence. The cows below, family above, they are designed for long dark winters. Although it's only 9:30 in the morning, we have already pedalled forty kilometres. Still no boulangerie. But wait, here's a rollicking downhill of 8% switchbacks for six exhilarating kilometres leading us into the historic valley town of Salins-les-Bains.

At the boulangerie, Cathie can't contain her excitement.

'I'll have a Paris-Brest,' she whispers to me as I approach the counter.

'No, make it a religieuse,' she says.

'Uumm, maybe a café éclair,' she reaches for my arm and points to the object of her desire.

The woman behind the counter wearing a chef's cap and apron smiles and waits patiently.

'Bonjour, Madame,' says Cathie. 'Je voudrais Tartelette Myrtille, s'il vous plaît.'

I order a framboise tart and we take our treats outside to eat in the sun.

'Is one enough?' I ask my beautiful wife.

She shoots me a knowing look.

'It is only a *tartelette*,' she says.

Salins-les-Bains has an underground salt works dating from the 13th century, still in operation today, although tourism brings in just as much revenue. Like many spa towns, it has a faded old world charm but is curiously empty, as if waiting for the next influx of people to wallow in the mineral baths. I've never been a fan of sitting around in metre-deep warm water with a bunch of senior citizens. I reckon a quick dip in a cold mountain stream is more invigorating than a few days in tepid pools with lion head fountains and mouldy locker rooms.

We locate the only café in town with outdoor tables.

'They have a choice of cakes on the counter,' I say.

Cathie kicks my ankle under the table.

I deserved that.

The rest of the morning is a slow meander through sleepy

villages - Pagnoz, Mouchard, Chamblay - in each we see more animals than humans. Sleeping cats, pecking chickens, doves, an acrobat of swallows. The terrain is flat and alternates between farm and forest. Time for some homespun philosophy.

'Do you want to hear my Zen of cycling,' I say, as I ride beside Cathie.

'Do I have a choice,' she replies, still unhappy with me because of my cake joke.

We continue in silence through the village of Ounans - two cats, a dove and a dog whining from behind a high fence. 'Come on then, let's hear it,' Cathie relents.

I take a deep breath. 'It's simple. For every uphill there is a downhill. For every headwind,' we both look at each other remembering the Mistral, 'there is a day like today.'

I steer around a pothole.

'For each pothole, an expanse of perfect tarmac. For every day of rain ... sunshine.'

Cathie smiles, 'And yet, the perfect lunch goes on forever.'

'Until we reach Belgium,' I say.

'So when it's bright and sunny, we should expect rain the next day,' Cathie says.

'Or during the wet slog, think only of tomorrow's perfection,' I add.

'Lovely,' Cathie says.

In Mont-sous-Vaudrey we stop for lunch at Le Petit Gourmand, a restaurant with solid stone walls, pink tablecloths and wicker chairs. The young waitress offers us a three-course special for sixteen euro starting with a large terrine and salad followed by roast pork and potato gratin that sticks to my sides and requires numerous slices of excellent bread to mop up the juices. For dessert Cathie orders fromage blanc and I'm offered a plate of four local cheeses. I sure hope there are no uphill slogs this afternoon.

At the next table, a couple have ordered frog legs. The delicacy is served in a sizzling fry pan. They don't look particularly appetising. The two diners attack them with gusto. The sound of sucking and lip-smacking can be heard. The bones slowly pile up on the spare plate. Soon enough, another fry pan arrives with a second batch of lovely little amphibians.

I like frogs. Alive and croaking in flower-filled ponds. Not on a plate. Not when only the upper joint of the hind leg is eaten, the rest discarded. The bones are now threatening to topple onto the floor.

'Remember the church we visited in Rome, with all the bones of long dead monks,' Cathie says.

'Piled on top of each other,' she adds.

She doesn't have to say anymore.

I remember the sign held in the skeleton hands of one monk. 'What you are now, I once was. What I am now, you shall be.'

I shiver. The same for humans as for frogs. Although, I hope I don't have the dead marrow sucked from my bones.

After lunch, I choose a quiet C road labelled rue val d'amour where four villages are closely entwined as if in ... love.

Cycling through a dense forest, I spy a single gravestone topped by a cross and ringed by pink flowers. Michel. 1949.

I have previously cycled through the town of Dole on my trip across France in 2012. I remember it as a village of narrow alleys, historic buildings and a delicious ice cream shop. My memory proves accurate and Cathie can't resist ordering a double scoop of absinthe flavoured glacé, distilled in Pontarlier, of course. 'If I can't drink it, I'll eat it,' she says.

The cycleway between Dole and tonight's accommodation at Rochefort-sur-Nenon is along a canal. This is the way I cycled three years ago. On that occasion, I arrived on a Sunday in a wild thunderstorm and was chilled to the bone. The young woman kindly started the central heater so I could dry myself and my clothes. I was the only person staying at the hotel. In the evening I wandered through the village cemetery where I saw the immaculately tended grave of a woman named Camille who died the year I was born.

After checking in to the same hotel, this time welcomed in sunshine by a middle-aged man wearing the checkered pants of a chef, I lead Cathie to the church grounds eager to show her how Rochefort looks after its pioneers.

Camille's grave has disappeared.

All of the graves are missing. I can't believe it. I wander the church grounds in shock.

'Perhaps you've mis-remembered,' says Cathie.

'They were here, behind the church.' I look up at the steeple, as if hoping for divine intervention.

Underneath our feet are freshly-laid pebbles. The first hesitant shoots of grass spring from the dirt where the graves once were.

'They've planted lawn ... over the top of Camille,' I say.

In the corner of the churchyard, I find five headstones stacked against a wall. Camille is not among them. How could a village remove its history, just like that? For grass? It's not like the French at all. Camille's headstone didn't even last as long as I have lived. They say you're dead forever. She's dead ... and apparently forgotten. I feel very sad.

'Come on, I'll buy you a beer,' says Cathie, taking my hand.

Over dinner, I ask Claude, the owner of the hotel about the missing cemetery. He looks pained.

'For ten years, they contacted the relatives to get permission to move the graves,' he begins.

'To where?' I interrupt.

'Outside of town. In the new cemetery. There was no more room near the church. Ten years ...' he repeats.

Claude continues, 'And two years ago, they began moving them, grave by grave, with respect.'

He sighs, 'It took a long time.' His brow creases, 'But for those who died in the war. They will stay near the church. Near the memorial.'

I can't begin to imagine how they moved the remains. Surely after fifty years, the coffins would have rotted leaving only the skeletons. To dig up so many and move them with the dignity they deserved. Claude glances towards the kitchen. I get the impression he'd rather be cooking than talking about this painful recent history. I'm pleased Camille has a new resting place.

Claude offers us a vast array of food at breakfast. He tells me today he must do his taxes. I suspect he envies us our regimen of cycling and eating without a care in the world. It's a sunny morning with mist on the hills and a traffic jam on the main road heading towards Dole. We take a side road and avoid such dramas. I love mornings like this. A clear sky, choice of atmospheric back roads, villages just waking up and nothing to focus on but the slow rotation of my legs and the glorious countryside, passing by at a human pace.

Authume is a village of no more than two hundred people, yet its immaculate gardens and well-tended public spaces speak of the pride of millions. At a fork in the road is a long stone seat under a flowering tree. I can imagine someone walking their dog to this point each afternoon for the birdsong and wide view of ploughed fields and a distant forest. Unlike many French villages, there are no *for sale* signs. Why would you leave?

Auxonne has an impressive church with a number of statues and carvings dating from the 15th century, a series of medieval ramparts attesting to its conflicted history as an outpost of Burgundy and a somewhat downtrodden Château from the 17th century. We spend an inordinate amount of time looking for the cycle path alongside the sparkling Saone river before giving up and following a farm road instead. We cross the river further upstream at Pontailler-sur-Saone but still find no sign of a path alongside its banks.

In the village of Talmay, I eat tripe for the first time in my life. It's a restaurant where those wearing business shirts dine in a back room while the workers and cyclists eat at the bar, even though we all choose the same menu - a thirteen euro bargain of saucisson for entree, followed by chicken and cous cous or tripe and potatoes for main course and ice-cream or fromage blanc for dessert, washed down with a 50 ml jug of rosé. We diplomatically choose one of each main course and dessert and share the plates.

My Dad loved tripe. Mum hated it. Dad was a foundry worker for most of his life. My mum stayed home and looked after the seven children. None of us had to eat tripe with Dad. Mum would offer two meals that night - tripe for Dad ... and a leg of lamb as the alternative. On a working class wage, Mum managed to keep the fridge stocked with luxuries like ham, cheese and fresh fruit and vegetables and on Saturdays Dad worked at a chook farm, so we had roast chicken at least once a week. What we missed in new clothes and modern furniture, we gained in good food. Dad insisted on his tripe, once a week.

Bits of tripe get stuck in between my teeth, but in honour of my old man, I finish the plate. I guess it's another reason to drink the jug of rosé.

My verdict on tripe? Mum was right.

Just when I think we've finished a long lunch, the waitress who has spent most of the afternoon flirting with the handsome truck driver at the bar, brings us a wooden tray adorned with seven types of cheese, from creamy brie to a pungent blue with a delectable goat's cheese in between.

'So, we've eaten mortadella, saucisson, chicken, tripe, seven types of cheese, ice cream ...' I begin.

'And how much further do we have to ride?' Cathie asks.

'Only a lazy thirty kilometres,' I say.

Cathie sighs. 'I walk into a restaurant too hungry to cycle anymore and walk out too full to cycle further.'

Our solution?

In Champagne-sur-Vingeanne, we park Bruce and Aiwa against an ancient lavoir wall, spread our jackets out on the soft green grass and recline under an oak tree. As Cathie sleeps, I remember being ten years old again and waiting at the front fence for my dad to return from his day at the foundry. He'd ride his bicycle downhill and without braking swerve into our front yard, through the gates which I'd opened. After he had a shower, he'd sometimes bring a watermelon downstairs and we'd sit in the back yard and eat juicy slices he carved, spitting the pips into the compost heap. He died fifteen years ago and in truth I don't think of him that often. Perhaps the tripe and sunshine as bright as childhood brought it all back.

The final twenty kilometres is ridden at snail's pace with both of us promising to eat only a salad for dinner. Our accommodation at Fontaine-Francaise is fabulous. Opposite an imposing Château and lake is the old Moulin, now turned into a B&B. We knock tentatively on the front door. It's early. The only sound we hear is the rush of water tumbling into the stream beside the mill. Madame comes to the door as if she's just woken. Perhaps she dined at the same restaurant as us? She directs us around to the rear entrance where we can leave Bruce and Aiwa in the garden. She offers us a soft drink while she rushes upstairs to prepare our room. We have time to look around. In the drawing room is a huge wheel once used for grinding the grain. Now a child's inflatable toy hangs from one of the cogs. The beams across the ceiling hark back to a more industrious past. It's cool and dark and timeless.

Our room is ready and what a chambre it is, with a long view downstream and the relaxing sound of cascading water coming through the open window. It has a huge double bed, polished timber floorboards and a bathroom featuring a sink chiselled out of white stone. All this and breakfast for cheaper than most hotels in Australia.

In the late afternoon, we drink Picon in a quiet bar and then go shopping for dinner, a picnic of brie, jambon, salad and a bottle of rosé to consume in the garden outside our bedroom window. If there's one image I retain of travelling in France, it's the ability to experience luxury at a bargain basement price. The quality and supply of simple food - wine, bread, meat and vegetables means a cyclist can dine in an ancient Moulin opposite a château dating from the Middle Ages. The château has five metre high windows, a double staircase and large dome, a garden planted with three hundred lime trees and a lake of lily pads bordered by stone walls. The Moulin is arguably in a better location, beside the stream, facing away from the busy road, a park opening up alongside the waterway to a line of ornamental trees. We dine like royalty for a few euros.

Madame offers us a large typically French breakfast - bowls of coffee, a basket filled with croissants and baguettes, a choice of confiture, a jar of yoghurt each and a plate of fresh fruit. Bruce and Aiwa are none the worse for sleeping outdoors in the garden as we set off once again under clear yet cool conditions. We cycle between rolling hills of wheat and canola bent slightly under the weight of dew.

In a field of wheat, a lone stem of canola towers high. I'm reminded of a recent landmark case in Australia where an organic farmer sued his neighbour who planted a nearby field with a genetically-modified crop. Sure enough, the GM seeds blew across the fence and infected his fields, rendering his high-price organic status invalid. To add insult to injury, he lost the resulting case. It seems as if the GM farmer had financial backing from 'major companies' to employ the best legal team while the organic farmer was left to fend for himself.

So it goes, little by little we allow corporations to dictate how our food is grown and what we can eat. The market doesn't care for health, only endless economic growth and increased production. Yet another reason to treasure the attitude of the French who eat seasonally and shop locally. The only market the everyday French country folk care about is the numerous cheese, fish and meat stalls open in the town square each Wednesday. The town market, not the market of bankers and financiers and faceless corporations.

As if to prove my point, near Occey is a scatter of free-range chicken and turkey farms. In each large paddock of six, the animals roam free outside a wooden barn with the wide doors flung open. The birds scratch in the dirt, peck for worms and flap and squawk. They are birds, not prisoners. At night, they'll return to the barn to roost. But in the sunshine, they are doing what their ancestors have done for centuries. We'd do well to remember that next time we buy our meat.

On the D140, we follow a ridgeline and finally, after thirty hours of cycling in the famed wine region of the Cote d'Or, we see a vineyard, a small patch of gnarled vines on the side of a hill. Half-way up a long 7% climb, we stop for Cathie to retrieve a chocolate from her panniers. She feels a bonk coming on and she knows I'll never refuse a sweet treat. As our backs are turned against the wind, a herd of cows wanders to the fence to investigate. I walk close and notice that each has a four-digit number stapled to their ear. Cow 3136 is particularly inquisitive, poking his large head over the fence. I say hello and he tilts his head slightly in response. I wonder why he must be given a number not a name? I decide to call him 'Sam.' Sam and I have a chat for awhile. I do most of the talking. He listens intently, nodding his head and occasionally stooping down to munch on the lush grass. As I continue up the hill, I hear a bellow from a distant paddock. I realise why Sam has a number rather than a name. I don't fancy eating Sam for dinner. But Cow 3136? No worries.

Aujerres is a town given over to swallows and one young boy on a bicycle. As we pass the Mairie, I recall I haven't seen another person in the previous three villages, just the ever-present swallows. We haven't passed a boulangerie in fifty kilometres.

We climb into a dark forest and see signs announcing the source of the Aube river, somewhere amongst the tangle of undergrowth and tall impenetrable trees. I'm very excited, knowing we'll be following this stream for the rest of today's long ride. It's a lovely downhill to the village of Auberive with an impressive château and an open café. We buy fromage, pain complet and make ourselves a sandwich at an outdoor table, tearing the white-rind cheese and bread apart with the gusto of a fifty-eight kilometre hunger. As the church bells ring, we order coffee and a cannelle.

Today is the anniversary of the end of World War Two and a platoon of senior citizens walk home from the village War Memorial where they have left garlands of flowers. We sit at the table for longer than we should because I'm intrigued by the shopping habits of the village. A middle-aged couple in sensible walking shoes and long overcoats carry a picnic basket filled with baguettes, a cheesecake and a salad. Another man leaves the shop with two bottles of wine and a bar of chocolate. An old man carries a cardboard box containing a cake to his Renault van. Then a man goes and ruins it all by buying a kilo of carrots.

And so begins the afternoon ramble through what I dub the

'Aube ghost towns' - circled by swallows and littered with *for sale* signs in dusty windows. We pass numerous bars and auberges that don't appear to have opened in the past ten years. We see very few cars. In one village, three men clap and call 'bravo' as we pass, but that's it. We cycle for forty kilometres alongside the gentle Aube and I admire the permanence of stone. These villages have been built to last and they remain, long after the descendants of the original families have moved away. The Aube is a lovely river but it doesn't seem to have many friends as it flows through this sparse landscape. Every village is a huddle of pale stone houses, each with a halo of swallows.

After a one hundred kilometre day, we finally arrive at Lanty-sur-Aube. The owner of tonight's lodging is arriving home on her bicycle. She welcomes us inside and offers us beer and madeleine cakes. I eat three. She's very impressed with our journey and kindly speaks very slowly so we understand her French, or at least most of it. Tonight she is cooking us dinner which will be shared with eight members of her family who live in neighbouring villages and two fellow cyclists, one who speaks English she says, aware of the potential difficulties when family members get together. She demands we use her washing machine and shows Cathie a special drying closet in the basement. Our room looks over an immaculate garden of perfectly trimmed trees, two wood stacks each thirty metres in length and a small vineyard.

At dinner, Madame carefully arranges where we should sit, with the English-speaking Claude and Dominque next to me and Cathie respectively. Before Madame has a chance to introduce us, Claude has done the honours. He and Dominque are from Metz and Claude is celebrating his retirement with a three day cycling trip of the region.

'It is an excuse to be outdoors,' he says.

We are served pâté campagne with salad to start and the characters of the family take no time in revealing themselves. Jean-Paul, the uncle wears shorts and a work shirt and whenever anyone's glass is half-empty he jumps from his seat to offer a refill. Madame's son, Henri sits at the head of the table and tells long involved stories that Claude manfully translates where possible.

For the main course, Madame has cooked Cathie and I a venison stew in place of what everyone else is eating, blood and tripe sausages. Jean-Paul cheerfully announces that he shot the deer in the nearby mountains a few days ago. He watches closely as I take a bite. It's delicious, of course. He's even more impressed when I mockingly demand a taste of the sausage. The dinner table is hushed as Madame places a sausage on my plate. I take a small bite. It's certainly better than the tripe I had yesterday, so I take a bigger bite. Everyone claps. I offer to share my sausage with Cathie and she readily agrees. Jean-Paul says something in French and everyone laughs. Claude translates, 'You eat like the French but are not fat!'

I smile and answer with one word, 'Velo.'

Claude tells me of his cycling history, recommending Scotland and the New Hebrides as future routes. Dominique prefers the flatlands along the Danube river. I have to be careful not to drink too much as Jean-Paul seems to be hovering around my glass with alarming regularity.

By now, the excess of wine has worked its magic and everyone is laughing especially when Jean-Paul returns from the kitchen wearing a red wig. He doesn't say a word, just sits down and accepts all the sly digs I imagine are coming his way if only I could understand the language. Soon enough, Henri demands the wig. He slaps it on his head and the ribbing starts again. How can I resist? I delicately place the wig over my bald head and everyone cheers. It is as if I have become an honourary Frenchman for the evening - tripe and blood sausage, too much wine and a red wig. For the next half hour, we play 'pass the parcel' with everyone taking a turn of the wig.

Madame excels even her high standard with an wonderful dessert of custard flavoured with grand marnier. Madame's husband, the quiet and sensitive Gerard has baked a simple financier. He encourages me to dip the cake in the custard. The combination is divine. Proving once again why I love French cuisine - it's dippable!

Jean-Paul disappears again but I already know what he'll bring out next. I've been to many of these French dinner gatherings and around this time, someone always produces a bottle of Eau de Vie. The 'water of life' tastes anything but. Sure enough he returns with two bottles. Poire and Apple. Cathie pours a large slug and drinks it all. Everyone cheers. I limit myself to the poire - it tastes like rocket fuel.

And so it goes for another few hours. We are welcomed into this family as friends and despite the language difficulties, enjoy ourselves enormously. At midnight, we stumble up to our room. Madame will wake us early in the morning as another one hundred kilometres await. Oh dear.

The morning brings a hangover and the joy of freshly washed clothes. Madame shows how welcome we are in her fine home by offering us breakfast in the kitchen rather than the more formal dining room. Gerard brings out the remainder of his financier. Madame apologizes for the clanging of the church bells every hour during the night. I thought it was the pounding in my head.

They wave us off from the front gate into a day of cloud and a temperature that struggles into double figures. It's a wide open road with a hint of downhill for thirty kilometres. It's difficult not to switch off and dream.

Perhaps that's why I mistake a prison for a château.

We cycle up to the front gate to be met by armed guards and a few women waiting to visit their incarcerated husbands. It's not a castle keep but a watchtower. The high walls are not to defend against marauding armies but to keep the prisoners confined.

Clairvaux is a high-security prison in the former surrounds of the Abbey. In the grounds are buried the remains of the 11th century monk, Bernard, one of the founding fathers of the Cistercian order. I'm not sure how he'd feel about his present companions. I try to imagine what it's like inside these high walls. Would I want to be an inmate in an ancient building such as this or in a modern 21st century prison? Cold dark history or soulless metal and wire? The infamous terrorist, Carlos the Jackal spent time behind bars here, as did the notorious Claude Buffet who with a fellow prisoner took a nurse and a warder hostage. He killed them both in cold blood before being recaptured. He was sentenced to death and guillotined in 1972. The French continued this rather macabre form of execution until 1977.

The road remains flat, bordered by wheat and canola with glimpses of the fast-flowing Aube every few kilometres. We are cycling through a wide valley of farmland with nothing to break the monotony except a quiet village every five kilometres.

'I reckon we'll turn soon and have the wind at our backs,' I say.

'I'm going to kill you,' replies Cathie.

She knows it's unwise to ever tempt the wind. Sure enough, the road veers into the hostile breeze. At lunch we seek shelter in a tabac, the only place open for miles around. Five men and a ten-year-old girl sit along the bar. We order toasted paninis and beer at a table near the window, in the sunshine. No-one else is eating. The girl drinks her pink-coloured beverage and smiles at the exotic couple dressed in lycra.

Finally the wind turns in our favour, but I resist pointing this out, at risk of cold stares and nasty insults. We are pushed up a long hill. We're cycling on a narrow ridge looking down at the villages in the valley. Normally I'd prefer to be in the valley, but this wind is strengthening and we barely have to pedal. I cycle past what looks like a tombstone in a canola field. It worries me for the next kilometre until I call ahead for Cathie to stop.

'It looked to be in the shape of a bicycle wheel,' she says.

I shiver. I decide to ride back to investigate.

On a windswept hill on a long looping corner, Jacky Serindat died while riding his bicycle on the 11th September 2005. His family and friends have erected a tombstone in the shape of a bicycle wheel with black lines for spokes and an embossed picture of Jacky on his bike taking a corner coming down a mountain. He is smiling. It's a beautiful memorial.

More downhill follows, taken at a slower pace until we reach Vitry-le-Francois which has a lovely town square ringed by outdoor cafés and the church as its focal point. We walk into a bar and take a booth, the only people spurning the sunshine. One hundred kilometres is enough. On the television is a cycle race. The winner has just crossed the line and is now receiving his trophy, flanked by two models in short skirts. He leans down as they both kiss him. Cycling really needs to get its act together regarding the image of women - they are participants, not decoration. The Tour de France could start the process by dispensing with its yellow mini-skirt models after each stage.

We walk to the church and step inside. The first painting I see is of a semi-naked man holding the severed head of a rival. Prison riots, guillotines, severed heads, the barbarism of man knows no bounds.

Our hotel is undergoing extensive renovation with brightly-painted front doors surrounded by scaffolding. Our room is on the third floor at the rear, away from the building site. For dinner, we have a choice of pasta, pizza or cous cous. Remembering the meal in Annemasse, we choose the Moroccan L'Arganier restaurant. It's a wise move. The place is already full in the early evening and the owner seems to know all his customers. We share a chicken cous cous and a lamb tagine accompanied by a bowl of vegetables and an extra serving of sauce. We order pastries to take away and walk the quiet streets of Vitry. It's Saturday night, yet only a few teenagers are out, flirting and laughing around the fountain in the square. The girls preoccupied with their hair, the boys making as much noise as possible, that intense peacock dance of youth.

We eat breakfast in the only boulangerie open in town and I notice a sign in front of the croissants. *Croissant buerre.*

Aren't they all made with butter?

Please don't tell me the modern French baker uses margarine. Sacrilege.

We spend thirty minutes looking for the bike path out of town, reputedly alongside a canal. We find two canals but a combination of industrial fences and blocked streets means we can't get close enough to see if there is indeed a cycle path as Uncle Google promises. When we eventually navigate our way to the canal a few kilometres out of town we find a potholed overgrown service path. Non. In the village of Pogny a vide-grenier is in full swing. The French love their flea markets and we're forced to dismount and slowly walk past a cornucopia of vinyl records, microwaves, power tools, a technicolour of plastic toys, a library of books and the unwanted fashions from the past thirty years. For some reason known only to the French, they always bring their dogs along to the market. We trip on dog leads and brave the crowds before finally escaping down a side street. It's safer back on the N44!

In Chalons-en-Champagne, we park our bikes against the closed chemist shop next to a boulangerie. The gruff baker serves us an excellent millefeuille. He goes out to our bicycles and I assume he's going to tell me to move them away from the window. When he returns he explains in broken English he was worried they may get stolen. I wonder who would be desperate enough to pilfer two dusty bicycles and panniers containing dirty clothes and spare lycra?

Despite being in the Champagne region, we haven't seen many vineyards. Is it churlish to say that even the brilliant yellow of canola can get monotonous over a few hundred kilometres? After a lunch stop at Conde-sur-Marne - more children sitting at the bar of a tabac - we finally come upon sloping hills of vines. The plants are short and stout, slightly bulbous at the bottom after years of careful pruning. We pass an old shanty barn built of fibro and timber. On the side is the name of the owner - Moet Chandon. Gee, I thought the champagne industry was doing better than that. At the top of the climb we see the steeple of Reims Cathedral fifteen kilometres in the distance. It's downhill through vineyards all the way. Ironically we stumble upon a canal path just outside of town and follow it to the centre-ville.

Is it an unspoken rule that every cathedral in France is surrounded by cafés and restaurants with outdoors tables and chairs all facing the spire? Everyone appears to be drinking from flute glasses.

We order an overpriced drop of bubbly. I've never seen the attraction to be honest. I prefer my bubbles in an amber fluid. But when in Rome ... or Reims.

While I may be somewhat dismissive of the sparkling wine, I am overwhelmed by the majesty of the Cathedral. A church has existed on this hallowed ground for over one thousand six hundred years and witnessed the rise and fall of Kings and Queens; withstood siege by the British in the One Hundred Years War; celebrated liberation with Joan of Arc; hosted coronations of monarchs from King Henry the First in the 11th century to Henry the Second five hundred years later; was bombed by the Germans during the First World War and now stands before millions of tourists unbowed and glorious, although regularly wreathed in scaffolding as she is today. A skin of temporary planks and pipes cannot detract from its beauty. Boasting more sculptured figures than any other cathedral in Europe apart from Chartres, Reims has two glorious rosé windows over the main portal and, as if to prove its enduring legacy, a series of windows designed by the legendary French-Russian artist, Marc Chagall.

But perhaps my favourite story about the cathedral centres on one of the small statues dubbed the *smiling angel* adorning its exterior. Carved in the 13th century, the angel boasts a curly mop of hair and was 'beheaded' by a German artillery attack during the First World War. She fell to the ground and broke into several pieces. The remains were collected by the Abbot and stored in the cellars of the cathedral, only to be discovered a short time later and repaired and celebrated as an icon of the resistance - a symbol of French art damaged by German aggression. After the war, amid great ceremony, the smiling angel was restored to her place in 1926. She smiles forever more.

In the late afternoon, we check into our hotel a few hundred metres from the *smiling angel* and the *drinking tourists*. To my surprise we're given a delightful front room, three flights up with two metre high windows and a tiny balcony offering views down two impressive avenues. All for fifty-three euros. In this town, that's the price of a bottle of ordinary champagne.

Continuing my theme of eating stuff I wouldn't normally touch, at Restaurant Le Comptoir le Boeuf, I begin with bone marrow served alongside a smattering of Guerade salt and thin toast. What can I say? It tastes like soft salty fat. Rather nice actually. For main course I order lamb shanks and vegetables Provencale. You and me call it *ratatouille*. The waiter has the classic French face of drooping jowls, popping eyes and floppy hair. He does his job with grace and efficiency.

In the early morning, I watch a man cruising down the deserted streets on a foot scooter. He's dressed in a suit and tie and carries a briefcase. He zips past the Hotel de Ville and disappears from view, his little wheels ringing on the bitumen. We eat breakfast in a café and watch the city awaken. A street sweeper cleans the gutters, delivery vans hustle between bollards and drop their cargo outside locked doors while workers scurry to the office. Everyone seems to be carrying a take-away coffee.

After a few kilometres haunted by the howl of traffic on the D944, we escape into a series of lovely villages in the hills. The sign announcing each village also tells us how many stars they have attained in the *Villages Fleuris* Awards. Villers-Franqueux has one star, Hermonville and Cauroy both have two stars. I wonder if the citizens of Villers are jealous of Hermonville? Or do all the villages pitch in together and try to improve each settlement along the quiet D530? I'm particularly taken with the statue of a cyclist in Hermonville. Made of polished timber, he pedals along on a shiny silver bicycle with the stub of a cigarette between his lips. He's not wearing a helmet, of course.

I've been wondering if we are officially in the North of France, a region where the locals tend to be looked down upon by many French as uncouth and gauche. They've even made a movie about it where a cosmopolitan office worker is sent to the Nord on assignment. He and his family fear the worst, but are met with only kindness and assistance. The only differences I've noticed on past visits are the majority of people seem to be working class. As the son of a foundry worker, I see nothing wrong with that.

Back on the D944, the truck drivers are extremely patient, regularly waiting behind us until it's safe to pass. We feel guilty to slow them down so much but unfortunately there is no quieter alternative. The lovely town of Laon welcomes us with a six-storey nightmare of apartment blocks at the foot of the medieval village. I see this regularly in Europe and it never fails to upset me. Surely there are better ways to house the working population so close to a national treasure? Did the architect not think of the medieval jewel rising directly behind this monstrosity. Cursing aside, we begin a steep climb up into the Middle Ages, where despite their barbarism they knew how to design buildings.

Showing our usual sense of priorities, we eat lunch at the

Restaurant Le Parvis before visiting the Laon Cathedral. Food for the body before nourishment for the soul. The plat du jour is a delicious tagliatelle with fruits der mer. Excellent value in a lovely setting. And as usual I leave something behind. This time it's my treasured Alpe d'Huez riding cap which soaks up sweat and prevents sunburn. I pity the poor waiter who found it. When I return a short time later, it's hanging rather decorously from the menu board.

The Cathedral of Notre Dame Laon is a priceless example of Gothic architecture from the 12th century. Erected before its more famous namesake in Paris, the white stone interior appears to radiate light. We wander the hallowed halls gazing up at the rosé window bathed in sunlight, trying to imagine what a pilgrim of the 12th century would feel on first stepping across the threshold. Reverence. Exultation. Joy. Perhaps such feelings are not only reserved for the true believers. It's a splendid building. A village has existed on this prominent hill since the time of Julius Caesar and has witnessed the rise and fall of monarchs, housed Templars in the 12th century, been stormed in vain by Napoleon, endured the invasion of marauding Germans in both the 19th and 20th century and now - horror of horrors - looks down upon a travesty that is a camp of modern apartment blocks, washing fluttering from verandahs, abandoned cars on blocks, a service station offering two-for-one soft drinks and the perpetual hum of rooftop air-conditioners.

The pilgrim turns away and stares at the cathedral, wondering how it all came to this.

It's an easy twenty kilometre ride through the ever-present canola fields to the Tour de Crecy Hotel where the owner, a charming man dressed in a light blue shirt and grey trousers shows us a garage for Bruce and Aiwa and leads us up to our first floor room with wide windows opening out to a view of the Tower of Crecy, a circular brick edifice adorned with a working clock. Three o'clock in the afternoon. Time for a drink, surely? Above our window are a number of swallow nests. The birds go about their business oblivious to our attention.

Across the road is one of the strangest shops I have ever encountered. Although it's billed as a hardware, the interior is crowded with a bewildering display of items, all covered in a thin film of dust. It looks as if the store hasn't been opened in twenty years. All of the wares are from another era. Dolls with woollen knitwear, old metal children's toys, lampshades in lurid orange, metal watering cans, a skipping rope, a 1990 FIFA World Cup football. I stare into the window trying to date when the shop closed its doors for the last time. And then I walk past the front door and realise a man is standing behind the counter. Yet there are no customers. I wonder what the children of the town think of this? A shop full of toys and yet it would be a very brave person to step through the doorway. What shopkeeper doesn't replenish his stock? I peer in through another window. There are no lights on and it looks very dingy and uninviting. I really want to go inside but even I'm a little scared. Perhaps its best to leave the shopkeeper alone? Maybe he lost his wife in 1991 and hasn't been outside since then? I wonder if the prices are ... I run back to the store. There are no price tags on any of the goods. It is a ghost store.

The upper floor windows of the shop face our hotel room. I spend the afternoon looking across the square. Not a soul moves. The curtains remain closed. He may have locked up hours ago, but there still isn't a light visible from inside. A darkness of twenty years envelopes the building. Cathie tells me to come away from the window, to stop making up stories, to leave the man in peace. She drags me down to the restaurant for dinner.

I love a chef who offers an amuse bouche of pork fat and bread. It sets me up nicely for the duck and potatoes main course. The hotel and restaurant is run by a husband and wife team who seem to be always smiling despite the lack of custom on this quiet Monday evening. I wonder what the ghost store owner does for dinner? Cathie warns me that if I mention the store again, she'll lock me out of our bedroom and I can take my chances with the ghosts opposite. I offer her the last of the pichet de rosé. It's the wise thing to do.

In the morning, I jump out of bed and open the curtains. All is quiet in the square and in a certain store opposite. We load Bruce and Aiwa and set out under cloudy skies. Today is ninety kilometres of undulating back roads. I love that word *undulating*. It implies hills without the heavy breathing and wobbles. We have entered the sparsely populated North. The villages are quiet, most of the houses are built of brick instead of stone and the windows seem smaller. The shutters are closed. Perhaps it's too early in the morning.

We stop at Guise for a millefeuille. Guise is the location of the *Familistery of Guise*, a wonderful social experiment orchestrated by the industrialist Jean-Baptiste Godin who made his fortune in the 19th century by manufacturing the cast iron pan, still widely used today. Godin used his fortune to improve the social conditions of the workers in his factories by building a compound of living quarters that offered such luxuries as a school, theatre, swimming pool, laundry and a meeting house. He wanted to build a community for the workers, a place they could call their own. He was a socialist in capitalist clothes. Godin eventually converted the familistery to a co-operative ownership model, managed by the workers. I toast his good politics with an excellent cake and a cup of sub-standard coffee at the Guise boulangerie. The cooperative lasted almost a century after Godin's death in 1888, a significant achievement and legacy to the great man. Some of the buildings remain and are still used by the community of Guise.

Restored by cake and social justice, we cycle up and down hills, beside canola and wheat fields, through desolate villages until we reach lunchtime in Engelfontaine. There are no restaurants, just a small grocery store. The owner sells us salami and cheese but is out of bread. Oh dear. She tells her teenage son to lead us to what I suspect is a shop around the corner that may sell bread. He cheerfully runs alongside us on our bikes until the intersection. He points up the street. We ride a few hundred metres to a tabac. It does not sell bread. The barman tells me the nearest boulangerie is four kilometres away. He looks very sorry as if he's setting me an impossible task. I can't help but smile. In France, where villages are so close to one another, four kilometres seems a great distance. In Australia, the barman would have said, 'Just around the corner, mate.' Meaning twenty kilometres down the highway.

I'm about to hop back on Bruce when the smiling teenager reappears. He points to a red vending machine a few metres past the tabac. I investigate. Rows of baguettes await the insertion of a one euro coin. I don't know how we didn't see it. I don't know why the barman didn't tell me. Perhaps he thought I wanted cake. Or ready-made sandwiches.

Thanks to a friendly teenager, we sit in the town park beside the church and eat sandwiches.

The next town of Le Quesnoy is a medieval wonderland of high walls, moats and cobblestone lanes. We clank over the rough roads agog at such a peerless example of a tourist town without the tourists. The streets are filled with handsome young people cycling or walking home from school. They seem oblivious to the beauty of their hometown. I'm cheered to learn that the Tour de France will pass through here later this year. Maybe that will alert more people to its charms. I'm sorry we have already booked accommodation further north. I would like to stay in a town that over the last thousand years has hosted people with such regal names as Philip the Handsome; Charles the Bold; Jacqueline, Countess of Hainaut and Charles the Fifth of Spain.

Steven the Steady and Cathie Princess of the Cobblestones depart Le Quesnoy, vowing to return again in the future.

In contrast, the much larger and busier Valenciennes is full of clothing shops, sushi restaurants, fast food chains and a 'erotic shop' near the railway station. Too much commercial navel-gazing has crowded out the lovely Hotel de Ville. Whoever designed, or redesigned this town and gave precedence to the car over the pedestrian should be sentenced to a year in Le Quesnoy to learn how a village functions. A council which allows multi-storey carparks to be erected, either above ground or underground, signs a death warrant to their town. Only the Hotel de Ville will remain of Valenciennes in one hundred years time.

In the 11th century, this region was struck by a terrible plague. According to legend, the Virgin Mary threw an invisible cordon around the city which protected the people from the disease. Since then, once a year, the devout walk around the town in a fourteen kilometre circuit of faith, to give thanks for the miracle. The real miracle will be if Valenciennes can be saved from rampant commercialism.

We only have twenty-four hours left in our beloved France, so I have booked accommodation in a château for this evening. Before you go thinking it's a wasteful indulgence, the cost is half what I'd pay for a four-star hotel in Australia. The Château Aubry is located in the middle of a large park and is surrounded, like all good castles should be, by a moat. It's not a huge building and bears the scars of perhaps too many renovations and refits over the past six hundred years, but the current owners are doing their best to make it part of the village again, opening it up as wedding and conference centre. Bruce and Aiwa are immediately impressed as they get to stay in an old barn filled with antique bicycles and a horse-drawn buggy. We're shown upstairs to a small room with a lovely view of the garden, the moat and the hundred year old trees beyond. Ducks circle the château, the willows weep into the water and a circle of teak tables and chairs wait for guests on the perfectly manicured lawns.

Dinner is on the enclosed verandah surrounded by three-metre high plate glass windows and Doric columns. I order a Trappist beer and the waiter opens it at my table and we watch it erupt over the clean starched white tablecloth. Another beer and table covering is needed. I make a joke about the beer being so old as it's made by monks. It doesn't really translate, I'm afraid. Would it surprise you to learn I ordered duck for main course? It was excellent, cooked with a local honey sauce and accompanied by a sweet potato mousse and salad. There is a function in the drawing room where a host of well-dressed women are drinking champagne and eating canapes. Our young waiter - he of the spilt beer - is being run off his feet serving both the diners and the function guests. The senior waiter, an overweight man with a florid complexion and slicked back hair, spends most of the evening ordering the young man about rather than pitching in and helping. I think he needs a few weeks under the guidance of Jean-Baptiste Godin. That would sort him out.

After dinner, we stroll through the gardens.

'You should have a parasol,' I tell Cathie.

'And you should wear a top hat,' she counters.

I stub my toe on a rock and curse.

'I don't think we're suited for châteaus and elegance,' I say.

'Speak for yourself,' Cathie smiles.

Chapter Four: Belgium

Alas, the château charges ridiculous prices for a simple French breakfast, so we load Bruce and Aiwa and cycle around the corner to a café for petit dejéuner. It's a crisp cold morning and soon after leaving the château we arrive at the Petit Foret. A jogger is running out of the forest as we carefully steer our way onto the same path. The man looks at our panniers and points from where he's come, 'Paris, Roubaix!' I look down the path and see cobblestones. Immediately, I understand what he means. I call, 'Merci,' but he is out of range.

We have stumbled across the Trouée d'Arenberg, perhaps the most famous, or infamous section of the acclaimed Paris to Roubaix one-day cycle race. A two and a half kilometre stretch of hellish cobblestones first built in the time of Napoleon, it has been the scene of some horrific crashes including one in 2001 when the French cyclist Philippe Gaumont was leading the peloton. He hit the cobblestones at speed and ended up in hospital for six weeks with a broken femur.

Luckily for us there is a dirt path alongside the pave. This is where the fans stand to watch the one-day classic, thereby blocking any escape route for the weary cyclists. I slowly steer Bruce onto the cobblestones. It's bone rattling in the extreme and I'm going less than 10 kph. The racers charge through here at more than double that speed, on bikes with thinner tyres. In the Tour de France, mountains are categorised according to their difficulty - from an easy Category 5 up to the difficult Category 1 and the hardest of all, the Hors Category - literally translated as 'beyond category.' It's the same for cobblestones, only in an ascending order. It's no surprise to learn that the Pavé d'Arenberg is a Category Five, the most extreme. This section is so difficult because of the irregularity of the surface, partly blamed on the fact that fans have been known to steal a cobblestone. The council spends a fortune each year replacing the missing stones. It doesn't help the cyclists much. I steer Bruce back to the safety of the dirt. It's a quiet forest of birdsong for three hundred and sixty-four days a year. Followed by one day of madness.

I'm thrilled to learn that this section was first introduced into the Paris-Roubaix at the suggestion of a certain Jean Stablinski, a Tour cyclist who worked at a nearby mine. Astute readers will remember Jean from earlier in the book as being the first cyclist over the Col de l'Espigoulier, the mountain I climbed on the first day of this trip. A thousand kilometres further north Jean and my paths cross again. I don't think he'd mind me saying that I'd rather climb the mountain, for all its difficulty, than race along the dreaded Pavé. I'm even more pleased to see a small memorial to Jean at one end of the section.

We return to sanity and smooth surfaces with a cycle path leading us to Saint-Amand-les-Eaux where we stop at a café proudly boasting of American coffee. Perhaps, only in France would I see that claim as being a positive. We sit at an outdoor table opposite the historic white stone tower, built in the 19th century and housing an impressive forty-eight bells. The young waitress brings us a very acceptable cup of coffee. Suddenly, the bells begin ringing. Although 'ringing' is perhaps too kind and tuneful a word to describe the cacophony of noise that is unleashed over the peaceful town for the next two minutes. The bellringer must be tone deaf. It's a horror of clanging and discordant bashing.

'All that history and he only has one thing to do well,' I say.

'I like it! It adds a human dimension,' Cathie says.

I can see her point. By the end of the torture orchestra, I am smiling. If I lived in Saint Amand, I would certainly be anticipating each morning's recital. Heck, I may even sit in the sunshine, drinking American coffee in support of the tone deaf bellringer. I wonder if he has a hunchback as well?

And so we enter Belgium along a tree-lined bike path beside a wide canal, following lugubrious barges moving giant rocks. It's a peaceful passage through pockets of heavy industry and crumbling buildings that once were working warehouses but are now piles of steel and timber. It's the best way to enter the splendid city of Tournai, blessed with the Gothic Cathedral of Notre-Dame de Tournai and its accompanying belltower, quiet when we arrive. The belfry is the oldest in Belgium and is justifiably listed as a heritage site by UNESCO.

We sit at a café opposite the tower, perhaps awaiting the bellringing? Actually, being in Belgium, we're both eager to try a waffle. I know, it's a cliché, but on our last trip we had the tastiest waffles ever. This one is good, but perhaps a little light. And not enough cream. But then, there's never enough cream.

A woman riding a heavily-laden touring bike pulls up outside the café. She spies Bruce and Aiwa and comes across to introduce herself. Her name is Lotte and she's from The Netherlands. She tells us she's been cycling for a week and is planning to complete the Santiago de Compostella. She is a cycle pilgrim. Tournai, with its ancient church and tower, is a must-see along the route.

'My sister has cancer,' Lotte says, 'She's walking a section and I hope to join her and give support.' She smiles awkwardly, as if she's told us too much already.

'You have a lot of gear,' I say, changing the subject.

Lotte points to her left front pannier, 'My tent here. On the right, my sleeping bag. At the back is my food and cooking gear, On top, my clothes.'

She looks across at our two puny panniers each.

'We stay in hotels,' I say by way of excuse.

'I lost my job,' Lotte says, 'My husband lost his job also.' She sighs. 'So I decided to do this, alone to start, until I meet my sister.' She repeats the word, 'alone' and smiles.

We chat about routes and our bikes. Her Dutch bike is bright yellow and fitted with many extras. It's robust and strong next to Bruce and Aiwa, who both look like they're out on a weekend jaunt. Lotte can't resist ordering a waffle. The three of us sit in the sunshine, quiet, perhaps each living the journey of the other through what we've said. I think of her sister striding through the Spanish countryside, her eyes ahead on Santiago, yet glancing behind waiting for Lotte. I hope they meet up and fulfill their dreams. Lotte talks about her faith, they need to believe. She wishes us God-speed when we leave.

We walk around the ancient tower, not as pilgrims but because it's a lovely building that has stood here for centuries and seen the hopes and dreams of a million believers pass by. As I'm pushing Bruce I feel a strange vibration.

'Cathie, my bike is vibrating,' I say.

Cathie smiles. She thinks I'm making a joke about belief and the spiritual journey.

'I'm serious,' I say. 'I can feel it through the seat.'

'Have you and Bruce been touched by Lotte the pilgrim,' she says.

I wheel Bruce closer to her and say, 'Feel the seat.'

She rolls her eyes.

I grab her hand and place it on Bruce's seat. Her mouth opens.

'It's ...'

'Vibrating!' I say.

'Maybe there's a subway under the square,' Cathie says.

I touch Aiwa's seat. Nothing.

'It'll be fun to sit on,' Cathie smiles.

It seems to be getting stronger.

Then all of a sudden I remember.

It's not the peace and beauty of God's love.

I quickly unzip the top of my pannier and the noise gets louder.

'It's my beard trimmer,' I say.

When I shoved the bike lock back into my pannier after leaving the café, I must have pushed it against my trimmer.

We both giggle.

'God loves a man with a beard,' Cathie adds.

Whenever we've visited Belgium, we're told by the locals to try three things that 'Belgians make the best.' Waffles, chips and beer. For a nation that has so much trouble agreeing on anything - whether it's language, culture or politics, these are perhaps the only binding elements. So on this quick cycle through the country we have decided to put their claims to the test.

At lunchtime, I spy the Big Friterie across a busy four-lane highway. How can we resist. It only takes ten minutes to cross the crazy road. The joint is crowded with teenagers scoffing an obscene amount of chips. We take our place in the queue and wait. The big-hipped woman in the blue apron with her blonde hair tied in a bun has an interesting way of tossing the chips to remove excess oil. She tips our order into a large cardboard carton and we take it to the last vacant table. We are the oldest customers here by twenty years at least. The chips are crisp and crunchy with just the correct amount of salt. I score them nine out of ten as opposed to this morning's five out of ten waffle.

The beer will have to wait for tomorrow, because shortly after lunch we cycle back across the border into France through sleepy towns of brick houses and gardens growing potatoes and lettuce. Once again, we stumble across the Paris-Roubaix cycle path, only this section is covered with hard dirt and follows a canal all the way into Roubaix, past a smear of industry, kebab shops and car-choked alleys. We navigate as best we can into the centre-ville where the grand Hotel de Ville and an expansive Grande Place are surrounded by the crud of commercialism. Once again, the car and capitalism has scarred a town. The burghers of Northern French towns could learn a few lessons from their nearby Dutch neighbours on how to make their town centre more welcoming to residents and visitors. Perhaps a study trip to The

Hague. Or Groningen.

We cycle the six kilometres out of town to our Bed and Breakfast. Madame welcomes us into the tidy garage for Bruce and Aiwa and leads us to an upstairs bedroom with a view over the garden. It's been a grimy long-distance day and we can't be bothered getting back on the bikes for dinner so we walk to a nearby pizza joint. We're earlier than all the locals, as usual. What is it about the French that they dine so late while just ten kilometres north, the Belgians are sitting down to their evening meal at least an hour earlier. Does the sun set quicker just up the road? Do Belgians work harder and need to eat earlier? Or the opposite - are the French still at work and can only dine later in the evening.

I think it's none of the above. The French love their apéritif, their casual evening sojourn at the bar before thinking about the serious question of food. To them, the evening is a time to socialise over a long slow meal and drinks. It's the rest of the world who need to come around to this more relaxed and mature attitude to food and wine.

It's a pity our last meal in France on this trip is a pizza. Sigh.

I do love a cake for breakfast and Madame obliges with a pomme tart among the usual suspects of bread and croissants. On a cold cloudy morning, we cycle along a bike path in the centre of a quiet boulevard past elegant houses and tree-lined gardens. Tourcoing boasts a lovely neo-Gothic 16th century Church of Saint-Christopher and is possibly the quietest town I've seen on a Monday morning. There's hardly a soul about. A lone bus is parked outside the shopping centre, a woman on an e-bike rides towards us and a man in a long overcoat sits outside a café smoking a cigarette. Where is everyone?

Surely it's not another public holiday? I check the font of all knowledge and Google tells me today is Ascension Day. We celebrate our good fortune and Christ's rise to heaven by cycling through the centre of town unfettered by traffic and pedestrians.

Soon after crossing the border back into Belgium, the streets are lined with tabacs. Something to do with higher taxes for cigarettes, I imagine. It's a sad fact that far too many Europeans smoke. We follow a straight road through the border villages. The houses are rather grey and bleak, the road is potholed and the skies are threatening rain.

Welcome back to Belgium.

We come upon a *route barre* sign. The only option is a detour over a train line and along an unfriendly freeway. We wheel our bikes past the barrier and cycle over the unpaved section hoping for the best. A kilometre along, we cruise past the barrier on the other side and rejoin the main road, which features three car dealerships and two 'gentleman's clubs' both painted a lurid shade of pink. I have no idea why they're located in this industrial zone. Or perhaps I do.

The lovely town of Kortrijk is still asleep when we arrive. Boasting one of the largest car-free city zones in Europe, it's a pleasure to wander the streets on our bikes, not worried about holding up traffic or dodging impatient motorists. We cruise into the medieval town square, past the late-Gothic town hall and a belfry topped by a statue of Mercury. Not every building is old, but the vast expanse of the square seems to direct our gaze towards the beautiful and ancient and away from the modern and plain. I compliment the town planners on opening up such a space to people. Not that there are many people here this morning to enjoy its amenity. All the more room for us!

The confusion that is Belgium means the town is predominantly Dutch-speaking despite being only six kilometres from the French border. Which means by the time we find a café that is open on the square, we have no idea how to address the busy waiter. He obliges by speaking English and brings us two excellent coffees - goodbye France! - and an apple cake with cream. We share. Well, I probably eat more. On this holy day, Cathie forgives me my sins. It is a glorious square. And there's not a car in sight. Would it be sacrilegious to say it feels like we've ascended to heaven?

By the time we drag ourselves away from Kortrijk, its citizen have decided to wake up and begin riding their bicycles. And what better way to exit the city than across the wonderful bridge spanning the Lys River, each side flanked by the Broeltowers, the only remaining part of the medieval wall that once ringed the town. They are the perfect towers, each is circular with a single turret, featuring small windows, a tiled roof and an ornate steel flagpole. They were built to withstand invading armies. Although it must be said they were not always successful. The prize that is Kortrijk has been fought over since before the Middle Ages.

From the medieval pont to a sweeping new bicycle bridge which I cycle over twice just to enjoy the sensation of travelling on an expensive piece of infrastructure that was built only for the likes of Bruce and me. Ah, civilisation.

We cycle slowly along the river, regularly passed by Belgian road cyclists wearing Sky or Movistar jerseys and riding like they're rehearsing for this year's Tour de France. Bruce and Aiwa take a more relaxed approach. They are not sprinters but long-distance workhorses. They will still be going long after the road racing season has finished.

In the village of Zulte, we stop at the only tavern in town. It's crowded with extremely well-dressed locals. After church, the pub. A twelve-year-old boy is serving behind the bar. Surely that can't be legal. He takes my order for sandwiches but tells his Dad I want two beers. His Dad pulls the beer. Belgian beer. Yes, the Belgian Trappist beer is world-famous, but if I had to choose the country to cycle through exclusively for beer, it would be the Czech Republic first, Germany second and maybe Belgium would sneak in ahead of France on the podium of beer.

We're both naggingly unsatisfied by the toasted sandwiches.

'There's a bakery across the road,' I suggest.

Cathie reaches for my hand. 'That's why I love you,' she says.

A light cherry butter cake and a stodgy bread pudding are the prefect partners before an afternoon of cycling alongside the river contemplating the dietary problems of a country that boasts chips, waffles and beer as its favourite treats. No wonder they take to the bicycle with a gusto. They need to lose weight.

And then we arrive in Ghent, one of the most beautiful and underrated cities in Europe. It may lack the natural beauty of San Francisco, Sydney or Venice but the few square kilometres of Ghent old town is a wonder built from the Middle Ages. Much of the architecture from this period remains and is complimented by the largest car free zone in Belgium. I know I prattle on about this but if you remove cars from the centre of an old town, the remaining space is flooded by people and markets. Suddenly, what was once a polluted dangerous impersonal space becomes a place for humans. This afternoon we arrive to a city crammed with smiling citizens. There is a giant food market covering much of the inner-city. Hundreds of stallholders are offering everything from bratwurst to sushi. The locals and tourists are doing their best to eat the counters empty. No-one is looking over their shoulder before crossing the street. The pace is gentle and human-scaled. The only thing happening quickly is the consumption of beer. We park Bruce and Aiwa among a stand of hundreds of bikes and join the throng on foot. While everyone is busy looking at the treats on offer, I spend my time gazing open-mouthed at the splendour that is the Ghent skyline.

Within a ten minute stroll is a list of awe-inspiring buildings beginning in the heart of Ghent which houses the Gothic St Bavo's Cathedral displaying the masterpiece by Jan van Eyck, *The Adoration of the Mystic Lamb*, a multi-panelled extravaganza featuring Christ, the Virgin Mary, John the Baptist, singing angels, Adam and Eve, pagans, Jewish scholars - the whole gang is here and looking down on today's congregation of snap-happy tourists and believers.

A few hundred metres away is Saint Nicholas Church, another Gothic pile of slender turrets and a single medieval tower which if you climb to the top looks across the square to the Belfry of Ghent, the tallest tower in Belgium, topped by a gilded dragon. I love a city where I can gaze from bratwurst on a roll to gilded dragons. And not just any dragon. This one is believed to have originated in Norway in the 12th century before making an arduous journey with the Emperor of Constantinople to the Aya Sophia where it stayed for a century before returning to Bruges and finally ending up atop the belfry here in 1384. I hope my bratwurst isn't quite so well travelled.

And so it goes for the rest of the afternoon. Medieval building, photo, beer, building, bratwurst, beer, bridge, photo and finally back to Bruce and Aiwa as the rain starts to fall and clears the streets of thousands of people. They all have the same idea which is to head to the pub. Luckily, Ghent has as many pubs as it does memorable buildings. Places to remember, places in which to forget.

We cycle down a friendly bike street and across another ornamental bridge to our accommodation for the evening. I have booked it through AirBnB and been given directions via a number of rather cryptic text messages. Following these leads, I fish the key to a set of imposing double doors from a letterbox, open them wide and then locate another key hanging from a wall in a plastic bag with a note telling us to walk through the courtyard, past the twenty skeletons of old bicycles, up the ramshackle stairs to the top floor flat. We do as directed and find ourselves in a splendid, and splendidly untidy, apartment overlooking a canal. It's a mess. A three-day old baguette moulds on the kitchen table, clothes hang from the walls, books are scattered on settees and tables and a note informs us to 'make ourselves at home.' How? By cleaning? There is no bed, just a lounge that converts to two single mattresses on the floor. The bed linen is a technicolour scatter of blankets and throws and I wonder if the owner has any idea how to furnish a place for paying guests?

AirBnB is accommodation anarchy. Earlier in this trip we stayed at Vaison with Brigitte who allowed Cathie access to a beautiful house at 11am and offered her lunch and wine while she waited for her stupid husband to climb Mont Ventoux. Brigitte was a goddess of a host - kind, thoughtful and available. She became a friend with whom we have corresponded during this trip.

But the flip side of internet start-ups is this place in Ghent. The owner, a young woman, is spending the night with her boyfriend and renting out her apartment to us. Fair enough. God knows, young people today have it tough economically. But surely AirBnB should issue a list of guidelines to their hosts? You know, simple stuff like don't leave stale bread on the kitchen table for a week; provide linen and blankets; learn how to use a vacuum cleaner. This is couch-surfing at a cost. A pity, because the apartment is wonderfully atmospheric. It reminds me of a painter's studio - a light-filled open-plan space alongside a canal.

The rain falls harder. We had planned to eat in, but there's no way either of us is going near the kitchen. We may well be attacked by a nuclear-proof arsenal of cockroaches. We shower, shrug into our waterproof jackets and take Bruce and Aiwa out, sans panniers. We're off to the pub. It's a Belgian ritual, I believe. There are so many pubs it's hard to choose. The Backdoor; De Bierwinkel; Hot Club de Gand and Defoo are all tempting by name if not by nature, but we eventually decide on the one with the silliest name possible, 11 Pop Up. I have no idea what it means either in English or if there is a Dutch translation that makes more sense. But it does offer an impressive array of beers, many brewed by Trappist monks. I sincerely question the calling of monks who spend so much time brewing ale as tasty as my Ramee beer, served in a jug. Is it eight hours brewing, eight hours praying and the rest of the evening sleeping off the stresses of both? I admire their dedication and order another jug along with a ham and cheese omelette, followed by a waffle with extra cream.

'How long do you think we can stay here,' I ask Cathie.

'Are you scared of returning to the apartment,' she smiles.

'Nah.' I say. 'Well, yeah.'

'Have another beer,' she says, 'It'll help you sleep.'

'And provide antibiotic properties to fend off the diseases we're bound to catch by sleeping on the floor?' I add.

'It's not so bad,' Cathie says. Although she appears to be in no hurry to leave this warm friendly pub either.

Yes, I'm exaggerating. And yes, we survived. AirBnB loses its last B as there is nothing to eat in the kitchen, not for humans anyway. We load Bruce and Aiwa, return each of the keys to their hiding places and cycle back to the centre of town. It's crushingly early and the only place open is McDonalds. Just as I'm about to scream, I notice a line of old men waiting outside a café next door. It's called Exki and opens in five minutes. We join the end of the queue. Wow! What a place. It's gives meaning to the word 'green' both in the colour of the decor and the servings it offers. Croissants, fair-trade coffee, bio bread - the lot for five euro. Plus organic yoghurt and fresh fruit. I go back for seconds. Damn it, I almost consider staying here until lunch. Within ten minutes of opening, Exki is crammed to the rafters. McDonalds next door is almost empty. Sitting next to us are two middle-aged American tourists. They tell us they went to McDonalds on their first day in town, but haven't been back since. They've been here a week.

Full and fulfilled, we complete another cycle tour of Ghent, including the lovely square of Sint Veerleplein where the streetlights are connected to the children's hospital on the other side of town. Whenever a baby is born, the lights in the square flash to announce the arrival. What a lovely simple gesture of solidarity and optimism. On that note, we slowly turn the handlebars to face north and follow the canal path out of town.

What is medieval and timeless in the centre of town fades to the industrial and brutal on the outskirts. An oil refinery, a rusting power station and numerous hulking barges and trucks inhabit the dead zone of industrial Ghent. Luckily, there is a cycle path through the detritus until we reach the safety of the suburbs where newly built brick houses with impressive espalier gardens are plonked haphazardly along quiet roads near green meadows. The overwhelming aroma is of mud and cow. I wonder how long the farms will last. Surely they're too close to Ghent to survive. We follow the N458 past satellite towns, windswept and rather featureless, in a semi-world of urban and rural. We pass an old church with a single elegant steeple beside a newly erected funfair of dodgem cars and a carousel. A kilometre further on we're back among the cows and goats.

It's only a few minutes to the Dutch border. We're leaving Belgium as we arrived, confused and a little lost. Where is the quintessential Belgian? Does he live on a sprawl of farmland in a newly built brick and tile house or in a medieval apartment in one of the most beautiful cities on earth? Does he or she speak French or Dutch? Or

English? Do they want to be a single country or the parliament for all of Europe? Is the only connection between a dairy farmer in his Flemish field and a bureaucrat in Brussels the beer they drink? Urban or rural. Cosmopolitan or suburban. European or Belgian. I doubt these questions will be answered within my lifetime. The Belgium we have cycled through is perhaps a microcosm of the European project. Is it one continent of like-minded people? Or a bunch of nations tired of invading and killing one another? Can they reconcile permanently, or will the troubles in Greece be the flame that burns the edifice to the ground? Which will leave Belgium with a lot of shiny new buildings that once housed the hopes and dreams of a greater Europe. In the future will they be an attractive museum piece, or the beating heart of Europe.

Chapter Five: The Netherlands

We trundle into The Netherlands on a cobblestone lane beside a canal. How very appropriate. It's a short cycle through low-lying fields. The poppies are blooming and the smell is of new mown hay and cows. At Ijzendijke, there's a memorial to thirty-seven British and Canadian engineers killed in an accident in 1944. I can't read Dutch but get the impression it was a flood or similar natural disaster rather than through German aggression.

We stop for lunch at a hamburger joint. The attractive blonde woman at the counter can't speak English, which is unusual in The Netherlands. A man behind me helps with the order. They don't have any burgers left. We make do with chips and chicken nuggets. It's hardly an inspiring introduction to Dutch cuisine. As we're eating, a well-dressed man comes inside and asks if those are our bikes leaning against his plants. Oops. I apologise profusely and move them. He tells me I can park them anywhere on his front cobblestone entrance, just not leaning on his ornamental plants. He can't understand that our bikes don't have stands. All bikes have stands! At least they do among the sensible Dutch. I move Bruce and Aiwa across the road to lean against a lamp post. He smiles and walks off shaking his head. Bikes without stands. A nonsense!

The sun comes out from behind a flotilla of clouds as we breeze into Breeskens, a town we cycled through last year on our zigzag route between St Malo in France and Prague in the Czech Republic. The next ten kilometres will be the only duplication in routes, deliberately so because we wanted to return to the medieval recreation that is Middelburg in Zeeland.

We cycle onto a ferry to take us across the channel to Vlissingen. It's a large boat with space for hundreds of bikes on the lower deck. After setting off from the wharf, the ferry captain slams on the brakes as a sailboat cuts across his bow. The ferry dips and shudders and an amateur sailor never realises how close he came to being squashed.

We cycle off the ferry and take a wrong turn that, by chance, leads us along the dyke protecting Vlissingen from the North Sea. It's a wide path, suitable for pedestrians and cyclists. We stop at a memorial to the Allied invasion on this beach in late 1944 when a force of English, French, Scottish and Dutch troops came ashore and met heavy resistance from the Germans. Fighting raged in the town for three days before the Allies were victorious.

It's a lovely town with a long and continuing maritime history due to its strategic location where the Schelde meets the North Sea. It's popular with 'ship spotters' because nowhere else in the world do large ships pass so close to the shore. Today most of the old salts appear to be eating seafood and drinking beer at outdoor restaurants. We cycle slowly along the cobblestone streets dodging people more interested in menus offering cod, plaice, squid, sole and the local favourite, mussels. Can't say I blame them.

Confusingly, we pass a statue of a man dressed in a blue jacket with cream trousers and yellow shoes. His hair is neatly parted and he looks uncannily like Donny Osmond. I can't imagine what this has to do with the sea-faring life and unfortunately can't find any plaques to enlighten me. Perhaps Donny has a cabal of admirers here in far-flung Vlissingen?

We arrive in Middelburg and easily find our accommodation, the same B&B we stayed in last year. The owners, Sam and Simon have renovated a typically narrow Dutch house into three flights of luxury. Bruce and Aiwa are carried down to the cellar to spend the evening among the Australian and French wine. Bruce promises to be on his best behaviour.

After exchanging lycra for cotton, we walk the streets of Middelburg. The centre of town is largely car-free and we find our way to De Mug, a pub offering seventy brands of beer, including their own brew. Cathie orders a bitter and I choose an amber ale. Both excellent.

Much of Middelburg was badly damaged by the German bombing raids in 1940. The authorities have gone to great lengths to recreate the medieval character of the town amongst the few remaining old buildings. It's a superb recreation. The 12th century Abbey has been converted into a museum and its clock tower, nicknamed Lange Jan (tall John), remains to give a focal point to the old village. We also walk around the former Town Hall, nicknamed Crazy Beth by locals because its clock is always just a little out of sync. It's an appealing building of mixed styles, the 14th century late-Gothic section facing the square is somewhat at odds with the Classical style of the other sides, reconstructed during the 17th century.

I'm a sucker for free alcohol. I admit it. The local Greek restaurant is furnished like a seaside café with fishing nets and starfish hanging from the walls and the taciturn waiter brings us both a glass of ouzo with which to begin. We order more food than we should, avoid the retsina in favour of Greek beer and watch the teenagers opposite holding hands and giggling. Young love. I reach for Cathie's hand.

'I need that hand to grip the knife,' she deadpans.

'My life my love my lasagna,' I say.

'That's Italian, not Greek,' she laughs.

'My life, my love, my souvlaki doesn't really work,' I say.

'Does for me, I love souvlaki,' Cathie says, before returning to her vine leaves.

In the morning, Simon excels with a huge breakfast, prepared early just for us. The old wooden dining table is cluttered with breads, fruit, yoghurt, eggs, ham, cheese and bolus, Cathie's favourite cake, a cinnamon-flavoured round doughball that is absolutely delicious. Simon brings another for me. Lovely man. We chat about the importance of an accurate weather report. Not just for cyclists but for innkeepers as well. It seems they experience weekly cancellations largely based on the weather report. So if the bureau forecast rain for the coming weekend and it doesn't arrive, Simon suffers a financial storm while the town basks in sunshine.

No chance of sunshine today as we retrieve Bruce and Aiwa from their cellar. The rain falls in a fine mist, making the cobblestones shine like polished brass. As always in The Netherlands, I carry a piece of paper in my pocket with a list of numbers indicating which bicycle route we should follow. I call it bicycle-bingo. The country is criss-crossed with numerous paths and the only safe way through this maze is to follow the numbers, even if you're sure you should be heading left not right. The numbers never lie. This morning they lead us through a bevy of lovely villages, along quiet canals and between high hedges on cow farms.

All the way to Veere, a picturesque town on the edge of the inland lagoon, Veerse Meer. We circle the streets. It's the perfect Dutch town. A white-painted old-fashioned lighthouse, a small lake with an island duck hide, a simple church and ornate town hall, a canal where numerous sailing craft are moored. And friendly locals who look up at the rain and wish us a good day. Pity the bakery isn't open yet.

A short distance from Veere we come upon the famous Oosterscheldekering, a nine-kilometre storm surge barrier that helps protect the Netherlands from the might of the North Sea. I can barely contain my excitement, rushing ahead of Cathie to take a photo of what the American Society of Engineers listed as one of the Seven

Wonders of the Engineering World. Okay, so it's not the Pyramid of Giza or the Hanging Gardens of Babylon, but it is an impressive display of man's struggle against the natural elements. And in 2015, it hosted the finish to the second stage of the Tour de France. We're riding on the road of champions. Only much slower.

The barrier consists of sixty-five giant pillars with sixty-two steel doors, each forty-two metres wide. As I cycle past each section, I'm reminded of a huge mechanical shovel operated by large hydraulic arms which drop into the water and hold back the sea or open and regulate the flow of water. The long line of white circular pillars is surprisingly beautiful in the misty rain with the gulls screeching overhead and the dark water lapping ominously against the sixty-two shovels. This being The Netherlands, we have a wide lane all to ourselves to enjoy the scene. Cars and trucks slosh by on a separate road, their headlights vainly leaking through the drizzle.

This wonder was opened in 1986 by Queen Beatrix with the simple yet heart-felt words, 'The Delta Works are completed, Zeeland is safe.' In 1953, the infamous North Sea flood swept through this gap and killed one thousand eight hundred and thirty-five people. The flood covered nine percent of Dutch farmland, thousands of animals perished and many buildings were destroyed. The Dutch, being an industrious and inventive population, vowed the sea would not cause such havoc again. Originally, a dam was proposed but this would have caused the inner sea to lose its salinity and consequently lead to the death of many marine animals and the demise of the fishing industry. Protests ensued. Eventually a compromised was reached. The barrier can be opened to allow the North Sea in during times of calm and closed during storms to keep the population safe. A very Dutch solution.

And today, I'm cycling - no, I'm being blown across the marvel that rose from that disaster. On my own lane, I wander from side to side, peering over the edge to the massive steel gates, designed to last two hundred years. A plaque at the end of the barrier states confidently that, 'Here the tide is ruled by the wind, the moon and we the Dutch.'

Given our inaction on climate change, perhaps the prediction is a trifle optimistic. Although if anyone can combat the effects of this impending man-made disaster, it's the wise and thoughtful Dutch. As if to remind me of that, we pass under the swooping arms of numerous wind turbines. It's the closest I've ever been to these elegant monsters. They are being blasted by a ferocious wind and the sound they make is like a jet taking off every ten seconds. But no-one is out here, just the seagulls and we passing cyclists. Despite the wild conditions, if I was given the opportunity to cycle that barrier again, I'd do it in flash.

We're pushed by the gale to the boathouse at Burghsluis which has a café with a flashing neon sign announcing they're open. I can barely control myself from running to the front door. Inside, I strip out of a soaking jacket, gloves and balaclava, just so the owners don't think I'm a bandit on a bicycle. Time for the greatest Dutch invention apart from the surge barrier - apple cake! It's delicious. I quietly take off my shoes and feel my socks. Today is a two-sock day, so there's a lot of squelching to be done on the immaculate timber floor.

In fact, the weather looks worse than it is, with the flags stiffening in the wind and patches of water puddling on the deck. Four road cyclists walk in, utterly drenched, one is shivering uncontrollably. The owner gives them a large plastic tray on which to put their wet gloves and scarves. They hang sodden jackets next to ours. They look much wetter and sadder than us because on road bikes they lack the protection of mudguards. At a faster speed, the water shoots up from the road and leaves a bandicoot stripe of mud along their jackets. They are nervous of sitting down in the clean booth but the owner just smiles and tells them not to worry. Looks like apple cakes all round!

With the wind at our backs, we cycle along the dykes all the way to Zierikzee.

'If we pedal faster, we'll get there quicker,' I say.

Cathie looks at me as if I'm an idiot.

'And if we pedal less, we'll get their slower, Mr Obvious,' she says.

Zierikzee was one of the towns devastated by the 1953 flood. It has rebounded from that disaster to be a prosperous and welcoming place. We can't resist a restaurant with the name 'Same same but different.' We sit on high stools and order Indonesian soup and a chicken noodle dish. Perhaps the only good thing that has come from an Imperial past is the infiltration into the former Empire's food culture by the citizens of the colonies. The soup is sensational. I recall the best meal I've eaten in my previous visits to Amsterdam was also Indonesian. Perhaps the cry should have went up in the colonies - 'Give us our freedom and we'll give you our recipes!' It would have lead to a less blood-stained past for all we former Imperialists.

On this blessed biking day, the sun makes a brief appearance after lunch as we cruise into the village of Noordwouwe. We're early and the owner of the B&B isn't home so we retire to the pub around the corner where a serious billiard competition is in progress. Lots of studied frowns while chalking cues. And absolute silence, except when some buffoon dressed in lycra trips over a bar stool. Who put that there?

My Trappist westmalle tripel ale is described as having a 'complex smaak.' I can only agree. Cathie orders a coffee and another slice of apple cake.

'That's your second apple cake of the day,' I say. I know, stupid of me. The beer loosened my tongue.

'What's your point,' she says, her voice low and flat. Even the billiard players appear to flinch.

'Noth ... nothing, I was just ... admiring the amount of cream,' I stammer.

Cathie pushes the plate towards me.

'That's it. We go halves or I'm not speaking to you again on this trip,' she says.

'It's three thousand kilometres to Norway,' I say.

'So you'd better eat some cake,' she flashes a smile, 'Or prepare for a very long silence.'

I eat the cake. It's delicious. Any country that serves apple cake in pubs has my enduring affection.

Our room in the B&B overlooks a garden and the exceedingly pleasant hosts have a communal fridge where beer is a paltry one euro and chocolate two euros. The bed pulls down from the closet, the room has underfloor heating and there's a washing machine in the laundry. Oh yeah, and Lianne, our host makes superb tomato and meatball soup which I eat after Cathie cooks us both a dinner of cheese omelette.

'This soup really is sensational,' I say.

'Almost as good as the omelette,' Cathie responds.

When will I ever learn.

I love the Northern European breakfast. Is it the chilly weather or the earlier start that signifies the difference between a Dutch or German breakfast and the Mediterranean variety? Do the Italians and French eat lighter in the morning because they have dined later in the previous evening? The Latin countries seem more interested in cigarettes and coffee in the early hours than their Germanic cousins who choose eggs, cheese, ham and heavy breads. Today's variety is so large it takes Lianne and me three shuttles from the kitchen to bring it to the table.

Yesterday's rain has disappeared in the night and been replaced with a clear sky and radiant sun. There is a 'cat crossing' sign at the entrance to the first village we cycle through. We see neither felines or people. Sunday.

I had trouble leaving the room this morning, not only because of the tremendous hospitality but the football team I support was playing in the Cup Final in Australia. Eight am in Europe is an afternoon kick-off in Australia and Sydney FC were one game away from the Championship. I'm always torn at these moments between my life 'at home' and this slow-cycling adventure. Where does my heart lie? In the team I've supported since their inception or on the road ahead, the warm sun and the promise of apple cake.

I started watching the game. Sydney FC looked disjointed and clueless, despite their stellar season. The sun streamed brightly through the window. I thought of the eighty kilometres, the canals we'd ramble alongside and I knew I had to choose the moment here, not twenty thousand kilometres away. If I'd been in Australia, I would have been in the stadium and every sense would be focused on the game.

But I just couldn't do it here, with my wife quietly reading a book and waiting. I sighed, packed my panniers and we pushed Bruce and Aiwa out the front door. My son Joe texted me the score two hours later. Oh well, at least we made the final and qualified for the Asian Champions League. You can't win them all.

The village of Scharendijke should perhaps be called Scharen*dive* because everyone is in a wet suit on this sunny Sunday. I'm astonished at the number of overweight men wriggling themselves into the sealskins. Snidely, I wonder if they need diving weights. But who am I to judge? I can barely swim and these intrepid locals are diving into the frigid waters of the North Sea. I'll stick to the relatively safety of Bruce on the canal paths.

We cycle across the dyke on Brouwerdam with the calm waters of Grevelingen to our right and the sea to our windswept left. In the sheltered estuary, fishing boats are moored in long lines and winnebagos gather around the small beaches. Seaside is wind surfers and even more winnebagos, unafraid of a little breeze. The Dutch are industriously going about enjoying their Sunday.

Once over the dam, we detour to Ouddorp in search of food. It's a lovely village with a square crowded with cafés. I count five with outdoor tables and chairs. All are closed. What! Surely they can't all be in church? The bells ring as if to question my assumption. Cathie pokes her head into one café. The owner tells her he opens at midday for lunch but not at this heathen hour for apple cake and coffee. The pious sing another hymn and we pagans cycle ever onwards.

In Stellendam, we find salvation and cake at the only café in town. We sit in comfortable outdoor chairs and contemplate the amount of cream cradling our apple cakes. Heaven.

'How long have we been cycling,' Cathie asks.

'A few hours,' I answer.

'I mean how many days,' she says, rolling here eyes.

'Oh, it's twenty-four days since we left Le Ciotat,' I say.

I know where she's heading. It's taken us a little over three weeks to finally get into the swing of this trip. The mistral and long days in the Champagne region made it difficult to settle into the necessary rhythm of long-distance cycling. Without wishing to sound like an old hippie, the tenor of the trip is as important as the landscape through which we're cycling. Here in the Netherlands, we are at ease. The most-bicycle friendly country in the world has brought a constant smile to our faces. Nothing matters only the next few kilometres. We are in the flow.

After cake, we cross another dam with giant sluice gates. It's astonishing standing above these mechanical monsters, trying to comprehend the amount of pressure they can withstand from the North Sea. I imagine every child in The Netherlands grows up wanting to be either a footballer or an engineer, boy or girl.

'We are the Dutch and we can hold back the sea.'

We cross more canals and dykes before racing downhill off a bridge towards an oil refinery port. A giant wind turbine rotor swoops above us. It's so close, I instinctively duck. I'm thrilled to be able to ride amongst so much working industry. In my home country, industry is often closed off, the domain of trucks and men in hard hats. In The Netherlands, everyone is given space - walkers and cyclists can wander between swooping wind turbines, swinging bridges and steaming barges. Rozenburg is marooned on an island in the river Maas. It's very quiet and rather bereft of character with a treeless shopping centre where a few kids ride their BMX bikes across the expanse of cobblestones. Only one shop is open, a Chinese take-away. From the majesty of windmills to the banality of fast food.

But it's a sunny Sunday afternoon and on the other side of town, we roll onto a ferry which, for a pittance, takes us across the Nieuwe Waterweg, one of the busiest shipping canals in the world. Opened in 1872, it allows Rotterdam to remain a vital port, linking the Rhine River flowing into mainland Europe with the North Sea. Such is its value, there are no tunnels or bridges across its twenty kilometre length, just this ferry. Here, cargo is more important than cars and people.

We cycle parallel to the waterweg, racing container ships and battling a headwind. There are lots of cyclists out here, from lycra-clad racers to old men in mock leather coats pedalling creaky bikes in an endearingly haphazard fashion. At Hoek van Holland - literally the Hook of Holland - we celebrate our arrival with yet another apple cake in a café. We amuse ourselves listening to a group of Dutch speak their native language. It reminds me of verbal ping pong - a friendly rhythmic bounce with only the occasional guttural whack. The language reflects the people - pleasant, easy-going yet solid and unflinching.

In the late afternoon, we check into the B&B. The blonde-haired woman with a single tattoo on her left wrist - yes, it's a bird - happily shows us how everything works in our tiny room. If you open the bathroom door the light and fan operates, if you close it and there is no movement, they both turn off. If you push the two buttons and lift, the fly-screen retracts. Pull down ... you know the rest. Simple. There is a communal area at the front of the house, furnished in bright purple and polished wood with deep lounges and expansive windows from which we can see the actions of the working port. In the foreground is a grassy park leading to an elegant tilted glass roofed restaurant on the beach. Cargo ships churn out of the canal and head towards the open sea while across the water idle cranes wait for Monday morning. In the distance, the wind turbines continue their slow graceful dance. It's a fine view with so much activity beyond these plate-glass windows. I pour a beer, grab a handful of free chocolates and flop into the lounge. What a lovely guesthouse. I can forgive any lodging with small rooms if they offer a free drink and a large bowl of chocolates. I'm easily swayed by beer and sugar.

I'm even more convinced I have discovered nirvana when Cathie raids the fridge and cooks a delicious cheese and ham omelette. She also finds a bottle of rosé for five euro. It's a bargain. We spend the evening watching cross-sea ferries cruise past our window and get slowly drunk. Let me rephrase that - we fend the teevening waching pips curse sloely paste out windo and git quikly dunk.

Which explains why I sheepishly admit to the blonde-haired woman in the morning that I broke one of their wine glasses. The table moved! She remains as happy as she was yesterday and tells me to forget it. She also refuses to charge us for the eggs we used to make an omelette. If you're ever in Hoek van Holland, may I suggest an evening in the Gestrand Bed and Breakfast. Only try and act more responsible than a certain Australian cyclist.

It's a cloudy day and a kilometre after leaving town, we're cycling among sand dunes beside holiday parks dotted with cute white single room holiday cabins. Rabbits hop from the path into the spinifex dunes and it's hard to believe we're ten minutes ride away from the capital of The Netherlands, Den Haag or The Hague.

Is there a greater transport pleasure than riding a bicycle into a major city in The Netherlands? We have our own path, the traffic lights seem to always work in our favour and we can cycle slowly and admire the uniform three-storey buildings that make up this fine town. It also gives us more time to choose which café we'll stop at today.

The waitress hands us the menu and we spend a long time trying to decide which coffee and cake to order. When she hears our accents, she says, 'Why don't I make you a flat white. And the carrot cake is great.' She spent a year waitressing in Melbourne and knows the Australian preference for flat whites. The Hometown café in The Hague makes the best coffee in Europe. There. I've said it. We talk with Mila about her experiences in Australia. In short, she loved the country and hated the motorists. 'Don't they understand that tonnes of metal ... can kill,' she says. She tells us about the laws of presumed liability in The Netherlands. Simply put, it's assumed that the operator of the larger vehicle is at fault in any accident. The result? Truck drivers are extremely careful around cars and cyclists, motorists are vigilant around cyclists and pedestrians and The Netherlands has some of the safest roads in the world. 'It's not about punishment, just respect,' she says.

We cycle around the corner to the Peace Palace, where the International Court of Justice resides. It's a lovely building built in a Neo-Renaissance style at the beginning of the 20th century that has witnessed some landmark adjudications in the field of International Law. It was here that the massacre in Srebrenica was ruled as genocide; a ruling was passed that the Japanese government should cease slaughtering whales for 'scientific purposes' in the Southern Ocean; that the construction of the Wall along the West Bank by Israel is a violation of International Law; and perhaps most famously that the United States had violated International Law in supporting the Contras in their fight against the people of Nicaragua. While the Court has some remarkable successes, in the last two cases you can see if a powerful country like the USA or Israel wish to ignore the ruling, not much can be done. Don't you love it when the mainstream media talk about 'pariah states' and yet fail to highlight the abuses of civil rights meted out by Western powers? One law for the wealthy and ... well, that's all that matters in some places, apparently. Long may the Peace Palace reign. We can only hope that all of the rulings of the Courts within its fair walls are implemented.

And now back to the peaceful world of cycling.

It's an easy ride to Leiden, a university town of canals, old buildings and the birthplace of Rembrandt. Unfortunately, his house no longer exists but the city fathers make do with a statue of a young boy looking at a sculpture of the great man. Yet again, the centre of town is dominated by people and bicycles. The town seems to be remarkably prosperous and almost totally consisting of handsome young people. Universities do that. And who can not love a town that has over one hundred poems by famous writers written on building walls? Poems by a diverse bunch from William Shakespeare to E.E. Cummings to the Japanese poet Basho are represented and not all are in English, although translations in Dutch and English are offered on a smaller plaque nearby. Some of the poems fill the complete side of a two-storey building, others are smaller and surrounded by a creeping ivy or a painting as a frame. The project has proven to be so popular that other towns in Europe have adopted the idea, most notably Sofia, the capital of Bulgaria. A win for the poets!

We cycle away from Leiden past a series of houses ringed by a canal no wider than a metre. Each house has its own small arched bridge. The effect is startling. I feel like I'm passing a toy town, everything is shrunken in scale, the type of village a child might design. The houses are simple one-storey brick constructions with large windows, all with white trim and neat gardens featuring bonsai-style trees. It's impossibly cute.

The rain starts to fall as we arrive in the area of tonight's accommodation. We're staying with a teacher friend who lives on an island. And yet we are miles from the sea? I soon understand what she means though as we search for the café where we're supposed to meet. It's a water wonderland of narrow canals threading thin veins through nursery farms. We cross many tiny bridges and follow an endless circuit of bike lanes and soon enough, we are impossibly lost. It's a little Venice of farmland. Eventually, we knock on the door of a house and the lady tells us where to locate the café. It's close to the old windmill, only a kilometre away. Ha! We still get lost making our way to the café which is closed. Oh dear. We sit in a glasshouse out of the rain and I text Michele. She answers that her husband will be along soon in his boat. One of their three boats. Sure enough, Nop putters into view along a canal, under an arching willow tree and adroitly pulls up beside the dock of the café. Bruce and Aiwa are stacked aboard as Nop expertly turns the longboat on a dime and takes us to their island home.

Nop is a genial man with a sailor's beard and a cheery disposition while Michele is friendly and relaxed. They show us around their island, bordered on two sides by canals three metres wide and on the opposite sides by canals you could jump across. But that would only get you to another island. I'm having trouble getting my head around so much water, so well managed amongst the numerous nursery tree farms for which the area is famous. Michele and Nop have built a haven here - with fruit trees, a large greenhouse, a workshed for Nop and enough open space for their students to regularly pitch a few tents. They are such dedicated teachers they host their students, even during school holidays.

After a lovely dinner, Nop takes us out on the boat again for a cruise among the waterways. It's a beautiful evening with the sun setting over the low fields, its last rays streaming through the arms of the windmill. We putter along the main canal and come upon a hand-operated lock. Nop carefully steers us into the chamber before handing me the rudder and jumping onto the dock. With a long pole, he closes the back gate behind us and with considerable strength opens the front chute. I steer haphazardly out of the chamber once Nop casually jumps aboard. I feel like shouting, 'Look, Mum I'm a sailor.' Pity I go and ruin it all on the return journey when I run into an overhanging bridge and damage the foghorn. Nop smiles indulgently. He's used to dealing with rash children.

He tells us the history of this land, explaining that it was originally a peat forest. When the trees were removed to dig up the peat, the land became unstable and was regularly flooded which rendered it dangerous for habitation or farming. So began the building of numerous dykes and canals in order to control the water and reclaim much of the flooded plains. Once stabilised, houses and farms were reintroduced and now the area is again profitable and full of life. An environmental disaster to triumph in the space of one hundred years.

As we fall asleep, I notice there isn't a sound outside. We are truly on a deserted island, here in the middle of farmland Europe. In the morning, we learn that it's Nop birthday. Michele gives him a book on beekeeping, perhaps the only thing missing from his impressive array of skills. I envy any man who can hammer a nail or operate a drill. As well as building this house and being a science teacher, Nop is presently studying for his Masters Degree in Physics. A Renaissance man, indeed.

Michele must leave early on her boat. She stands at the rudder and waves us goodbye, puttering slowly east to where her car is parked a few hundred metres away at the nearest cross roads. Soon enough, we've loaded Bruce and Aiwa onto Nop's longer boat and set course for the same car park. Today we have a one hundred kilometre ride, including traversing Amsterdam on our bicycles. I'm sure we're going to get lost in the big city. Nop has given us some rudimentary directions. The stay with Michele and Nop, albeit short, has recharged our batteries, such is the idyllic nature of their island paradise. We both give Nop a big hug before he drives to school.

While we're loading our panniers onto Bruce and Aiwa, a woman deposits her rubbish bin at the crossroads, ready for collection. She looks at our bikes and begins a series of very straightforward questions. She's not rude, just uninterested in pleasantries.

'Where did you come from?'

'Where are you going?'

'How long will it take?'

'Did it rain in France?'

I load my panniers and patiently answer each enquiry. Soon enough, a man arrives on his bicycle. He stops beside us and listens to each of my answers, cocking his head slightly, perhaps unsure of my accent. Occasionally the woman says something to him in Dutch. To the unwary, the Dutch can seem a little brisk and forward. But I understand it's their desire to speak plainly and clearly, particularly in their second language.

Twenty questions later, Cathie and I begin the slow journey north. Luckily the wind is in our favour and soon we're barrelling between canals, counting the number of geese in the fields. I imagine they migrate here from the North. Maybe I should have asked the lady a few questions of my own. Do the geese return to the same paddock each year? With the same partner? What type of geese are they? Do they ever get shot? Next time, I'll be ready.

The morning unfolds with our bicycle-bingo paths leading us between canals, dykes and through small villages. Hundreds of children are cycling to school. On one incline, four teenage girls stop to allow a row of dairy cows to cross the path. After the cows have gone into the field, the girls race past us laughing and shouting into the breeze. The bikes they ride are big and sturdy but they handle them with ease. I'm pleased to see they're dressed in street clothes, not a school uniform. I hate the way young people are forced to dress by a particular code as if the school is so insecure of their teaching methods they have to impose strange restrictions on their students. Values, morals, and tolerance are important. Not dress codes and petty rules.

We join the Amstel river. Don't you love a river named after a beer! Or perhaps it's the other way round? No matter. The water is choppy in the wind and numerous sailboats bob at their moorings. It's been a morning of scudding clouds and after forty kilometres, we deserve apple cake. And pecan pie. Both with extra cream.

On the way out of Amstelkerke, I spy a bike shop. We enter and I buy my fourth pair of waterproof shoe covers. I admit it. I'm an idiot. A fool. I believe what is written on the label of products. If the woman behind the counter says these shoe covers are waterproof, will keep my feet warm and are long-wearing, I'll hand over my credit card with an optimistic grin.

While I'm doing this, Cathie tries on a pair of waterproof pants. The woman says they're 100% waterproof and breathable. I try on a pair. Thirty minutes later, we both walk out of the store in our new pants. We are impregnable.

Five minutes later, the rain pours down. One of us yells 'Ha!' at the sky and ploughs on. The other suggests we seek shelter because no matter how waterproof our clothes, this is one mighty storm.

I hereby apologise to the owner of the splendid two-storey house near Amstelveer for camping under their rear deck. We were only there for twenty minutes and we didn't sit on the garden chairs. We watched the rain tumble down and make short work of your lovely purple tulips. And then we rode away, still in our new gear, still not sure if it works or not. But we're dry. That's because the sun is shining again. Truth is, I think the pants will work quite well. My previous three pairs of shoe covers haven't worked so I don't really expect this pair to, but at least they might keep light showers at bay. But a long day of rain? Not a chance.

We follow the Amstel through the suburbs of Amsterdam. I remember my previous visits. I have a Dutch publisher for my young adult novels, so I've been here a few times as their guest doing author appearances in schools and interviews with newspapers. It's a lovely town of narrow five-storey apartment blocks overlooking canals, wide avenues with blue and white trams, the drivers ringing the bell whenever an unwary pedestrian looks the wrong way. Bicycles easily outnumber cars and the townfolk have a number of beautiful parks to escape the noise of the city. Of course, every first time visitor heads down to the garish red-light district to see scantily-clad women smile from behind plate glass windows. It's a horrible tourist trap littered with shady types standing outside coffee shops dispensing pot instead of caffeine. Once is enough.

Better to stick to the leafy canals, the Van Gogh museum or the beautiful Vondel Park, a green escape in the heart of the city. On my previous visits, I've performed my work in a number of schools. The teachers and students were an optimistic friendly bunch who all cycled to school and were mystified when I told them stories of Australian children being driven to school by their parents. They regarded this as an embarrassing loss of independence. I could only agree. What self-respecting teenager wants to spend an hour stuck in a traffic jam when they could be cruising around with their mates? It's not the Australian kids fault of course, just a tragic loss of faith by their parents.

In what other country can visitors with limited knowledge of a city, cycle from one side of the metropolis to the other and barely have to stop for a traffic light? The cycle paths are crowded and we're regularly overtaken by hipsters texting on phones, or statuesque women with long hair, jeans and high boots. No-one is wearing a helmet except us. We breeze past numerous cafés and restaurants, scoot across arched bridges, past hundreds of moored canal boats and under leafy tall trees at a gentle fifteen kilometres per hour. All we have to do is follow the bicycle signs to the railway station. It's that easy. In no time at all, we're behind the station waiting for a ferry across the lake. And this being Holland, it's a ferry reserved for cyclists and pedestrians and is free. Over fifty bikes and their riders enjoy a brisk trip across the IJ. On arrival in North Amsterdam, Bruce and Aiwa politely wait for the locals to disembark. It's safer that way. We trundle off the ferry and within a few minutes the city is gone, replaced by open fields, farms and the comforting smell of cow manure. We can't be more than five kilometres from the red light district, the drug cafés and the bustling downtown of Holland's largest city. Extraordinary.

It's a lovely afternoon ride in the sunshine with a tailwind pushing us all the way to the small fishing village of Monnickendam where we stop at the café De Zwaan for soup, toasted sandwiches and a beer. It's a pleasant spot with outdoor tables arranged on a street corner overlooking a narrow canal crammed with moored wooden sailboats. It's very quiet, with only the occasional car rumbling over cobblestones and a man scrubbing the deck of his boat. A dog trots unhurriedly across the road and considers whether we're worth investigating but decides to wander off to the port in search of amusement.

We hop back on our bikes and pedal along the dyke to Volendam, a beautiful village which suffers rather badly from tourist-overload. After cycling past the old marina, we dismount and walk between shops selling all manner of tat - *I Love Volendam* sweaters; clogs; Dutch football jerseys and most striking of all - huge wheels of cheese covered in brightly-coloured wax. The famous town of Edam is just up the road and Volendam can't resist profiting from its prefered location by the sea.

Ice-cream cones seem to be winning the battle for the tourist dollar today with every second person licking a double-scoop. Which is another way of saying I had one and Cathie didn't!

Eventually we cycle away, but not before dodging a gang of Japanese visitors who seem intent on taking numerous photos of a small garden gnome outside a seaside house. I have no idea of the relevance of this particular gnome, but it's selfie central for our Asian visitors. I understand we all have our particular whims while on holiday. I have been known to photograph the insignia of obscure European football teams. Oh look, there's FC Volendam! Its crest is a sailing mast under full sail stuck into half-a-football. Surely that's worth a snap.

After one hundred kilometres as the sun begins to drop over the IJsselmeer, we arrive in Hoorn where we're greeted by the owner of our B&B for the evening. She is a woman about my age who lives in a neat suburban two-storey brick house with the upstairs rooms allocated to guests while she lives downstairs. I would describe her as a 'prickly' character.

'Did you cycle through Amsterdam today,' she asks, by way of a greeting.

'Yes, it was lovely,' I reply.

'You didn't stop at the Van Gogh Museum,' she says, assuming the worst.

'I've been there before. It's wonderful,' I say.

'It's worth a second visit.' she says.

'It was a pleasant ride along the dyke from Volendam,' I say to change the subject.

'Horrible town that. I suppose you liked it?' she asks.

'Well ...' I begin.

'Where are you going?'

'To Norway, hopefully,' I say.

'Hhhmmm,' she says. At least I think that's the noise she made.

'Where did you start?' she asks.

'Marseille in France,' I answer.

'The French can be so difficult,' she pronounces.

They're not the only ones I think to myself.

Cathie and I go upstairs to our large and pleasant room with a view over the side garden. We look at each other, not knowing how to react.

'Maybe she's not Dutch,' Cathie says.

We have never met a Dutch person we did not like. Until today.

When I go back downstairs to move the bicycles to the back yard, the owner asks me for my driver's licence. I know it's a requirement in some countries for guests to provide formal identification, but I've never been asked this before in The Netherlands. I go upstairs and get the licence. She copies the details and tells me that breakfast is served at 9 am.

I've had enough.

'We won't bother. We need to leave earlier,' I say.

She is flummoxed.

'It's free,' she says, 'part of the room charge.'

'I understand,' I reply,' We'll just have to go without.'

Silence.

I pick up the licence from the table and begin to walk away.

'I can make it for 8:30,' she calls.

Normally I'd be gracious and say 'thanks for being so

considerate,' but I don't really want to be in her company for another second.

'Thanks, but we're leaving earlier,' I smile.

'8 o'clock,' she says. 'That's the earliest I can do it.'

I really want to say no, but that would be churlish, so I thank her and scamper away before she can say anything else. I leave my swearing to our bedroom. Cathie understands.

Breakfast is saved by the German couple from the room opposite joining us early in the morning. The owner dutifully provides us with a tasty assortment and we chat to the Germans who are driving around the north for a week. They have a small dog and spend the day taking him on long walks along the dykes. He chases seagulls while they stroll behind. The husband sighs and says, 'Once we took our children on holidays, now we take the dog.' Like Cathie and I, they are victims of the empty-nest syndrome. What to do when the children grow up.

It's raining as we cycle back through town. Children huddle in puffy jackets and pedal even faster to school. I suspect it's the rain making them hurry not an urgency to study. On one path our way is blocked by a herd of milking cows returning to the fields after doing their duty in the shed. A bunch of teenagers text and barely raise an eyebrow as they wait for the path to be cleared. Cathie and I take photos and marvel at the seamless nature of Dutch rural life where bikes, cows and commuting come together.

We spend most of the morning riding alongside cow fields, keeping a close eye on the wind. We're trying to gauge from which direction it's blowing because in a hour or two we have a thirty-one kilometre straight cycle across the famous Afsluitdijk, another Dutch engineering masterpiece that separates the IJsselmeer from the North Sea. We'll be exposed to the elements on this causeway. Will they be friendly or hostile?

After forty-five kilometres we cycle into Den Oever, the town located on the North Sea side of the dyke. We need cake and coffee before beginning the crossing. I suspect the wind will be in our favour and thankfully, the rain has stopped. All the cafés in town are closed. The only place open is a restaurant hosting a conference, due to begin in thirty minutes. There is one spare table and the waitress kindly allows us to sit and eat while they're waiting for the delegates to arrive. Business suits and lycra don't match so we scoff the delicious apple cake and prepare for the cannonball run across the dyke.

We're in luck. The wind is behind us. Without pedalling too hard, we settle into an average speed of twenty-eight kilometres per hour, much faster than our usual pace. It's a wide flat path separated from the roadway. The sun comes out and we gaze across the lake to the horizon. It's magical. Once again, I'm overwhelmed by what the Dutch have created. Constructed in the Great Depression, the dyke closed off the Zuiderzee, a salt-water inlet of the North Sea, turning it into a fresh water lake called the IJsselmeer which is fed by run-off from the polders and the IJssel river. Locks and sluices were built to allow overflow to be discharged from the lake in times of flood.

It's the most exhilarating ride on a flat road I've ever done. The dyke to our left is covered with white and yellow daisies and we're sheltered from a windswept ocean. There are parking bays at regular intervals for motorists to stop and enjoy the scenery. We join them at one viewpoint. Everyone has the amused expression of children. It's an engineer's playground.

Too quickly our adventure on the dyke is over. We coast into Zurich (no, not that one!) and pull up outside the Da Steenen Man Hotel. There is no stoneman present, just a jovial bartender behind a long wooden bar and two workmen repairing the billiard table. We order fish and chips and an Amstel beer and settle in to watch the slow methodical craftsman replacing the green felt of the billiard table. If they check the level once, they check it twenty times. I wonder if they'll ever be happy with the outcome but finally they agree and place the heavy wooden top back on the slate and felt.

After lunch the winds are much more fluky, changing directions at whim. I feel like a tacking sailor, turning left and right to avoid their bluster. Harlingen is a lovely seaside town with large fishing boats in the harbour and sleek new ferries at the terminal. It has a green-domed art deco lighthouse and just enough old sailing boats in the marina to speak of a long history on the water. In fact, the village was given city rights as far back as 1234.

We continue on to Franeker and eventually find our hotel just outside of town. We lock our bikes downstairs and walk to reception. I give the handsome gentleman behind the counter our name.

'Oh yes, we have a problem,' he begins, 'There has been a mix-up.'

After five minutes of circular discussion, I find there hasn't been a 'mix-up.' He just didn't allocate our room from the on-line booking I made two days ago. He asks us to wait and he'll 'resolve the mix-up.'

There's that word again.

Whenever these rare incidents happen, I've been bumped into a better quality room because the hotel feels sorry for the predicament. Alas, we're finally given a room on the ground floor at the end of a long corridor. It should have a sign on the front announcing 'for emergencies only.' Still, I guess we're away from the rest of the guests and their snoring.

We return to Franeker for dinner. It's a splendid old town of cobblestone streets, canals and a town hall from the 16th century. Built on a street corner, the town hall has arched windows and crenellations rising in front of an imposing tower. It's one of only three buildings in Friesland on the list of Top 100 Dutch Historic Sites. A worthy addition.

The Grand café lives up to its name with plush lounges, large photos of Dutch life, the evening sun streaming through tall windows and waiters dressed in pressed white shirts. It undermines this atmosphere by playing the Bee Gees over the sound system but as there's nowhere else to eat in town, we ignore Barry and his high voice while we order. We're still searching for the definitive Dutch meal, apart from apple pie. I choose chicken with brie and Cathie opts for baked fish. I'm not sure how Dutch the meals are, but both are excellent and accompanied by the tastiest rhubarb relish I've eaten. It's served in a large bowl like a vegetable, not a garnish. Which is fortunate because we eat it all. The waiter spies our empty bowl and asks if we'd like a refill. Cathie shakes her head and I say yes. The waiter decides to bring more anyway. And another bowl of chips even though we haven't finished the first serve. Wow. A restaurant that offers refills! Perhaps this is the essence of Dutch food? Comfort food served in large bowls with tasty garnishes and the ubiquitous chips. And cheap beer. Pity the music has degenerated from the Bee Gees to the Moody Blues. But I'm not leaving this table, even if they play Barry Manilow.

We sleep soundly in our isolation tank and line up dutifully for breakfast. A long relationship with hotel food tells me some items should be avoided in the morning. Scrambled eggs left in a heated pan; fruit salad that has more juice than fruit - it's probably out of a tin; and white bread. Today, I stick to hard-boiled eggs, brown bread and cheese. I slip a few cakes into a brown paper bag for later in the day.

It's sunny yet cool and the school children are out in force on bicycles again. They race past us with the abandon of youth. We pass farm houses where one large section is the barn and the smaller area is the living quarters for the family. I imagine the walls are thick.

'How many famous Dutch people can you name?' I ask.

Cathie rolls her eyes. So begins another extended game of displaying our own ignorance.

'Van Gogh,' she begins.

'Guus Hiddink,' I counter.

'Are you going to name every famous footballer,' she asks.

'He's a coach, but ... yes, I was.' I answer.

'No footballers, okay!'

'Rembrandt,' I counter.

We both cycle slowly, our minds wandering the museums of the world trying to remember who else is Dutch.

'William de Kooning,' Cathie says.

I'm impressed.

'Dick Van Dyke,' I say.

'Ha! Just because he has a Dutch name doesn't mean he's from Holland,' Cathie says.

'*Van* and *Dyke* is good enough for me,' I say.

'He's American,' Cathie says.

I know she's right.

'Hans ... the weapons inspector,' she says.

'Hans Solo,' I blurt out.

'Dick Van Dyke and Hans Solo, is this the best you can do?'

'Hans Blix!' I say.

'Well done, but on reflection I think he's Swedish.'

A cow moos from a distant field, the birds sing and a lone cyclist rides towards us. I wonder if I should stop him and ask for help.

'M.C. Escher,' Cathie adds, 'And Vermeer, the painter.'

My mind is blank.

Cathie is smiling. She's thought of someone else. Someone I should know.

'He's not a footballer. He's a writer,' she says.

I dodge a pothole on the path and scan my memory.

'One of your favourite books,' she adds.

This is torture.

'You bought his latest before we flew here,' she adds.

'Of course! Geert Mak,' I say.

'Bravo!'

Geert Mak is perhaps the foremost journalist of the age. His seminal book 'In Europe' plots the story of the continent in the 20th century - a history seen through the eyes of common people, not the leaders and warmongers.

Church bells toll to signal midday and lunchtime and a good reason to cease our 'famous Dutch people' game. We stop outside a pub which has no customers and is playing mindless British pap, sorry, pop music. I always find this a little disconcerting in Europe. Surely music is as culturally important as literature, art and football? And yet, all we hear is English pop from the 60s and 70s. The globalisation of our lives continues apace.

The bartender pours us beer and I notice a Groningen football jersey on the wall. I attempt to start a conversation with him about their recent successes. Somehow, he switches this to talk of the All Blacks Rugby team. I hate rugby. Sigh.

But he does offer us the best hamburgers I've ever eaten. He lists the ingredients - chilli, egg, spices, sambal oelek and good quality meat with a warmed bun, mustard mayo and lettuce. It needs nothing more. In a small village in the province of Groningen I have stumbled across prime Dutch cuisine. Cows and colonialism have combined for this perfect lunch. I forgive him his interest in thugby.

We arrive very early in Groningen and locate our apartment in the centre of town overlooking a canal. The lovely receptionist tells me they don't have a garage for Bruce and Aiwa as the apartments are scattered all across town. So I lug both bikes up three storeys of typically narrow and steep Dutch stairs. Our apartment is sensational, a mix of Asian and Industrial design with big windows looking over a canal and a line of cafés. We have two large lounges, a fully-equipped kitchen, a shower that takes me thirty minutes to work out how to turn the taps on and a rear balcony on which we can hang our washed lycra. It costs a bomb, but tomorrow I'm working at the International School in Groningen, so the taxman can help us pay for one night's indulgence.

We go for a walk around town and are gobsmacked by the number of cyclists. There are very few cars. It's a curious sensation. There is so much activity, but very little noise. Everything moves at a human pace. The sidewalks are wide with space for pedestrians and bike parking. Every bike has its own wheel lock and bike stand, unlike Bruce and Aiwa. Whenever we cross the road, it's easy to make eye contact with oncoming cyclists. We still have to rush to get across because there is so much two-wheeled traffic, but it all seems much more human. I'm astonished. It's not only quieter but there is so much more space. In most streets, there are no parked cars, so vistas open up in front of us.

Perhaps the one image we have of big cities is the noise and chaos of traffic - the blasting of car horns, the jostling of taxis picking up passengers, the heft of buses pulling into a stop. In Groningen all of that is removed, replaced by people and bicycles. It's a glimpse into the past, the present and the future.

Groningen will be the template for all our cities when we've finally given up the car addiction. The 180000 residents of Groningen own 71,000 cars and a whopping 300,000 bicycles. Studies have shown that bicycle journeys make up to 59% of all trips within the city boundaries. All this has ocurred because the local authorities have progressively weaned the citizens from their dependency on cars by providing bicycle friendly infrastructure and simple design rules preventing cars from ruling the streets.

I maybe too old to see this happen in my own backward country, but I'm pleased I got to see it here in The Netherlands.

If there's hope for civilisation, it's in the bicycle.

After wandering in a satisfied daze for an hour, we take a seat at an outdoor café and order two beers and watch the world go past at 15 kph.

Cathie takes a sip of her beer and pulls a face. 'I don't know why I ordered a spelt beer,' she says.

'Did you think it would be healthy,' I ask.

'I don't know.' She takes another sip. 'I like spelt,' she says.

'I like chocolate,' I add, 'but not in my beer.'

'It's hardly the same. Spelt is a grain, after all.'

'Try my dunkel,' I say.

She takes a nervous sip.

'Excellent,' she says.

'We could swap,' I venture.

'Nah,' she smiles, 'It's an acquired taste.'

'Yeah, one I hope to never acquire,' I answer.

A cyclist races past, dressed in lycra, piloting the largest cargo bike I've ever seen. It's the Hummer of bicycles. He's followed by a man doubling his girlfriend on the rear rack while pushing her bike along with one hand and steering his bike with the other. Such dexterity.

Cathie smiles, 'We could try that tomorrow when I get tired.'

As we continue our beer-tasting jaunt around the globe, I notice the large number of people being dinked on bicycles. It reminds me of when I was a teenager. We'd always be giving each other a lift. Cycling in Australia is considered too dangerous now for such childish past times as dinking. Here it seems a matter of course to carry two people on a bike. And everyone who is being offered a free lift is smiling. Childhood. It's a nice place to be.

The next day I cycle a few kilometres to the International School of Groningen. I spend the morning reading my poetry to teenagers. For the past twenty-five years, I have made a comfortable living as an author of books for children and young adults which, in turn, has led me to visiting schools all over the world. I'm always humbled that a bunch of teenagers are interested in what an old man has to say about poetry. Students like Maarten, Tomaz and Cornalie - just three of the many I met this morning - display an optimism that never fails to impress me. I leave the school certain that the future of the world is in good hands, if only we adults would work a little harder to allow these young people to have more of a say in their future.

I'm sorry to be leaving Groningen. Perhaps I'm just displaying my own prejudices, but the locals seemed to be a content and serene bunch - all that cycling has got to help. If I have one slight criticism of the town, it's that the authorities need to build even more bicycle parking garages. The city is overrun with bicycles. Yes, it's a good thing, but existing facilities are buckling under the strain.

We cycle away from Groningen along a wide canal where huge ocean-going container ships are being built. I'm astonished at the size of these hulks. The canal looks hardly big enough for them to make their way to the sea once they're built. And where is the sea?

In the next village, Cathie and I pull off to the side of the road to allow a school excursion to pass - thirty teenagers and two teachers are cycling in an orderly double file. No-one is wearing helmets, everyone is talking all at once and the teachers smile and nod as they pass serenely by.

In the early afternoon, we arrive at the curiously named Oude Pekela, our stop for the evening. It appears to be a village without a centre. We cycle in ever-decreasing circles looking for a town square and perhaps a row of shops. Nothing but one lonely grocery store. I had hoped for one last apple pie before leaving The Netherlands early tomorrow morning, but there are no cafés in town. We make our way to our lodgings on the outskirts of town. It's a tourist park of simple wooden cabins and lush grass for campers. We've booked a room in the main house. The owner, an effusive woman in her forties, takes us upstairs and proudly displays the room. It has a wooden kayak attached to one wall and a giant map of the Dutch coastline, should we feel inclined to use the kayak to go exploring? She shows us where the only restaurant in town is located and after a quick shower we hop back on Bruce and Aiwa and pedal through the empty streets for dinner. Alas, our last Dutch meal will be ... Chinese.

Chapter Six: Germany

As a welcome into our fifth country of this trip, I've loaded a new app onto my smart phone. It's called Komoot, and appropriately, is designed by a German firm. Komoot bills itself as a GPS navigation device for cyclists and walkers. Wisely, it offers a region for free before you have to buy. You simply load your origin and destination into the web-site and select either walking, road bike or hybrid bike and Komoot maps the best route. We've chosen hybrid and it's downloaded the map onto my phone and will now direct me without the need for phone reception and therefore at no cost. I like it already. Despite the rather mechanical female voice, we've called her Marlene. I'd willingly follow Marlene Deitrich wherever she commanded.

Unfortunately, Marlene can do nothing about the weather. We set off in full wet weather gear with the temperature struggling to reach double figures. Marlene proves her worth almost immediately by taking us down a flower-lined narrow path between canals. It's barely wide enough for two bicycles and is stained with duck droppings. The white flowers brush against my leggings. It's a lovely farewell to The Netherlands, which I hereby dub the most sane country on earth. Bicycles and windmills - two ancient inventions which will power our future. The Dutch are masters of both. I was so impressed, I wrote an article for The Guardian on what our politicians could learn from the Dutch. Perhaps cheekily, I suggested I accompany two significant Australian anti-cycling politicians on a 'fact-finding mission' to The Netherlands. I'm still awaiting their response.

Once into Germany, the land holdings appear smaller and the canal disappears. The only constant remains the weather and the large number of cows in the fields.

'What's the collective noun of calves,' I ask Cathie.

'A slaughter of calves?' she says.

'A doom?'

'A banquet!'

'A vacant?'

'A huddle?'

Fortunately, a village looms ahead, diverting us from our morbid wanderings. Time for German cake! The village is appropriately named Weener and welcomes us with a clearing sky and a large bakery. Before entering, I open the door for a lady trailing a very long extension cord from the bakery out to her sausage van. She's the wurst lady and is open for business with a line of Saturday shoppers already waiting. We sit in the warmth of the café with our cinnamon apple donuts watching her dispense a seemingly endless supply of sausages to the villagers.

Because of the magic of Marlene, this morning is a constantly changing platform of cycleways - quiet back roads, sandy trails and hard packed dirt taking us between small villages and through forests and open fields. Despite her mechanical voice, I love her already. We have already learnt to trust her decisions. Even though the road may point firmly ahead, if Marlene says turn right, we do as she commands and are inevitably rewarded with a scenic cycle through an old forest or beside a gushing stream. She really is a marvel.

I know what you're thinking. We're being chaperoned around Europe by modern technology.

Absolutely.

If Marlene keeps us off main roads and offers quiet country lanes, who am I to argue. I'm here to see the countryside, not endless highways. At Westoverledingen, Marlene directs us to an old rail trail. Cathie loves rail trails. She smiles and reaches for my hand. We unsteadily hold hands and cycle slowly along the dirt path. The birds sing in the forest and as we round a long slow bend a deer bounds across the path. Wow!

'It's good to see there is still wildlife in Europe,' I say.

'So they can be shot by a French man who wears a red wig,' Cathie giggles, remembering our dinner a fortnight ago in Lanty-sur-Aube. I still don't understand the wig.

We arrive in Barssell at lunchtime. The weather has improved and with sixty-five kilometres already completed, I'm in the mood for German food. The first restaurant is located at the port on the river. It has wide windows and lots of customers. It looks promising until we see the name - Texas Grill. It may offer authentic German food, but we want bratwurst not 500 grams of steak. We cycle into town and find a budget option. The woman behind the counter has a tattoo of a swallow on her wrist and wears a heavy metal t-shirt. We order kraut salad, bratwurst and chips. Somehow, she forgets to bring us the bratwurst so we make do with cabbage and chips. Well, we said we wanted German food. The beer is excellent.

After lunch, we cycle past a farmhouse with a sculpture of three storks, one carrying an infant in a pouch. Someone has just had a baby. For the next five hundred metres, scores of old baby clothes are strung along the power lines - cloth nappies, pyjamas, one-piece suits, little shirts and trousers - every few metres. The parents must have raided every Red Cross store within a hundred miles to find so many clothes. They flutter in the breeze and remind us just how joyful the arrival of new life is for a community.

The farmland of cows and open fields are replaced by nurseries boasting an infinite variety of bonsai trees and espalier designs. Alongside the floral art are rows of azaleas, rhododendrons and hibiscus or pine trees shaped as pom poms, stately rows of Tuscan pines and avenues of arid desert pines. It's a smorgasbord of ornamental trees and shrubs and it goes on for miles. I can't believe all of Germany has a need for that many Tuscan pines?

It's a relief to escape *Gardenland* and enter Bad Zwischenahn, a resort town that housed the largest Luftwaffe airbase in northern Germany during the Second World War. Consequently, the town was heavily bombed near the end of the conflict. The airbase is now a golf course which I find rather amusing. The town survives as a tourist destination for locals from nearby Bremen and Oldenburg. The lake is suitable for swimming and boating and supplies the restaurants with eel which is smoked and touted as a delicacy. We have coffee and cake while admiring the bullrushes lining the banks of the lake. A lone sailor in a sleek polished wooden boat sets off across the water. With that headwind, I don't like his chances of making the other side before sunset. Perhaps all small boats should be fitted with pedals?

There are even more nurseries as well leave Bad Zwischenahn. *The Big Bonsai* has acres of trees sculptured into a myriad of shapes - elephants; storks; prancing horses; one pine looks like a waiter trying to carry eight plates; two shrubs appear to be dancing across the lawn.

Further on we pass a stark white timber and glass building called the Explosives Wellness Centre. Underneath this title is an advertisement for beer. I'm not sure of the calming properties of explosive wellness, particularly when mixed with beer. Perhaps you need this combination after spending all day trying to turn a shrub into a giraffe?

After another day of over one hundred kilometres, we arrive at our guesthouse just outside of Rastede. The owner is a gruff man who dutifully informs us of our obligations to arrive at breakfast at the appointed hour. He also tells us the restaurants are just a quick walk up the road. It's the road from which we came and we saw no restaurants. We take Bruce and Aiwa for a pre-dinner pedal. It's five kilometres to the town centre. The only inexpensive German restaurant is booked out.

Sigh. Persian or Chinese?

The Safran restaurant is a good choice. A welcoming decor, friendly waiter and cheap beer. We order a Chicken Barg with buttery rice and a delicious Lamb Ghormeh Sabzi, a fragrant stew perfect for dipping bread, of which we've been given a large pile. I love the way restaurants in Germany always offer the local beer, not the generic variety. We order two more glasses of Oldenburger pilsener. I couldn't be happier.

On the way home we cycle past the Rastede Schloss, a welcoming two-storey castle with eleven upper-storey large windows, four chimneys and surrounded by a stark forest. After I finished counting the windows, I checked my smart phone to discover it's owned by the Duke of Oldenburg who is married to Princess Ameli of Lowenstein-Wertheim-Freudenberg. They have three little Dukes and a Duchess.

I'm always highly amused by titles. Simply being born to two people allows young Alexander von Oldenburg, the first born of Christian and Ameli to call himself a Duke for the rest of his life and to pass on this prestigious pile of pretentiousness (if you'll pardon the preponderence of Ps!) to his heirs. While the intelligent hardworking kid, let's call him Gunther Schultz, who lives down the road has to work his heart out to get a job or attend university and buy a home.

Perhaps I'm being unfair. Maybe Christian and Ameli open their castle regularly to the townsfolk for fairs and conferences and parties. Maybe Gunther spends most of his afternoon kicking a football with Alexander on the regal lawns. Maybe dear Gunther will marry Duchess Katharina and move into the Schloss.

Oh look, rising above the castle now is a flying pig.

We're welcomed in the morning by sunshine and hard-boiled eggs. Perfect. It's a lovely Sunday free of traffic as Marlene leads us once again along country lanes and down hard-dirt trails in the forest. Within the first five kilometres, we pass two stone war memorials and a cemetery set in a grove of trees, the sun filtering through the leaves onto the five-metre high white cross.

We also pass signs for three cafés and alarmingly each offers a special deal on cake and coffee. We reluctantly cycle onwards. With one hundred and ten kilometres to cycle today, stopping so soon is indulging just a little too much. The village of Brake on the Weser River is a quiet ghost of docks and locked factory gates. Even with Marlene, we get lost trying to locate the path along the river. We eventually give up and follow the road to the ferry crossing. Four cars, ten cyclists and a pedestrian board for the short journey across river. As usual, I hold out my hand full of coins and hope the jovial ferryman will take what is required. He does even better. He takes all the coins from my hand and returns us a single shiny two euro coin. Any less weight on a bike is a good thing.

On the far bank at Sandstedt, a dog show is in full bark. The arena is surrounded by hundreds of identical tents, as if an alien race has landed and set up base here by the river. The dogs prance around the enclosure led by their overweening patrons. The sound is deafening. Not the barking dogs but the accompanying disco music. Has there been studies done showing that dogs like disco? Or are the organisers trying a little too hard to rev up the crowd. Doof doof music on a Sunday morning is not my slice of heaven. Aliens indeed.

We retreat around the corner to a bakery where my heavenly slice is sugary, buttery and yeasty. I've forgotten its name but it had me dancing and clapping much more than any disco music could hope to achieve. The route detours away from the road and takes us along a lovely brick paved bike path through a glade. I'm always a sucker for sunlight through trees. Although the path is rough, once again we have reason to thank Marlene for her wise guidance. We emerge from the forest into a wide field of freshly-slashed grass. The birds are singing, the sun is shining, a stream gurgles nearby and a distant plane leaves a wisp of vapour across the sky. On a hill is a white-painted church of muscular proportions surrounded by an immaculate cemetery.

We've been in this fine country for twenty-four hours and are still waiting to savour true German food. The last village we cycled through had two Italian and a Turkish restaurant. After sixty kilometres, in Beverstedt we must settle for Italian as it's the only place open. I know Germans have a great affection for their southern neighbours. In summer, Italy is swamped with German tourists eating them out of pizza, pasta and gelato. Perhaps a few enterprising Sicilians have decided that summer is not enough. Consequently, every town has a touch of Rome and a spice of Istanbul. But, I'm in Germany and want German food! Maybe tomorrow.

Having said all that, the big-boned fräulein with her hair knotted in a long ponytail serves me a magnificent bowl of penne arrabiata. She is as cheerful and sparkling as sunshine on the Isle of Capri.

And now, dear reader, I need to enter somewhat seedy territory in this travel memoir to alert you to an activity Cathie and I do each morning and sometimes after lunch. Skip over the next paragraph if you are squeamish.

We retire to the bathroom and rub a buttery creamy substance on our bottoms. Not each other's bottoms, I hasten to add although I regularly offer. Chamois cream helps avoid lycra rash and is essential on long-distance touring. A dab on the inner thigh and a helping on the ... ahem ... sit bones and we're primed to cycle another one hundred kilometres, no matter what the temperature. It doesn't leave a stain and is a magic potion as far as I'm concerned. After pasta, we lather up and feel like new again.

A kilometre away from Bremervorde, I hear Freddie Mercury booming out a rhapsody. Across the road a teenager is slumped on the grass. He's drunk or has been struck down by Freddie's high notes. A minute later, we come across two young people in what can discretely be called a 'mutual affection wrap.' As Freddie gets louder, the bodies start piling up. Another man staggers along the footpath towards us. We take to the relative safety of the road. Two more drunks sway across the road. Either there's a mass party happening nearby or Freddie's operatic qualities have turned the town into a bunch of swaying zombies.

Finally, we arrive at the music festival. Hundreds of young people and those old enough to know better are bouncing along to Freddie. Bremervorde has been fought over these past one thousand years because of its strategic location between the Bremer and Weser rivers. Now it appears to have surrendered itself to the excesses of alcohol and thundering 70s rock. 'Mama, just killed a man' ... indeed. A few kilometres up the road we come upon three men pushing a go-kart full of beer. One of the men has a long trail of toilet paper coming out of his coat pocket. He's wrapped the excess around his neck and chest. He hears me approaching and shakily moves off the path. We both smile - me at his wedding train of paper and he at the world.

It's an easy flat road all the way to Stade on the lower Elbe river, where our lodging is situated just outside of town. Stade has a turbulent history, ruled by the Saxons, Swedes and Danes who coveted a strategic slice of the Elbe. In modern times, heavy industry has blighted some of its charms with Airbus and Dow Chemical setting up factories on the Elbe. Where there's industry, there needs to be power generation. In the dirty decades of last century, Stade was home to both a nuclear facility and an oil-fired power station.

Germany is now hailed as the world's first major renewable energy economy with a large percentage of its power generated by wind, biogas and solar. The decommissioned dirty fuel stations of Stade are testament to what can be achieved in a short period if governments have the will. Meanwhile in my country, our numbskull of a Prime Minister has called coal 'good for humanity' and said it has 'a big future.' Consequently, we are the biggest emitters of greenhouse gas per head of population in the world. A shameful record.

Which makes me very happy to be on my human-powered bicycle trundling through the holiday streets of Stade to our hotel where we're welcomed by a young man who shows us up to our first floor room. I draw back the curtains and see a wild deer grazing in the paddock. After a quick shower and lycra rinse we walk to the hotel restaurant, following a busload of senior citizens. Luckily, they're diverted into a large dining room at the rear while we get the front room all to ourselves. We order two excellent dark beers and I can't resist the house special - a pound of white asparagus. Cathie chooses a dish of three different fish fillets and boiled potatoes. Finally, we are eating German food. I love how Europeans eagerly await the white asparagus season. When it arrives, every restaurant has a 'spargel special' devoted to the luscious vegetable.

Asparagus has been sought after since ancient times with the Emperor Augustus creating the 'asparagus fleet' for transporting the vegetable back to Rome while the Egyptians decorated their buildings with asparagus-inspired friezes. Grown in Germany since the 16th century, I'm pleased to learn that half of the crop is still sold in roadside stalls and at country markets. My white gold comes served with a hollandaise sauce and is wonderfully delicious. It's an enormous plate of vegetable, so I gallantly offer Cathie a few tender threads. She responds by dumping boiled potatoes dripping with butter on my plate. We couldn't be happier.

Monday morning and the first person we see on the bike path is a young woman in moleskin trousers and a riding jacket leading a large brown horse. She smiles broadly. We will be spending the day riding our favoured steeds. In the fields beside the path, I spy a duck, a dove and further on a rabbit hiding in the long grass.

Near Drochtersen, in a fenced enclosure beside the river is a flotilla of bright orange lifeboats, each one on its own trailer. A cross between a hard plastic submarine and a tug boat, I wonder how it would be to be set adrift in a raging ocean in this enclosed coffin. While they look buoyant and watertight, I get the impression they'd roll 360 degrees in big waves. Do they come with seatbelts? Further along the wharf is a drill area where one of these boats is attached to a launcher at a 45-degree angle, ready to be dropped into the river.

We follow a path strewn with sheep droppings beside a dyke, slowly overtaking the lumbering container ships heading to the North Sea. We have to stop every few hundred metres to open another farm gate to prevent the sheep from escaping. They munch the grass and ignore us. We arrive at a narrow creek with a raised drawbridge. From our vantage point, I can see the ferry we have to catch to cross the Elbe. But our path is blocked by this raised bridge. The sign tells us it begins service at 10am. It's 9:45. Sigh. We park Bruce and Aiwa against the fence and watch the large ferry come into dock and unload its cargo of cars and motorcycles. It begins the return journey at 9:55am. But as it takes off across the wide Elbe, I notice another ferry is already half-way across the river steaming our way. As if on cue, a man cycles up to the the operating post opposite our bridge. He wears an official uniform of orange overalls and a peaked cap. He takes something from his panniers and throws it to the sheep who have all come to the fence in expectation. A morning treat. He climbs the stairs to the control tower and immediately begins lowering the drawbridge, just for us. We mount our bicycles and wave as we cross the bridge and cruise down to the Elbe, just in time to cycle aboard the ferry. We're joined by a hulking mass of Winnebagos and Harley Davidsons.

The motorcyclists pull up beside Bruce and Aiwa and give them a nasty fright. Such a cacophony! The six men get off their bikes and remove their helmets. They have bad haircuts and large beer guts. One of them has his name 'Horst' stitched onto the sleeve of his leather jacket. They all have tattoos.

Cathie hands me the lip gloss and says, 'I dare you to apply it while these blokes are watching.'

How can I resist? I make like Marilyn Monroe and pucker.

Horst and his mates don't even notice. They are too involved in looking at each other's hogs. What is it about men and motorbikes? Half-way across the Elbe a few motorists get out of their cars and start taking photos of the motorbikes. One stumbles into Bruce so involved is he at getting the right angle.

I'm pleased to cycle off ahead of the hogs and motorhomes. We have a lead for all of thirty seconds before a blitzkrieg of heavy artillery rumbles past. Shudder. The bikies go off to drink beer and eat schnitzels. The weedy Australian cyclist with lip gloss and lycra slowly cruises into Beidenfleth where a lovely café has a lunch special of potato and leek soup.

After lunch, for the first time since the rigours of Mont Ventoux, I hit a fatigue wall. No amount of creamy soup can starve off the accumulated tiredness of two thousand kilometres. I consider lying down in a grassy paddock and falling asleep until summer but we still have fifty kilometres to go. I share a chocolate bar with Cathie. It's a cloudy cool day, perfect for cycling. Marlene has chosen a delightful route between open fields and through numerous sleepy villages. I decide to ignore my lethargy and appreciate the countryside. Chocolate always helps.

As we cycle into Wacken, two foals canter alongside our road. On a lamp post, someone has attached a cute birdhouse. Ahead of us, a young man rides a motor scooter so underpowered Bruce almost beats him up the hill. This is not what I expected from Wacken - the home of the world's largest metal music festival. *Wacken Open Air* is attended by over eighty thousand headbangers each year, hosting bands with such wonderful names as *Grinning Sinner*, *Grave Digger*, *Primal Fear* and my favourite, *Gutbucket*.

I admit to going through a Black Sabbath and Led Zeppelin phase when I was a long-haired spotty teenager, so I can see the attraction of Wacken. I'm particularly taken with the Open Air logo which is a bull's skull painted on a fifty metre high tower in town. Opposite the tower is a tattoo parlour, although it's closed for the season. That's more like it - skulls and tattoos, not birdfeeders and foals!

As if inspired by *Cannibal Corpse* and *Sweet Savage*, the sun finally comes out and we breeze downhill all the way to the Kiel Canal. Of course, there's a cycle path beside the canal and we jauntily follow a number of yachts under motor power heading home from a day on the North Sea. The canal is ninety-eight kilometres in length and allows container ships and pleasure craft to sail between the Baltic Sea and the North Sea, avoiding the potentially treacherous route around the Danish Jutland Pensinsula.

In the late afternoon, I'm feeling much livelier and celebrate with a superb rhubarb cake and a beer at a kiosk beside the canal. As I'm spooning a slice of cake into my mouth, a giant vessel powers along the canal, not fifty metres away. I'm staggered by the size of the ship ploughing through such a narrow canal. This behemoth belongs on the ocean not steaming past fruit orchards and cow meadows. Astonishing! I'm always excited by industrial machines like this cargo ship because I can't operate them myself and I have little idea how they work. They are baffling and beautiful at the same time.

After crossing the canal on a dinky ferry, we arrive in Hamdorf, a village that looks too small to have a hotel. The Inn is easy to find but the front door is locked and it looks very dark and desolate. I knock loudly, not really expecting a response. A gruff old man comes to the door. I suspect he's been dozing in a back room. He leads us across the car park to a separate building. We've been given a large apartment for the price of a cheap hotel room. I'm impressed. The old man smiles benignly at our surprise. He even forgives me for asking twice if the hotel is serving dinner tonight. He repeats opening time is 6pm. He shows us where to lock Bruce and Aiwa in the garage next to ten rental bikes. They look brand new and unused.

Dinner is a huge surprise. What was a sleepy village gasthaus with no-one around an hour ago is now a full restaurant on a Monday evening. They have kindly reserved the only spare table for us. We are also the youngest diners. Nearly everything on the menu that we can translate is fish. Cathie orders the drei Gegrillte Fische - salmon, redfish and cod - accompanied by a huge bowl of boiled potatoes and horseradish. Real horseradish! I also order three grilled fish, but I'm unable to identify what they are other than extremely tasty! My side dish is a bowl of vegetables and asparagus.

In Australia, we claim the freshest seafood caught in the cleanest waters and yet much of what is served in restaurants is tasteless and bland. There is something to be said for centuries of knowledge on how to cook certain foods. I order a Flensburger dark ale and Cathie has a riesling and this perfect meal costs only thirty euro. No wonder it's crowded on a Monday.

Breakfast is at 7:30am not 7am, so why are two Australians dressed in lycra standing outside the hotel, waiting and watching the approaching dark clouds? Because they think their hunger will wake the owners. Alas it does not, so we return to our lovely room and watch the cows breakfasting in a grassy meadow. When we are finally admitted, we eat a rather large amount, perhaps to compensate for the extra thirty minutes? I love the variety of a German breakfast, with my current favourite being a soft-boiled egg on a roll with cheese.

The dark clouds and breakfast have vanished as we set off on a cool morning, heading directly north. The village of Hohn is well-catered for with cafés, service stations and a hair salon. A lady in a grey overcoat and bright red shoes waits outside the hairdresser. I fear she will have a longer wait than we did at breakfast. It's still very early and there are few people about and hardly any traffic. Perfect for cycling. We follow a tree-lined farm road of cows and large timber barns. It's songbirds and cow bellows with not a mechanical sound to hear apart from the whirring of bicycle gears and the rub of tyres on asphalt. Dare I say it? Not a puncture in 2,000 kilometres of cycling. My gentle steed Bruce is not like my previous bike, Craig who delighted in getting punctures almost as often as Cathie and I eat hot meals. Yes, I'm exaggerating but not by much. I loved Craig, but I love Bruce's reliability even more. Touch wood.

Kropp has a very busy backerei so we stop for a danish and a coffee. Unfortunately, it's a franchise bakery, so the cakes are a little sweet, but we eat them anyway. Despite it being only one week before summer, all fifteen diners have heavy jackets slung over their chairs. Everyone is wearing 'outdoor' clothing - it's been adopted as winter apparel for everyone from teenagers to pensioners. I guess visiting the local café is going outdoors?

A fighter jet zooms overhead a few hundred metres above ground. His wheels are down, yet he doesn't land at the nearby base. He guns the engines and does another loop. He does four screaming loops in the time it takes us to ride a few kilometres. If we hitched a ride with him, we'd be in Norway in a few hours. Each time the pilot approaches the landing strip, I imagine he looks down at the Burger King restaurant on the main road and considers strafing the installation - not to hurt anyone, but to be rid of the eyesore.

The Schleswig Airfield was a base for Messerschmitt fighters in World War Two. After the Allies took control at the end of the war, it became a vital component in the 1948 Berlin Airlift, with planes ferrying supplies to the Allied section of the fractured city after the Soviets had closed the road link between Berlin and West Germany.

At Schleswig, Marlene takes us on a lovely detour through the grounds of the imposing Gottorf Schloss, situated on an island in the

Schlei, a narrow inlet of the Baltic Sea. It's a muscular four-storey building with lines of windows on either side and a circular turret at the rear. Unfortunately, someone has decreed a car park should be placed at the front of the building, so the sightlines are disturbed by Mercedes bonnets and BMW roofs. I much prefer the rear of the estate which has a expansive patch of grass, a lake with a statue of a man wielding a large wooden club and stepped gardens leading up a hill. We follow the path beside the gardens and within a few minutes we're back on a lonely country lane. We cruise through numerous villages in the afternoon, all of them quiet and without restaurants or cafés. Oops, it's lunchtime and yet again, we have forgotten to pack a picnic from the breakfast offerings.

For the past hour, we've been following green bicycle signs and yellow walking signs. When we pass two young people with backpacks and a pet dog, I realise we're on a pilgrim trail, one of the many scattered throughout Europe, all heading to the Camino de Santiago in Spain. I'm constantly amazed at just how many people are now setting out along the Way of St James, looking for inspiration or forgiveness or revelations or perhaps just wanting to escape the humdrum of their daily work. Who can blame them. Walking is relaxing and healthy ... and almost as much fun as cycling.

We pass a cute pilgrim's hut, built of rough-hewn logs in a field. On the hill is a church. The pilgrims always choose a pleasant route and I bet they're smart enough to carry their own food. I'm starving. It's 2pm and there's no chance of a restaurant anywhere near here. Cathie and I eventually come upon a service station. Look away now, dear reader, as we scoff two pre-wrapped cheese sandwiches while sitting in a hard plastic booth, drinking machine coffee.

'Tomorrow, we'll raid the breakfast hamper,' I say.

'The place we're staying doesn't offer breakfast,' Cathie answers.

'What?'

'Or dinner.'

'Oh.'

'But it does have a kitchen, so I'm cooking.'

'Cheese omelette again?'

'Is there a hint of sarcasm in your voice.'

'I love cheese omelettes.'

'Tomorrow we'll stop early for lunch.'

'Tomorrow we'll be in Denmark.'

Jurgen is an amiable man approaching retirement age with a motorcycle in the garage and a wry sense of humour. The lodging he offers is the ground-floor of a house just outside of Flensburg. When I hand him the cash for the apartment, he doesn't even bother to check it, just stuffs the notes into his jacket pocket. He lets us use his washing machine and we decorate the apartment with hanging clothes. In the late afternoon, we catch a bus into Flensburg. After a month at the slumbering pace of bicycles, I'm hanging onto the railing at the speed of public transport.

We alight in the centre of town and the first thing we see is a simple yet captivating fountain that shoots an arc of water a few metres into the air from a variety of angles. It's so simple yet I could watch it for hours. Except my beautiful travelling companion wants cake and she wants it now. The raspberry tart is washed down with an excellent macchiato.

We follow the pedestrian arcade down to the port. There are lots of second-hand shops in town, some old-fashioned dusty places with serge jackets and brocade dresses as old as I am, others much more swish selling designer labels at prices that don't look 'second-hand' to me. Flensburg has the rather curious distinction of being home to the last Nazi government in Germany for one week after Hitler's death and now is home to the largest erotic mail-order company in the country. Lingerie and fascism, dildos and defeat, sex toys and swastikas.

Despite this, it's an attractive town of old stately buildings and a captivating waterfront with a church rising on a hill on the far side of the port and wooden clippers tied up at the boardwalk. Men sit and fish on the old wharf. I wonder if there's a waterside town in Europe that doesn't have a group of old men sitting, fishing, smoking and watching the world go by? They appear to be doing a lot of casting but with little luck. We retire to a pub for a Flensburger dunkel and consider whether we need sex aids and the latest erotic video? We decide on a block of local chocolate instead.

Tomorrow we leave Germany. It's been a pleasant series of one hundred kilometre plus days across an area of the country that is rarely visited by tourists. Marlene has guided us away from the busy roads and taken us through bountiful fields of green and across numerous rivers and streams. While the north doesn't have the wow factor of castles and vineyards offered by the Danube or Rhine routes, I'm always impressed by the cycling infrastructure, the food and beer and the friendliness of Germans. Tomorrow we enter Denmark.

Chapter Seven: Denmark

The morning dawns cold and cloudy with a strong chance of rain. We eagerly dress in freshly-washed lycra with an extra layer, just in case. The best way for a cyclist out of Flensburg is not to enter in the first place - that is, we take a rather long ring road that leads us into Frøslev, a Danish border town of two pizza restaurants, a Red Cross store and a hair salon. I'm expecting much better cycling infrastructure than we're currently offered. We chug along a stretch of road with the bicycle path separated only by a noise ribbon. Fortunately, the cars give us lots of space. We are a long way from Copenhagen, the capital of cycling.

The houses are painted white and stout in frame and the fields are a patchwork of canola and cows. In many ways, this reflects our eating habits on this journey - grain and dairy. Passing through a quiet forest, we hear gunshots, four quick blasts. Hunters? A few hundred metres ahead a deer is stencilled on a roadsign, warning motorists. Until I become a vegetarian, I can't blame hunters for catching their dinner. It's more than I do.

Is Aabenraa the first town in the index of a World Atlas?

In fact, I later learn that the residents argued forcefully to retain the double A when the central government wanted to change it to a single letter. They feared losing their status at the top of the index. We cruise down a hill to the large and expansive bay bookended by a coal-fired power station at one end and oil refinery tanks at the other. In between is a marina brimming with luxury craft and a fine stretch of white sand.

The town rises to a gentle hill where the main street is a cobblestone arcade of pedestrians and a ridiculous number of clothing stores, all displaying the new season stock on the street. It's like cycling through a fashion warehouse. Polo shirts are selling for 300 kroner which is $60 Australian dollars - twice the price they sell for in my homeland. A print t-shirt costs 400 kroner. I'm no fashion icon, but I wouldn't be seen dead in either of these shirts that I fortunately can't afford to purchase. We're struggling to find a café among all this obsessive retail.

Finally we locate a likely candidate down a narrow lane where lots of teenagers are hanging out, chatting and texting. It seems more canteen than café, but serves a delicious nutty danish pastry and a good coffee. The young man behind the counter is a gentle giant with fine sandy hair and a light blue shirt and grey trousers. He's dressed much older than his age. His haircut is equally conservative. He speaks very good English and is extremely polite. I fill my pocket with unfamiliar cash and coins. For the next few weeks, we'll be dividing by five to work out how much everything is relative to the Aussie dollar. I'm hopeless with Maths.

Our exit from Aabenraa is mercifully quick. One minute we're crossing a main road and cycling down a suburban street and the next we're saying hello to the cows again. We enter a forest and the road steepens rapidly. There is no traffic. At the top of the rise is a lovely village called ... Rise. It commands the high ground with a beautiful stout white church built in 1857. At least that's what it says on one side of the steeple. The other claims an earlier ancestry of 1788. It's set in a peaceful cemetery of flowers and shrubs and immaculately tended graves.

The next village of Mjols has a rather curious street sign displaying a boy holding a rope which is tied around the neck of a snail who is sitting on a kart. I assume it's to warn motorists of the presence of children? But such cruel children? I ride slowly through the village, just in case.

We turn on to the main road and our heads slump. No shoulder and a noise strip that is almost at the edge of the road, meaning we have to cycle on the dangerous side of the white line. Most cars and trucks give us space. I stop beside a canola field and study the maps for an alternative. There isn't one. It starts to rain heavily and the wind whips into our faces. I'm getting well-drilled at pulling on my rain pants and wet-weather booties in double-quick time. Ha! No such thing as bad weather only a poor choice in clothing, as Billy Connolly famously said. We battle the elements until it's time for lunch. This morning, we remembered to pack sandwiches left over from breakfast, so we walk past the lonely pizza joint in Agerskov and sit under a shelter near another stout white church and cemetery. This church is older than the one in Rise, although I'm tempted to circle the steeple to check for conflicting dates.

After lunch, we pass a series of farms with large long barns. Pigs. Factory farming at its worst. Denmark is the world's largest producer of pork, killing an astonishing twenty-eight million pigs each year. I love pork as much as the next carnivore, but the practise of locking these intelligent social animals in cages for their entire life is shameful.

For a country that rightly trumpets its liberal human rights policies and high standard of living, I wish Denmark would extend a little of that freedom to its most profitable animal.

The afternoon is spent gritting our teeth at the increasing headwind as the weather alternates between rain and bursts of fragile sunshine. It all has a rather numbing effect. There are few villages and the road follows a straight line through flat fields and past more pig jails.

We're relieved to enter Ribe, our destination for the evening. Wow! What a town. Reputed to be the oldest town in Scandinavia, it's perhaps also the most attractive town in Denmark. We find our lodging easily in the main street of the village. The yellow painted black-timbered building dates from 1668 and has the crooked walls and floor to prove it. The tall blonde woman warns us to duck our heads as she leads us along a corridor to our upstairs room at the rear of the building. The Danes were evidently much shorter in the 17th century. Our room is small but cosy with a lovely four-poster bed and has a view out to the garden, where the woman tells us tomorrow Audi will be filming an advertisement for one of their luxury models.

We quickly wash and change into street clothes to explore the town. As we step outside, the sun shines to welcome us to an afternoon in a town established over one thousand three hundred years ago. The narrow streets are filled with impossibly cute stone houses, all painted an alluring shade of gelato. The words *yellow* and *orange* barely suffice. I'll have to revert to nature - sunflower, lemon, ochre, apricot - each house is a masterpiece decorated by black-painted exposed timber and red-tile roofs. There is hardly anyone about. I spend the afternoon taking endless photos of sunlight beaming on stone walls. The Cathedral - the oldest in Denmark - is a mish-mash of styles, reflecting its long and troubled history from Viking to Romanesque to Medieval. Stories abound of tragedy - on Christmas Day in 1283, one of the towers collapsed, killing numerous worshippers. In 1580, the town burned to the ground, yet the Cathedral was spared. In 1643, a violent storm surge forever remembered as 'The Great Drowning' flooded Ribe. Eight thousand people perished. The water reached as high as the pulpit.

We leave this tale of disaster to survey the restaurants. Most offer fish and chips but the prices in this tourist town are astronomical, so we settle on lasagne at an Italian eatery. The beer is equally expensive but has the appealingly silly name of Fugslang, so I can't resist.

At 8pm every evening in spring and summer, a town crier walks the streets of Ribe. We join him and thirty other followers on this clear sky evening. He's a slight fellow wearing a long black overcoat, carrying a pointed staff and sporting a mischevious glint in his eye. He also wears a sailor's black cap and a short grey beard. For over an hour, he provides a potted history of the town, spoken in both Danish and English. This being a very old town, his monologue is of floods, fires, witches, death by plague and the assorted disasters wrought by God's will.

At one point, he stands in front of a grassy mound and tells us of the legend where all the victims of a medieval plague where thought to be buried. No-one was sure if it was true or not until one evening when a storm uprooted a large tree that had grown there for centuries. The tree fell and unearthed hundreds of skeletons, proving that sometimes legends are true.

As he wanders the town, he points to the oldest bass relief in Denmark; the oldest town hall in Denmark; the oldest church in ... you get the idea. It's a lively presentation and I get a real appreciation not only of the history of this beautiful town but of the jaunty happy language that is Danish. Judging by the responses to his monologues, most of the audience are Danish with just a few English-speakers. It's a cool evening, early in the season. I imagine he gets hundreds of devoted followers in high summer.

As he leads us through the streets he calls loudly in Danish for the residents to prepare themselves for bed, even though the sun still hasn't set. Oh well, it's a show for we tourists. I later learn that there are four criers - all bearded and suitably sailor-like - who offer this informative and free service to visitors. Ribe has discovered that it's not tourist tat but history that will attract visitors. Long may it continue.

The following morning, Jens the B&B owner talks about his love of Arsenal in the English Premier League. We discuss Arsense Wenger versus Jose Mourinho over ham and cheese and brown bread. He's kind enough to retrieve his air compressor from the shed so I can pump up Bruce and Aiwa's tryes. Except we have presta valves and the adaptor doesn't fit. No matter. Jens rushes next door to get another fitting from his neighbour. I compensate for the many kilometres we still have to cycle by over-inflating the tyres. Jens tells us this courtyard will be filled with luxury Audis in a few hours and he's been forced to close for the whole day. He smiles and let's us know he's charging Audi for the privilege. Perhaps enough to take him to London to see his beloved football team? He also tells us the town burghers have enacted stringent building laws stopping him from fixing his sloping walls and floors. History trumps modernity. I can't help but agree.

As we leave town, I notice many of the houses have a vase or an ornament in their front window. It's a lovely homely touch that implies a welcome. It also draws the eye to the vase rather than into the house, so acts as a pleasant way of maintaining privacy.

Today we're cycling directly east, ably assisted by a tailwind. We rocket through towns with four-letter names, as if the locals couldn't be bothered coming up with anything more complicated. We leave Ribe and cycle through or see signs for Gram, Brem, Seen, Birk and Fole. We eventually break the four-letter barrier by cycling into Rødding for cake and coffee.

Back on the road, we smell a large pond of waste water suspiciously near a series of barns. Pigs don't smell but the collective run-off of factory faming can be toxic. Despite its high standard of living, with a whopping ninety percent of the population classified as middle-class, Denmark has one of the highest cancer rates in the first world. The comprehensive welfare system means they also have modern treatment facilities and a high survival rate, but I wonder if there's any connection between their excessive consumption of factory-farmed pork products and such a poor health indicator?

Three horses gallop along a ridge. They turn into the wind and thunder downhill. In another paddock, a herd of cows slumber. On a narrow path, a group of walkers hear us clattering behind them. They step aside and wave us through with wide smiles. The wind is so strong, we decide to push on to our destination of Christiansfeld before lunch.

We trundle through town at precisely midday and sheepishly pull up outside the Brødremenighedens Hotel. I'm sure we're too early to check-in. Across the cobblestone street is the Honningkagebageri café. The town is famous for honey gingerbread cake and here is its spiritual centre. How can we resist? We lean Bruce and Aiwa against the wall and enter the café, a simple place of white furniture where mothers and their children indulge in the town speciality. There is one spare booth. We order a traditional slice and one with added chocolate mousse. I love a shop that offers large chunks to sample on the counter. The bakery has existed here since 1802 and as I look out the window and down the main street, I notice the town buildings are of a similar honey colour.

Christiansfeld was founded in 1773 by members of the Moravian Church. It has recently gained World Heritage Status. At first, I wonder why. It lacks much of the wow factor of Ribe. But after an afternoon of wandering the streets, I soon change my mind.

First stop is the impressive Moravian Church, a long honey-coloured stone building topped with black roof tiles opposite a pristine square of green grass and ornamental lime trees. All the other buildings in town have red roof tiles. True to Moravian tradition, the church is characterised by its simplicity. The walls and long bench seats are painted white, the floorboards made from broad planks of Douglas pine and covered in a light dusting of sand and the low-hanging chandeliers, dating from 1777, each hold four candles. The effect is one of simplicity and austere devotion. Unlike most churches which tend to be long and narrow with pews located a long way from the altar, here a simple lithurgy table is located in the centre of a long side of the building. It's slightly raised and has only one chair for the priest. The bench seats for the congregation are placed lengthways. There is much less emphasis on the heirarchy of the clergy. While the church can hold one thousand worshippers, the current Moravian population of Christiansfeld and surrounding areas stands at a little over three hundred and fifty.

Established in the 15th century in the present-day Czech Republic, the Moravians arrived here in the 18th century and were given special dispensation to start a religious community by King Christian the seventh. His patronage assured the citizens of religious freedom, tax and customs concessions, exemption from military service and a substantial investment in the infrastructure of the town. The grateful citizens responded by naming the town after the King.

The other main buildings of the town are the nearby brothers' and sisters' houses - imposing brick and timber structures where the men learned a trade in the workshop rooms and young women were taught the basics of knitting, spinning and weaving. The Moravians were skilled artisans with their communal workshops featuring a piano factory, a baker responsible for the delicious honey cake, a chandler's, a cigar and tobacco store and a bookbinder. The hotel and café are still owned by members of the church.

The Moravians established a communal social support network

which extended to building a large apartment block for widows and single women. This division of the sexes extends to the beautiful cemetery located north-east of the town, dubbed 'God's Acre.' The deceased are laid to rest in the same way as they sit in the church, with the brothers on the left hand side and sisters to the right. All the headstones are identical, symbolising equality before the Lord and in death. The headstones lie at a slight angle to the vertical and the inscriptions always face to the east and each is numbered, listing the order of deaths in the town since the first one on September 26th, 1773. It's a serene location, all the more majestic by the uniformity of the graves and the whispering presence of the surrounding lime trees planted when the cemetery was first planned. We spend a long time wandering the gravestones. While I may not want to be buried away from my beloved, I can see how this structure emphasises community above all else. It's a theme echoed throughout this wonderful town, deserving of its World Heritage status.

Our room in the hotel is on the first floor and is characterised by a large ornate heater in one corner and photos of early pioneers on the walls. It's a welcoming space with high ceilings and tall windows. The Moravians regarded hospitality as a virtue and so constructed this hotel initially as a simple guest house in 1773. Since then, it has been extended on four occasions.

Its most prominent role in Danish history occured in 1864 when the armistice was signed by the Danish Colonel Kaufmann and the Prussian Lieutenant Colonel Stiele allowing for the cessation of Holstein and Schleswig to Prussia. This was a huge loss for the Danish people. It lead to great introspection, perhaps best characterised in the phrase of the Danish poet H.P. Holst, 'what was lost without will be found within.' From that moment, Denmark would focus its attention on building a robust though perhaps inward-looking social democracy. Danish folk traditions were celebrated, one language was installed and the poets and writers looked to create a distinct cultural heritage free from the Pan-Germanic past. In defeat, Denmark looked inward and found a unique place.

In the evening, we wander the streets searching for Danish food. Our hotel offers roast chicken and boiled potatoes or Australian beef at a similar cost to a five-star restaurant back home. Eventually we find a cheaper alternative named Mad-Paletten opposite an Aldi supermarket. When we enter, the smell of roast chicken is overpowering. There are no other diners, just the portly owner and his young female assistant. We both order the chicken dinner, not expecting much.

I don't know what the owner puts on the bird but this is the best chicken I've ever eaten. The skin is golden brown and crispy, the meat succulent and the chips are accompanied by a few slices of pickled cucumber. I'm almost tempted to eat the bones. I'm not sure if this is Danish cuisine but it tastes great and is reasonably priced. As we eat, a steady stream of locals come in to pick up take-away orders. This is the most popular place in town.

We walk home along Lindegade Street. A boy rides his bike over the cobblestones, he lifts himself out of the seat to avoid the shudder before adroitly jumping the gutter and continuing along the footpath. A woman carries plastic bags full of groceries in both hands. She smiles at the boy and turns down a narrow side street. It's a lovely town. Who would have thought such uniformity of design could survive for centuries without being ransacked and changed utterly under the guise of modernity. Christiansfeld is a working example of how we can live among a fragile history yet recognise its power and beauty. Long may it never change.

We leave Christiansfeld under the threat of rain and join the long straight Route 170 all the way to Kolding. This road should be the default template for all trainee road builders. Although it's only one lane in each direction, the lane is very wide and bordered by a noise strip. On the outside of the noise strip is a metre-wide section for cyclists. Although we are on the same road as cars, I feel relatively safe because of the simple inclusion of a noise strip. Certainly it would be better to have a separate bike lane, but if that can't be achieved because of budget or land constraints, then I'd be happy with this.

We reach Kolding much earlier than expected. Located at the head of the Kolding fjord, the town is the seventh largest in Denmark. Apart from the glittering waters of the fjord, the most prominent attraction is Koldinghus, a Danish royal castle from the 15th century. Now used as a museum, it sits on the lakeshore with a suitably regal bearing. In the Napoleonic Wars, soldiers from France and Spain used it as a barracks in the freezing winter of 1808. They burnt whatever they could find to keep warm. Much of the castle's furnishings were sacrificed. It was this and perhaps the intake of too much alcohol to keep them warm that caused a fire, significantly damaging much of the building. The Spanish soldiers had enough, they defected and returned to warmer climes.

While the war between Denmark and her allies against Sweden and England proved a stalemate with no territory lost to either side, Sweden once again invaded Denmark in 1813. This time the Swedes were much more successful, forcing the Danes to relinquish control of Norway. It was a significant precursor to their loss of southern lands to the Prussians later in the century. In the space of sixty years, Denmark had been humiliated in two major wars and lost a significant proportion of its land. No longer would they be seen, or see themselves, as a military power.

North of Kolding we cycle through rolling farmland of cow paddocks and wheat fields. On a rise just outside the small village of Almind, we pass a non-descript blue building with a red door. Alongside the building runs a gravel track to a barn at the rear. On the front of the building is a sign announcing the Tucan Swingers and Wellness Club. I can't believe my eyes. A swingers club among the cows and wheat fields? I stop and take a photo. No-one is around, it's much too early for any self-respecting 'swinger.' Cathie and I stand on the road, giggling like school children.

'Can you imagine Magnus, the cattle farmer sitting down to dinner with his wife Ingrid and suggesting that after dinner, instead of watching Borgen on television, they head down to the Tucan for a piece of action,' I say.

'And what if they run into their neighbours, Frederik and Clara at the club,' Cathie says.

'Do they talk stock prices or whips and lashes,' I say.

Cathie shivers, 'I guarantee there are more men than women as members. Scores of seedy blokes in the dim light.'

I punch Tucan Club into my smartphone and sure enough the website features a scantily-clad model suggesting I become a member. The owners are Torben and Mie, a handsome couple in their forties. They proudly announce that Tucan is the only swingers club in Denmark and comes complete with a 'fully equipped disco with vibrating sound, fancy light effects and a sexy gogo dance pole.' All behind the rather staid blue facade ringed by wheat fields. I still can't understand how they get clients among the farmers and small town workers of rural Jutland? I'm not sure if this is what H.P. Holst was meaning when he wrote about the Danes needing to find something within to compensate for their losses at war.

Onward to Vejle, once billed rather disconcertingly as the

Manchester of Denmark. I suspect because of its long history of manufacturing and industry, but what can you say about a town that has one of the largest chewing gum factories on earth. Welcome to Stimorol land! The town itself is cut off from the fjord by too much industry and port facilities hogging the shoreline. We make our way through the traffic to the pedestrian mall which is cluttered with clothes shops. Once again, racks of garish men's shirts take pride of place.

We park Bruce and Aiwa in a bike rack and attempt to choose from a cluster of cafés. Clothes and coffee seems to be Vejle's preoccupation. We enter the Baresso café and are surprised to find they offer 'flat whites' - the Australian café mafia has reached Scandinavia. We order two excellent coffees and cinnamon buns. The price gets my heart pumping almost as much as the caffeine. I look around the café at the other customers. There must be a model convention in town today. They are all staggeringly beautiful. Blonde hair, white teeth, tall, slim, sparkling eyes - and that's just the men! We slink a little lower in our chairs.

Since we've entered Denmark, the roadside poles and fences have been cluttered with election posters. Most of the candidates are extremely handsome. Politicians, thankfully, are not usually elected because of their physical attributes. As ignorant visitors, we're baffled in trying to understand which candidates we'd vote for, given the chance. The wild-eyed female blondes represent the 'People's Party' - a bunch of right-wing nutters. The handsome bearded men and attractive yet serious women with short hair are part of the Liberal Alliance, a centre-right group. The nerdy types in suits and button-down expressions are in Venstre, the mainstream conservative party. Perhaps the only party that seems to have a broad range of candidates - appearance-wise - is the Social Democrats, the centre-left party currently in power before this election. The Prime Minister is Helle Thorning-Schmidt who is a dead-ringer for Birgitte Nyborg from the hit Danish series Borgen about a female Prime Minister. Like Nyborg in the series, Thorning-Schmidt cobbled together a number of centre and left parties to form a coalition government.

I'm betraying my own prejudices but if I had the choice I'd vote for the Socialist People's Party or the Red-Green Alliance - good looking candidates and attractive policies - what's not to like?

We wander downhill to St Nicolai Church, a red-brick Lutheran place of worship dating from the 13th century. We want to visit the famed Haraldskær Woman, a bog body found near here, dating from 490 BC. The bog woman was discovered in 1835 and has been pored over by scientists ever since. They have concluded that she was about forty years old and was almost certainly the victim of a ritual sacrifice. Her neck had a faint groove as if someone had applied a rope for torture or strangulation. She was buried naked with her clothes consisting of a leather cape and woollen outer garments placed on top of her in the peat bog.

Alas, after entering the small church we discover that she has once again been taken away for more forensic examination. I wonder if she will ever be laid to rest, here in the glass-covered sarcophagus in Vejle or buried in a nearby graveyard.

We cruise downhill to the fjord and rejoin the 170 which takes us all the way to Horsens in the late afternoon. Just in time for yet another excellent cake and coffee and to load up with supplies because tonight we are staying in a farmhouse on the outskirts of town. Through the wonders of AirBnB, I've booked an entire top floor of an old wooden farm building for a pittance. The handsome owners, Anita and Per have done a splendid job of renovating the space which offers a lovely view of lush fields and a distant forest. As if on cue, once we're safely inside it starts to rain heavily.

The rain disappears by morning, pushed east by a strong wind which buffets us along a quiet hilly backroad all the way to Lake Mossø, the largest freshwater lake in Jutland. It's home to osprey and the much rarer white-tailed eagle, both of which are hiding out of the wind this morning.

The rain returns as we reach Skanderborg. We seek shelter in the modern town library on the shore of Skanderborg Lake. The place is bursting at the seams with children running around and laughing, parents drinking coffee in the café and old folks trying to make sense of it all. A woman wearing a blue uniform greets us at the entrance and welcomes us to the Skanderborg Children's Literature Festival. The woman tells me the festival is in celebration of the writer Ole Lund Kirkegaard, a local author who tragically died in 1979 and is regarded as one of Denmark's finest writers for young people. His books are still in print and continue to sell in high numbers, quite an achievement forty-odd years after his death.

Unfortunately, the books and the readings by other prominent authors are all in Danish, so I can't make any sense of it. Like many children's writers, Ole Lund began his career as a teacher, reading stories to his students. His books often trace the childhood of an anti-hero, a weedy shy boy who struggles to make sense of the world. In short, an every-boy. In his relatively short career, he produced numerous titles that remain children's classics in Denmark, including his biggest hit 'Gummi-Tarzan' - the life of a shy skinny untalented boy named Ivan Olsen. Six of his books have been adapted either for the screen or theatre. He died in the most tragic of circumstances. Coming home late one night after spending the evening drinking at an inn, he passed out in the snow and died of hypothermia. He left behind a wife, two children and a grieving nation of literature lovers. It's a testament to the power of his stories that he remains so revered and honoured here in the region of his birth.

We retire to the café for waffles and chocolate cake at eye-poppingly expensives prices. I hope the profits go towards the library buying more books. It's a beautiful space with large double-storey windows looking over the lake.

Skanderborg is invitingly clustered around the south side of the lake and today has closed off the main street and erected a stage for bands and entertainers later in the afternoon. A metal band starts to tune up. We jump on Bruce and Aiwa and pedal north.

At Stilling a batch of houses hug the shoreline of the lake, all with fetching views of the two hardy kayakers plowing into the wind near the point. And I thought it was tough on a bike. We wobble along through the morning until we reach Aarhus, which achieves a balance between being a working port and opening up the waterfront to the residents. Marlene takes us through a very hip inner-city precinct of cafés and bars, packed at midday on Saturday. Here, everyone is good looking *and* well-dressed. Even more striking is the ARoS Kuntsmuseum, a spectacular ten-storey art gallery topped by a large circular rainbow-coloured plastic skywalk, fittingly dubbed *Your rainbow panorama*. I'm sure the museum is filled with great art, but I'm quite satisfied to stand below and watch the people walking around the colourful skywalk. This single installation has helped boost the museum's attendance so it's now the second-most visited gallery in Denmark. I wonder if they'd let me ride Bruce around the circular pathway?

Aarhus is an attractive city, the second-largest population centre behind Copenhagen. It's a hub of research and development and higher education, which explains all the handsome young people riding past us on hipster bikes. Much of the docklands have been converted into residential and shopping developments and the area is flooded with people wandering the narrow laneways. Bikes easily outnumber cars and there's a joyously relaxed attitude to the city. Maybe it's just me, but everyone seems to be smiling. Perhaps they've just walked around the circular skyway? Marlene leads us on a merry trail through the dockland streets. We ride very slowly, looking up at all the warehouse apartments we'd like to live in if we were young and Danish and ready to sign with a modelling agency.

I'm so relaxed I unwittingly pull out in front of a car crossing an intersection. I hurriedly apply my front brakes which fail to grip. Luckily the woman behind the wheel stops and my back brakes hold just enough to prevent a longer, less-pleasant stay in Aarhus. I wave my apologies and stop on the footpath to do some brake repairs. So much for Bruce and reliability. After a few adjustments we get moving - and stopping - again. The bike path follows the waterfront into the outer suburbs of the city. Time for lunch. We take a sidestreet down to the water and follow a sandy path to a bench seat overlooking a long curve of beach. Cathie unpacks our sandwiches prepared earlier at breakfast. A fast ferry leaves the terminal at Aarhus.

'Do you think it's heading for Ebeltoft?' Cathie asks.

'Nah. Copenhagen,' I reply.

We look across the bay to a small village on the far side. I wonder if that's Ebeltoft, our destination for the evening. I check Marlene. She tells me we still have fifty kilometres to travel.

'I reckon it's going to Ebeltoft,' Cathie smiles.

The rhythm of today is a strong wind bringing sunshine followed by a storm which is soon replaced by sunshine. We slip in and out of wet-weather gear and remain grateful the wind is behind us. We take a pleasant forest path through fields of canola down to Kalø Vig, a magic sweep of bay where teenagers fish from a wooden jetty while their younger brothers and sisters play among the sandhills. There are no adults around. Black or grey timber houses are spread around the inlet. They are very small, just a few rooms, but each has large windows and a front verandah opening out to take in the majestic views.

The Danes are obsessed with summer houses. Although the majority of the population is wealthy enough to be able to afford month-long holidays in Italy or France, most people choose to spend it no further than a few hundred kilometres away at the seaside in their homely little shacks. It's a curious phenomenon that seems to hark back to the desire to find happiness and contentment within the borders of their own country. Some would say it's insular, but I prefer to think it's a heartfelt celebration of their love for the homeland and the tolerant society they have built over the past two centuries.

It reminds me of Australia thirty years ago, where everyone was content to hang out at the seaside and eat endless tubs of ice-creams and drink cartons of beer. And then we discovered Bali. Perhaps the Danes' affection for the summer house runs deeper than food and drink. It signifies independence and solidarity, a place where the whole population can gather on an equal footing. Of course, the term 'summerhouse' is misleading. The Danes have such an affection for their second home that they use it all-year round as a weekend retreat. The uniformity of design of the houses stems from the fact that all new development in these coastal areas is heavily restricted. Those lucky enough to own one of the over 200,000 summerhouses existing today are unlikely to sell because there's limited opportunity to get back into the market. The black timber shack across the road from the cove is worth a fortune and the owners are wise enough not to attempt to extend or redevelop the site. Enjoy what you have. Don't rock the boat. How very Danish.

The sun comes out and we find a kiosk serving ice cream and coffee. We sit on a bench seat and watch as thirty people - yes, I counted - line up to buy a cone. It's the longest line for ice-cream I've seen outside of Roman tourist hotspots. Most of the customers are big beefy blokes all ordering double-scoops. Around the corner is Kalø Slot, the ruined castle founded in 1313 by King Erik the Sixth to counter the rebellions taking place in Jutland. Built on an island, it's connected to the mainland by a five-hundred metre man-made embankment. It's now just a ruin of red brick pockmarked with graffiti and one crumbling tower set on a majestic expanse of paddock where cattle still roam freely, giving the daytrippers endless photo opportunities.

We cycle on to Ebeltoft, home to the largest wooden warship still floating. The black and white Jylland was built in 1860 to assist in the naval blockade against Prussia. Alas, she has been a much more worthy tourist attraction than warship. With pale timber masts and gold decorative brocade, she is an attractive ship, worth her weight in tourist dollars for the settlement.

Our hostel is up a steep hill and looks like a cross between a

Soviet holiday park from the 60s and an environmental dream-home-turned-bunker. A square of low grey brick buildings, each topped by earth roofs surround a central space where we comrades should gather to discuss the next five-year-plan. Instead we retreat to the kitchen and cook pasta and drink beer. One day soon we'll have a Danish meal. Or perhaps we already have? Ice-cream anyone?

If you believe Sunday is the holy day, then surely we have been blessed with a perfect road this morning leading us to the village of Draby where a white dog with distinctive black highlights sleeps on the street corner. All of the sudden the church bells toll. The dog wakes and barks incessantly. No-one is around. The church mimics the dog's colour scheme perfectly - a glorious white building with flashy black touches. Next door is a barn painted by the same artist who loves his black trim. We leave the dog and the bells waking Draby and cycle through a quiet forest.

This really is a lovely road - from forest to field to village punctuated by regular views of the sea. Our speed is Sunday slow as we take in the countryside. To complete the magic we enter Rugard, a village centred on a large duck pond. Whichever way you enter the town, a stop sign makes you appreciate the beauty and tranquility of the pond. The narrow road circles the water bordered on one side by a forest, on the other by the few remaining town buildings including an exceptionally long and immaculate black and white single storey barn. It's the supermodel of barns, so perfect surely the farmer doesn't let his cows wander in without having a wash first. The narrow road skirts between the barn and a stream fringed by tall trees. I can't resist turning around and cycling through the village again. We still haven't seen a human this morning - just dogs and ducks.

Near Høbjerg, we come upon our first Danish castle, complete with its very own tunnel entrance. We ride through, even though it's apparent this is private property. Katholm Castle was built of simple red bricks in the 16th century in the Renaissance style. Wilhelm Dinesen, the father of the celebrated Danish author Karen Blixen spent much of his childhood here. It's a rather severe three-storey pile at the end of a long gravel driveway bordered by painted white stones. I much prefer the long, low red and black barn off to the right. It looks much more lived in somehow, even if it's only by pigs and cows.

As we take our leave of the castle and pedal up a hill through a beech forest, we're overtaken by a bunch of cyclists. They've chosen the perfect road for a Sunday criterium. We follow them, rather more slowly, all the way to Grenaa Harbour and an open cake shop. If you're ever in this pleasant seaside town, I can heartily recommend two cakes - the Brunsviger is a jam tea cake topped with brown sugar and the Kakoa Snitte is, as the name suggests, a chocolate slice sprinkled with coconut. We consider placing a second order but make do with ogling the Trekant, a huge chocolate-smeared pizza slice. Well, that's what it looked like anyway!

We wobble down to the fishing port to inspect Grenaa's fleet which seems equally divided between recreational and industrial fishing. As we're leaving, Cathie spies a seafood restaurant.

'It's just opened,' she says, 'I can see people inside.'

I glance at my watch. Midday.

'But we've just eaten cakes,' I say.

'It's a chance to finally eat some authentic Danish food,' she answers.

'So you're suggesting lunch purely as a cultural experience.'

'Exactly!'

Cathie hops off Aiwa and leans her against the wall before walking across to inspect the menu. She turns and smiles.

Looks like an early lunch. For research purposes only, of course!

Even at this early hour, the restaurant is nearly full. The smiling blonde waitress hands us the menu. Cathie chooses the 'Shooting Star seafood platter' and I indulge with the 'Seven types of fish' plate. We recognise a few of the offerings - salmon, plaice, shrimp. The other types of fish remain a mystery. I'm pretty sure one is eel. It's not the dish I was expecting with all of the servings being cold, in true Scandinavian fashion, including a fish cake, roe, a fillet of whitefish and a pâté. It's all very tasty, but I'm yearning for something hot. Cathie's shooting star is predominantly salmon and shrimp and very tasty. It's a casual place with a nautical theme of fishing ropes and nets draped from the walls. We have a lovely view of the trawlers who no doubt provided much of the food on our plates. I mean, in our stomachs.

The afternoon ride is very quiet as we amble through a sparse and under-populated countryside. Just outside of our destination, we pass a beech forest. I stop to read a sign near the entrance to a walking trail. It tells the story of a local legend. In the 16th century, a nobleman promised his daughter's hand in marriage to a rich landowner. The girl had meanwhile fallen in love with a shepherd called Christian Skipper. The girl was forced into an unhappy marriage, but continued the affair with her true love. She had three children, a boy and two girls. When the husband found out about the affair, he killed the shepherd and put his head on a spike at this place, perhaps as a warning to all would-be romantics. The daughter died shortly afterwards, some say of sadness. Prior to her death she arranged for her three children to escape, assisted by the relatives of Christian Skipper. Before disappearing forever, each of the children planted a beech tree, in memory of their mother and her true love, the shepherd. The forest I now stand before grew from those first three saplings.

Lovely.

Our lodging for the evening is above a pottery shop in Fjellerup. The kindly owners, a hippie couple in their sixties, allow us to use their guesthouse kitchen to cook an omelette for dinner washed down with Danish beer. We have strawberries and yoghurt for dessert and sit out on the back deck listening to the quiet.

In the morning, the sky is cloudy with hopeful patches of blue as we cycle north. A few kilometres into a characterless forest, we come across a freshly-graded field. Newly-built chicken coops, each fifty metres long and raised a metre above ground are being constructed in regimented rows. I peek into one of the coops and see the cages are no bigger than an A4 piece of paper cubed. Coming from the coop are numerous pipes to ferry away the waste. One hundred metres down the road is a vast waste tank. This is not a farm but a chicken prison where the inmates will be worked to death in the space of a few cramped months. Coupled with their treatment of pigs, I'm beginning to believe the Danes are not quite as liberal and progressive on animal issues as they are in social policies. They should be commended for the latter and roundly criticised for the former.

A few kilometres further along the back road is an Army training area. The forest is fenced in with signs forbidding entry to anyone but military personnel. We really are hitting the highlights this morning. The whole place has a feel of being miles away from civilisation. The wind picks up and turns into our faces. It's a relief to reach the ferry at Udbyhøj. The ferryman is a wisened old chap with grey hair and stubble. Luckily for us he speaks excellent English and tells us where we can find food. We trundle off his vessel on the north side of Randers Fjord and head to the camp ground. We hustle to the front office and the blonde woman tells us she's closed but when she sees how crestfallen we are, she offers to make us a sandwich and fetch a coffee. White bread and cheese never tasted so good. We buy a packet of chocolate biscuits as well, just in case. Thus continues our culinary tour of Denmark.

We battle the hills and wind for another few hours, making very slow progress through the expanse of Danish farmland. Finally we speed downhill to Mariager, an idyllic village of cobblestone streets and timber-frame houses located on the Mariager fjord. With an impressive Bridgettine Abbey founded in 1430, a salt centre where visitors can inspect the old mines, a paddle steamer for cruises on the fjord and an old vintage railway open in summer, this is a town that lives off tourism. Today, before the peak season, it's very quiet. We eat lunch in the only bakery and trundle away. It's apparent our tired bodies need a rest day. We haven't had one since Geneva which was two thousand five hundred kilometres and twenty-eight days ago.

Tonight we're staying with Warm Showers hosts just outside of Hobro. Martin and Heidi are a handsome couple in their thirties who have a two-year-old livewire son called Wilhelm. Martin is an agriculture specialist at the local university and Heidi is a teacher. Heidi is pregnant with the baby due in a few months but it doesn't stop her cooking a splendid salmon dinner with potato salad. The salad is exceptional with every ingredient grown in their sizeable garden. Potatoes, asparagus, beans and radishes are carefully cut by Heidi and expertly mixed by Wilhelm who playfully throws an extra radish in because he likes the colour red.

We spend a pleasant evening talking politics - baffled in equal measure by news the Radical Party in Denmark is actually conservative and only 1% of pork in Denmark is free-range. They ask us questions on parenting. Is there a difficult age? Cathie and I smile. What can we say? Finally, Cathie says, 'No. Never. Children are our gift to each other. They increase the love in a household exponentially.'

After dinner we walk around the garden which overlooks a lake. Next door is the church with flowers and shrubs and lines of graves. I'm a little concerned to find empty plots among the ancient sites. Martin tells us that if the plots aren't renewed every twenty-five years, they can be 'reassigned.' He tells us the story of a neighbour who is mad at his life-long friend who died recently and 'stole' the best remaining plot, one he'd had his eye on for years. I'm surprised the tenure of the dead is so short without renewal. It's a very different view of the dead than we witnessed all those miles ago in Rochefort-sur-Nenon in France where they moved the cemetery, one precious grave at a time, no matter the ages of the graves.

The weather gods must have heard us talking about the possibility of a rest day, so they've sent heavy rain to accompany us north. Wilhelm buoys our spirits at breakfast by completing time trails with his plastic kart between the kitchen and the lounge room. The energy of the young. We older children serve ourselves oats, stewed rhubarb and yoghurt and contemplate how many kilometres we'll cycle before we're saturated. My guess is ten. Cathie, ever the optimist, suggests twenty. We shake hands with Martin and Heidi and Wilhelm waves goodbye before attempting one more lap.

The road winds across rolling hills through horse paddocks and the ever-present canola fields. The small village of Vebbestrup has more flowers in the cemetery than gravestones as a flight of swallows swoop around the steeple.

Soon after we enter Rold Skov, the second-largest forest in Denmark, home to an astonishing five thousand species of fungi, including the amazing Troll Butter fungi, a yellow scrambled egg slime that attaches itself to bark mulch. With such an intense appearance, it's little wonder the fungi has attracted myth and legend, usually to do with witches and trolls looking for revenge. As we enter the rough dirt path, our eyes scan the undergrowth. The forest is also home to numerous deer, badgers, fox and five species of hibernating bats. It's a rank dark place of fallen red leaves, mossy tree trunks and a heavy green leaf canopy, which for a while shields us from the rain. It's a wonderfully atmospheric ride with no-one else around along a ragged puddle-thick dirt road. Bruce and Aiwa start complaining loudly as grime gets into the gears and the disc brakes. We finally reach a small cottage, its chimney smoking furiously. Someone has put damp wood on the fire. We pull up beside Lake Oksso and look across the mirror expanse of water. The only sound is a songbird performing on a branch that's been washed ashore on the sand. Rold Skov was once the province of highwaymen and thieves, its dense forest and numerous trails a perfect spot to hide from the authorities. In the mid 19th century, the police rounded up hundreds of men in this forest. The court cases must have went on for months. Soon, all that remained were flora and fauna and those elusive fungi.

Bruce and Aiwa continue to moan under the weight of mud and grit so as we reach Skørping, I stop outside a house and borrow their hose to wash away the gunk. The owner comes out to investigate. She offers to fetch me a brush but I assure her a good rinse will do the trick. In the centre of town, we seek refuge in a bakery where the stocky owner sells us two excellent fruit bollers and two machine coffees. We stand at the window, slowly dripping on her tile floor. She also sells a staggering variety of 'trail mix' - nuts, raisins and seeds favoured by bushwalkers and other hardy folk. I'll stick to cakes.

We follow the 180 which offers us a separated bike path through villages with suitably guttural Danish names - Volsted, Gug and Ferslev. It's a flat land of muddy paddocks, newly-built aluminium barns, workshops and rust-coloured grain fields. Eventually we arrive in Aalborg. These Danes love their town names beginning with double A. I soon learn that this town has been voted by the European Commission as having the most satisfied citizens in the Union. Wow! I cycle slowly through the centre of town, expecting wide smiles and a jovial welcome. Oh well. In their defence, it is raining rather heavily. Perhaps they did the survey in summer?

We stop in the main pedestrian street. Yes, there are hundreds of clothes racks under the awnings but right now I want food not a garish blue and red check shirt. We wander into a café announcing fair-trade coffee. We're starving even though it's only 11:25am. We both order the rather expensive club sandwich. The waitress - one of the most satisfied people in Europe - ruefully shakes her head and says they don't start lunch until 11:30am. Five minutes. Surely, she'd just accept the order and the chef could wait until the allotted time to begin preparation.

No.

Oh.

So we wander down the street to café Baresso, which may have less ideologically pure coffee but serves us whatever they offer whenever we want it. And what we want are two excellent chicken and pesto paninis. Actually, make that four. The barista at Baresso (sorry, I couldn't resist), makes excellent strong coffee and within a few minutes we join the rest of the population in feeling hugely satisfied with ourselves.

'This coffee's much cheaper than down the road,' I say.

'Do you think it's because they use slave labour in Guatemala?' Cathie asks.

'Fair-trade always means higher prices. It's just debatable whether the extra goes to the workers who pick the crop,' I say.

'That's a little cynical.'

My first-world mouth is full of panini, so I take this opportunity to change the subject.

'If you're cycling in the rain for three hours, no barrier will prevent your feet from getting wet,' I say.

'Plastic bags?'

'It's a bit hard to cleat into the pedals,' I answer. 'And I'd look even more like the village idiot wandering through town with plastic bags attached to my feet.'

As you can see by this conversation, we're doing everything possible to avoid heading back into the rain. Aalborg is the home of Jørn Utzon, the architect famous for the Sydney Opera House. In 1957, Utzon unexpectedly won a competition to design the landmark building, set on the harbour foreshore opposite the iconic Sydney Harbour Bridge. Utzon's visionary plan was inspired by the simple process of peeling an orange - a complex set of spheres - although I prefer Clive James's description of the Opera House as 'a portable typewriter full of oyster shells.'

Alas, after gifting my country with one of its timeless landmarks, Utzon was dismissed by the conservative Liberal government who were concerned with cost overruns. The building was opened to much fanfare in 1973 and remains one of the most lauded buildings in the world. Ironically, Jørn Utzon never saw his visionary work in all its glory, such was the hurt of his premature dismissal. While the philistines may have won the initial skirmish, it is Utzon who is remembered fondly in Australia for giving us a building that changed the image of an entire country.

Aalborg also remembers their favourite son with the Utzon Centre, a set of buildings with dramatically curved rooftops glistening in the rain as we cross the Limfjord. I stop on the bridge to get a better look. It's a welcoming site, like someone has pitched a number of shiny giant tents on the waterfront and set up camp. Which is roughly the philosophy behind the project - here is a refuge for young architects to meet and discuss the future, to consider entering competitions to design landmark buildings in far-away lands. I hope they'll be treated better than their idol.

We pedal north, the rain continues and I think of how long I can stay in a hot shower when we arrive at our lodging for the evening. We've booked a 'cottage in the forest,' as it's described on AirBnB. Marlene, unaware of the driving rain, takes us on a four-kilometre detour via a forest track before arriving at the cottage. It's an austere log cabin set on a rise and backed by a dark forest. Hidden under a flowerpot is the key and in no time I have the log fire blazing and am eating the last of our chocolate biscuits and drinking Turkish Apple Tea which contains no apples and is not made in Turkey but is nevertheless warm and flavoursome. The answer to my shower question? Too long.

Jacob, the owner calls me to check we have everything we need and I ask him if we can stay another night. I explain that after so many kilometres, it's nice to have a washing machine and a fireplace and a well-stocked kitchen. It's hard to explain that I'm insanely excited to be watching Seinfeld repeats on the television. He readily agrees and offers us a discounted rate.

For the next thirty-six hours, we drink Danish beer, slumber on the soft lounges and eat copious amounts of food cooked in our very own kitchen. It rains steadily and I couldn't care less. We make one short outing to Dronninglund, the nearby town. I have a theory I want to test. Denmark is a rich country, so I imagine the second-hand clothes shops are full of quality items. Cathie needs a jacket. I assure her we'll find one. Sure enough, the first Red Cross store we enter has a black puffy jacket that is obviously last year's design, but in perfect condition. It is very cheap and very warm. Cathie gives me a sloppy kiss and excitedly puts it on to ride home. The rain stops for just long enough.

Reinvigorated after eight episodes of Seinfeld and a good lie down, we tackle the kilometres this morning as if we're cycling for the first time in months. Even the sun has risen to the occasion. After ten kilometres, we turn a corner and ... whoa, the sea is sparkling all the way to the horizon and Sweden.

The village of Voerså is threaded by a pleasant little stream with a kiosk on one side and an amphitheatre on the other. A row of sailboats float at the dock. An old man in brown corduroy trousers and a green cardigan walks to his mailbox to check for news from the outside world. Does anyone use snail mail anymore? Even our bills arrive by email.

We follow the lonely coast road all the way to Sæby, a newish suburb of brick houses with tile roofs and picket fences before entering the town centre. The bakery is closed and the only place offering food is the supermarket selling giant sugar bread for thirty kroners. We sit in the sun and scoff the lot. The north side of Sæby is crammed with enticing beach hyttes of black timber with big windows and indeterminate gardens. The hyttes are gathered so closely together it looks like a wealthy version of a trailer park. This is the Ikea of trailer parks - modern, modular and once you're in there's no way out! We cycle along a beach track, counting off the rock walls pointing towards Sweden every forty metres. I see a postman with bulging saddlebags, but as I get closer all he's delivering is advertising material. Sigh.

The Empire café in Fredrikhavn has lounge chairs and free wifi but severely overpriced weak coffee. Fredrikshavn has a cross sea ferry taking cargo and passengers to Gothenburg in Sweden. We choose instead the north coast route, a rather tedious path beside the main road until hunger leads us to a blue-painted take-away joint which offers a hamburger covered in salty gravy. I buy a Carlsberg beer as an antidote. The meal is like fast food the world over - salt, fat and too many carbohydrates. I recall getting three courses and a litre of wine in France for the same amount of money.

As I do my best to digest this lump of a lunch, I recall that Denmark is home to Noma, the gastronomic mecca regarded as the best restaurant in the world. We are a long way from Copenhagen. But surely a country's cuisine should be judged by what the everyman and woman eats at a simple family restaurant than what rich tourists and diplomats scoff in the nation's capital? It's why France and Italy are so popular, two countries where visitors can eat like royalty while paying a pittance. So far in Denmark we have paid a premium for rather uninspiring fare. The Danes are a smart enterprising people, yet they seem curiously uninterested in eating anything more than pork and cake and drinking rather uninspiring beer, if truth be told.

Gripe over, we set sail for Skagen, Denmark's most northern town. The bike track leads us through a wonderful expanse of sandhills, spinifex and bracken. Out to sea I catch glimpses of a line of container ships but always my attention is distracted by clear pools of water among the dunes and the many wading birds. We crest a sand dune and spy the white steeple of a church partially buried in the sand. Saint Lawrence Church, otherwise known as the *sand-buried church of Skagen* is a curious sight - a blindingly white steeple, crenellated at the top with two narrow windows devoid of glass, surrounded by sand dunes and spinifex. Underneath all that sand is the original church. Constructed in the 14th century, its precarious existence lasted until 1795 when the locals tired of digging the sand out from around its base and left it to the elements. A new church was built further away from the vagaries of nature. I wander around its base, mesmerised. The steeple looks to be tilting at an odd angle, as if emulating a certain tower in Pisa. But it's just an illusion caused by the shifting levels of sand around its base. It's not the tower that's wonky but the ground upon which I'm standing. Cathie and I spend a pleasant half hour admiring the odd vision of Christ's work here in the sand dunes and bracken of faraway Denmark.

Skagen sits on a promontory where the Baltic Sea meets the North Sea. Its history is tied to fishing and art. The fishermen arrived first and earned a fortune primarily from herring, although at great cost in loss of life. While the fish were abundant where the seas met, so was the wild weather. Shipwrecks and drownings occurred regularly.

In the late 19th century, a group of Impressionist painters were attracted by the seascapes, the afternoon light and the fishermen. They became known as the Skagen painters and included Michael Ancher, P.S. Krøyer, Holger Drachmann and Anne Ancher, the only member born here in 1859. She married Michael Ancher and they became the leaders of a group of artists who visited in the summer months. They painted large canvases of women dressed in long white dresses carrying parasols; of local fishermen dragging boats onto the sand; of the broiling sea and the endless sky.

Many of their works are in the local gallery, so after checking into our lodging, we spend a few hours wandering its generous halls. I love the Skagen painters, but then I'm a sucker for oversized brash landscapes peopled by peasants. I stand in awe of the three paintings of sailors dragging a wooden fishing boat ashore. Wait a minute ... one of those big beefy sailors with the beard and cloth cap is wearing a gold earring. In the 19th century? Surely not.

I walk across to an attendant and politely ask him to follow me. He wears a blue gallery jacket and an amused smile. I point to the bearded hipster in the painting.

'Did fishermen always wear earrings in the 19th century?' I ask.

He laughs.

'Absolutely. If they drowned and their bodies washed ashore miles from Skagen, there was an understanding that the person who found the body could take the earring as ...' he searches for the word in English, ' ... as a guarantee of a Christian burial. The earring was worth more than a burial, so there was an incentive to act honourably.'

I stare once again at the fisherman, his giant hands capable of handling fishing ropes and anchors, the heavy layers of clothing that would surely drag him to his death if he was swept overboard, and the one glistening earring that promised him a Christian burial. Sure enough, the next painting is of a family gathered around the dead body of a sailor, their pale faces downcast, the only light in the room from one frail window. The women lean close, the sailors remain upright, their big hands useless under the weight of so much sadness.

It's a great exhibition. If you're ever in Skagen, don't miss it.

Not content with wonderful painters and a sublime location, Skagen boasts a beguiling town centre of uniform houses with red-tiled roofs, white trim, yellow plaster walls and a white picket fence. It's like wandering through a theme park of yellow. Many of the houses were designed by local architect Ulrik Plesner in what was considered a National Romantic style. He's also responsible for most of the public buildings in Skagen including the hotel, post office, railway station, bank and hospital. Surely it should be renamed Plesnerville?

But that would take away from the marketing genius of a Danish couple who moved to New York in 1986. Henrik and Charlotte Jorst, perhaps missing their homeland, decided to enlist a number of Danish craftsmen to design a range of watches. They started selling them at fairs and hit upon the highly marketable idea of giving their brand an exotic European name. *Skagen* implied quality and sophistication. Within ten years, Skagen Designs Ltd was in the top two-hundred and fifty fastest growing privately-owned companies in the USA with sales approaching thirty million. Ten years later the profit was eight times as large. That's one way to cure homesickness.

Of course there is a Skagen brand shop in town with white-tiled floors, yellow walls and glittering display cabinets. Skagen the brand has nothing to do with the town, but how could they miss an opportunity. We tourists flock inside, perhaps expecting a glimpse of a lone watchmaker working in a back room, or a handsome designer drafting the new year's range? What we get is an immaculately-groomed woman with high heels and perfect skin offering me the chance to try on as many watches as I want. My current watch, a birthday present from Cathie five years ago stopped working only last week. So with her approval, I buy the cheapest Skagen watch I can find. Leather band, plain face, three hands - that'll do me. The woman wraps it in a natty box and tells me the company has just been taken over by an American clothing giant. Sigh.

After dinner, we follow our noses to the port. It stinks. Fishing trawlers the size of oil tankers float at dock. On a blue vessel registered as being from Bergen in Norway, a large silver pipe, one metre in diameter and ten metres long is hoisted alongside the deck. I imagine it's for a speedy unloading of the catch, a chute where thousands of fish fall to their fate as fish fingers or frozen fillets, if you'll pardon the f'ing alliteration! I try to imagine how long the ship stays at sea and how many tons of fish they net. I wonder if nature can keep up. The Danish fishing industry hauls in over one hundred thousand tons of fish every year and Skagen is the biggest port in the industry.

I remember the paintings of fishermen hauling wooden boats onto the sand. All that effort for a few hundred kilos of fish. Here the weapons of choice are sonar, fork lifts and industrial cranes. The fishermen no longer wear gold earrings as insurance. In fact, the process is so mechanised there are very few of them left. Along the old boardwalk is a line of red timber fish restaurants. All except one are closed. I imagine the smell has driven potential customers away. This is no longer a wharf, it's an industrial complex of ships and cranes and cold rooms and refrigerated trucks. And the customer isn't a walk-in tourist looking for a grilled cod, it's a fast food franchise with locations in hundreds of cities throughout the globe. This North Sea catch will travel much farther as fillet than it ever did as a fish.

We have travelled the length of Jutland so it would be churlish not to go the extra few kilometres to the very tip of the point where the Baltic meets the North Sea, the preferred spot of my favourite painters. We wake early on a glorious sunny day, leave our panniers in the hotel room and pedal unencumbered out to the car park a kilometre from the point. We leave Bruce and Aiwa next to a simple earthen-roofed kiosk and walk across the dunes. It's a lovely morning, just us and the twenty bird-watchers lined up on the largest dune near a tidal pool. Skagen Odde is considered the prime birdwatching spot in Northern Europe, particularly in the spring when the raptors hold court - sea eagles, golden eagles, buzzard, kites and falcon all squabble over who has the longest talons and who can dive the fastest. Their displays are observed by a hardy bunch of watchers armed with nothing more than expensive cameras, a thermos of coffee and a dog-eared copy of *A Birdwatcher's Guide to Raptors*. Each to their own.

A seal sits on a rock just off shore and languidly raises his head as we walk past. He decides we're not worth eating and goes back to sleep. We finally reach the point where the waters meet. It's a calm day. The sky seems to go on forever, mirrored by the sea. I walk to the apex of the sand where the east meets west, Baltic meets North. Tiddly waves, perhaps thirty centimetres in height splash timidly against each other. It's not what I expected. There will be no shipwrecks today. A lone oil tanker cruises past, the seabirds wheel overhead and I consider returning with an easel, canvas and brushes. What a beautiful spot. I can understand the birdwatchers spending their holidays here. Perhaps it matters little whether you see a buzzard or a kite. To spend time in this spot is enough.

Alas, we have a ferry to catch tomorrow at Hirtshals to take us to Norway, so we return to our bikes and pedal back to the hotel, where in my rush to pack I rip my panniers. Merde! Everything is unpacked and repacked with the ripped side now holding much less weight. I wonder if Bruce will wobble? Only as far as the nearest chemist where I rush in to buy a pack of large safety pins. Five pins along the ripped seam and the panniers are no longer saggy and open. Good for another thousand miles! As an extra measure I wrap an octopus strap around the bottom, just to take some of the weight off the pins. I found the occy strap beside a road in rural France all those kilometres ago. I knew it would come in handy one day.

We follow a quiet forest road. There is an increasing number of day cyclists passing us as the morning gets warmer. In a clearing is a lonely campground. I stop to investigate. A wooden log structure, like a narrow child's cubby house sits on one side, sleeping quarters for perhaps eight adults cramped together. There is no door, just a raised platform with a sloping earthen roof. It would keep the rain out. A few metres away is the kitchen, a campfire with a metal contraption holding a swaying skillet set above the coals. Next to this is a curious wheel and lathe. It takes me a while to identify it as a rudimentary log splitter for cutting firewood. A rusty saw is attached by a chain. How thoughtful of the authorities to provide shelter and cooking facilities for campers, all free of charge. And then I slap the first mosquito. Soon enough his buddies discover the exquisite vintage of my blood and they all crowd around for a drink. Time to leave.

Soon enough, we have crossed the spit and are now looking west over the North Sea rather than east towards the Baltic. It feels as if summer has finally arrived in Denmark, on our very last day here. I'm so excited, I consult the smartphone map and head towards the beach. We push our bikes through the soft sand to the water's edge.

'Do you think we could ride along the beach?' I ask.

'In the sand,' Cathie says.

'*On* the sand,' I answer.

'*In* your dreams,' she says.

I grip Bruce's handlebars firmly.

'Let's give it a go for a few hundred metres,' I say.

Cathie reaches for the camera and says, 'After you.'

I push off and pedal gingerly along the damp sand, navigating among the seashells. Bruce and I wobble valiantly along, like a drunk in a bar. After a few hundred metres my beach adventure sinks in the soft sand. I look back from where we started. Cathie hasn't moved. She waves. Perhaps the noise I hear isn't the squawk of a seagull, but the sound of laughter. Bruce and I wobble back.

'Lawrence of Arabia returns on a bicycle,' Cathie smiles.

'I just need fatter tyres,' I say.

Near Tversted, Marlene leads us down a lovely dirt path with glimpses of the sea as we wander between sand dunes and through the gorse and heather. We turn a corner and are confronted by a tide of cyclists ... a tsunami of cyclists heading our way. It's a 'fun cycle' which means beer is involved. We steer as far to the right of the path as possible as we're passed by scores, no hundreds of young cyclists. They are drunk. It starts harmlessly enough, people saying hello as we head valiantly against the flow, but those not at the front are by definition more drunk than their leaders. These stragglers wobble haphazardly past us, shouting in Danish. I'm sure they're saying 'you're going the wrong way!' There are as many women as men, equally intoxicated. We cross a bridge over a perky stream. We all must dismount. Boomboxes in baskets on handlebars blast doof doof across the dunes. Empty cans are thrown anywhere. What was a beautiful nature reserve resembles a litter dump. The revellers at the rear are dressed in fancy costumes - nuns and nurses for the ladies, nuns and Batman for the men. Empty beer cartons clog the path. We're increasingly forced off the track by sheer weight of numbers. I consult Marlene, but there is no alternative route. The tide keeps surging past us. I ring my bell constantly to warn of our approach. It makes no difference. These riders own the path for today. After thirty minutes of drunken mayhem, the tsunami subsides and we are again alone on a wonderful path leading through a mossy forest. We come upon two volunteers picking up beer cans. Both are riding mechanical trikes pulling large skips. The skips are nearly full.

Time for reinforcements, chaps.

Hirtshals, like many ferry ports is a town people only visit in order to leave. Ferries depart for Norway while fishing trawlers wait at the harbour. The trawlers are as large as those in Skagen. There's also a bevy of smaller trawlers. As we cycle slowly past one, three men work on deck, cutting fillets and putting them in plastic bags. I assume this is part-payment for their labour. A young boy works beside the men on the table. He looks up as we pass and smiles, holding up a bag of fillets, his trophy for the afternoon.

We divert to the port terminal. It's closed because all the ferries left hours ago. I walk to the three-storey office building, not really expecting anyone to be there. I push the double doors and they open. A young man at the counter confirms our tickets for tomorrow's boat. I ask him if today is a national holiday as everything is closed. He answers, rather uncertainly that it's Independence Day. I later learn it's actually Constitution Day to commemorate the signing of the document in 1849. It's also the date the Danes celebrate Father's Day. Two holidays for the price of one. Reason enough to get drunk and ride a bicycle through the sand dunes.

Our lodging tonight is in the basement of a house close to the port. The owner, a lady in her seventies welcomes us with gusto and leads us down the steep stairs to the bunker. It has chenille blankets on the single beds, a fading carpet and mysterious pipes running along the ceiling. On the walls are numerous photos of her family. She points out her mother, grandmother and her daughter. From the cardigan her daughter is wearing in the photo, I'd guess 1973. The young woman with chestnut hair and a winning smile is probably my age by now.

We eat dinner down on the wharf at the fresh fiske restaurant. We both order seafood plates which include smoked salmon, herring fillets pickled in sugar and spices, the ever-present fillet of plaice, shrimp, fish cakes, roe and a bundle of salty crisp chips. It's good value and quite tasty, although I've had enough of fried food over the past few weeks. After today's drunken encounter, Denmark is doing its best to leave us with a positive impression.

And what do I think of Denmark?

We've cycled the length of the Jutland peninsula but haven't visited the more progressive easterly island where Copenhagen is located. I've been to Copenhagen a few times previously. In many surveys listing wealth, happiness and contentment, Denmark ranks near the top of the pile. The people pay high rates of personal tax and yet maintain one of the best standards of living, proving the lie to all the Friedman economists. It's true the Danes have the lowest rate of personal savings in the EU, but this is largely because the State takes care of their welfare. They don't need to put money aside for unexpected illness or to fund their child's education. These are provided through taxation. As a society they have looked within and found what is workable and just. While the dogs of Friedman howl their nonsense of trickle-down economies and private ownership, thankfully the Danes have resisted such poisoned bait.

I admire the Danes. While they may be inward-looking and smugly content, perhaps it's because they deserve to be? The summer house is not so much a symbol of insularity as of satisfaction with what they've created. Why leave paradise? More than most, the Danes live in an almost classless society. A New Statesman poll found 90% of the population have a near-identical high standard of living. We should all aspire to such equality. If they can improve their culinary skills, I'd be tempted to visit more often.

While we've visited some magnificent cities, the countryside has been rather plain and repetitive. Wheat, canola or open farmland. We're mentally feeling a little dulled after so long on the road. Both of us talk of Norway and whether it'll jolt us out of our lethargy.

Chapter Eight: Norway

I'm always amused at how grown men get excited in the presence of ships and trains. Five of us, all middle-aged and holding cameras jostle for the best angle as the SuperSpeed One ferry slips into the dock. It's a blue and white behemoth capable of carrying the hundreds of cars and trucks parked behind the wire fence. Bruce and Aiwa are obediently waiting in Lane Thirty-nine, reserved for bicycles and a posse of rather large and intimidating Harley-Davidson motorbikes. The ferry unloads its cargo, including hundreds of Norwegian passengers who've travelled here to shop. Hirtshals has a large meat supermarket and apparently the stock is much cheaper this side of the strait. I checked the prices last night and deduced rather quickly that Norway is going to be hellishly expensive.

We're the first vehicles ushered aboard. Cathie and I pedal furiously ahead of a thunder of motorbikes. Bruce reacts rather peevishly by getting a flat tyre, the first of the trip, the moment we reach the gangplank. I manage to coax him into the bowels of the ship and we secure both bikes as best we can. We're all shepherded upstairs to vast decks littered with restaurants, bars and even more shopping. Despite this tacky array, I'm very excited to be crossing the Skagerrak. We choose a seat beside a large window and watch Denmark slowly recede.

An hour into the journey, I locate a young handsome Norwegian security guard. I ask him if there's any chance I can go below to repair Bruce's flat tyre. I'm expecting the standard party line of 'No, it's a safety issue.' He smiles and says, 'No problem.' His name is Leif and he escorts us down to the locked cargo hold and helps me manoeuvre Bruce into a safer area where I can work. Leif even offers to get me a bucket of water to make it easier to find the leak in the tube. He tells us when we've finished to find him on the upper deck and he'll secure the bike again. I fix the tube and Cathie goes to locate Leif. He's busy so another handsome young Norwegian named Henrik comes down. When he hears we're from Australia, he writes his phone number on a piece of paper and tells us if we have any problems along the coast road to call him. He has friends all the way to Bergen who'd be only too happy to help.

So often the first impression of a country influences your attitude. If this is a harbinger of what to expect in Norway, I can't wait to dock in Kristiansand.

We are given the honour of departing the ferry first before all the machinery starts up. We cycle into a cool sunny afternoon and within five minutes have located our hotel in the centre of Kristiansand. The receptionist is very friendly and leads us to our room which has a view over the rooftops to the sea and a scatter of uninhabited granite islands offshore. This hotel is above our usual budget but I managed to get a very cheap deal on a booking site so we're paying less than a three-star hotel in Australia. Breakfast is free.

We eagerly dress in street clothes and head out to get an exceptionally good coffee from the *Joe and the Juice* café around the corner, served by a hipster barista who smiles, a rare combination. We wander down to the foreshore where scores of young people are playing volleyball or football on the sand. It's like we've wandered into a supermodel summer camp. Blonde hair, white teeth, toned bodies. Two brave young men in swimmers stand on the boardwalk, pretending to dive into the water. Three hundred years ago, this area was cluttered with sawmills and rugged bearded descendants of Vikings loading ships with timber. Today, glass and steel apartment blocks circle the open spaces of the foreshore. I spy a bicycle repair station near a children's playground. It has a pressure hose for pumping tyres. I'm very excited. I can never get enough air into a tyre with my hand pump. I love Norway already.

We follow the shoreline around to the fish markets where sleek restaurants outnumber fishing boats. The markets are housed in recently redeveloped timber buildings painted yellow and red. We choose Restaurant Retti-I-Garnet simply because it has a menu that promises not to drain my bank account in a single sitting. We sit outside near a gas heater and gratefully accept a blanket each from the gorgeous blonde waitress. Surely every Norwegian can't be handsome? We order mackerel and trout with potatoes and cucumber salad and sour cream. It's hearty and delicious, with the mackerel having an oily flesh and crispy skin. It's much better than the seafood dishes we had in Denmark. I order two beers and consider emailing my bank manager for an overdraft. You want how much for a beer?

Over dinner, I list the unusual facts about Kristiansand - such as it's on the same latitude as Anchorage, Alaska and Leon Trotsky spent a year in exile here before fleeing to France and finally Mexico. Kristiansand is also the birthplace of the future Queen - the Crown Princess Mette Marit who you'll be shocked to learn is a strikingly handsome blonde woman. And, finally the Kristiansand Zoo is home to Julius, a male chimpanzee who was abandoned by his parents and lived with humans for a while where he learnt to drive a car and to paint. I wonder if he can ride a bicycle?

We return to our hotel and at midnight discover that a nightclub opposite our window has opened its doors to the supermodel brigade. They dance and drink and laugh until the early hours. We toss and turn and curse in rhythm.

A grumpy cyclist heads to breakfast, but is immediately cheered by the sign near the kitchen - *If you want to pack a picnic, ask us for suitable bags.* They're inviting us to steal food! Excellent. It's a huge smorgasbord of cheese, meats, fish, eggs and fruits. We fill our stomachs and our backpacks with treats. What a wonderful country!

Burdened with a few extra kilograms, we cycle around Posebyen, the old town of Kristiansand, a few blocks of low-rise wall-to-wall white wooden houses. For a city dogged by fire over the past three centuries, it's sad to see so little of its architectural history remaining. Posebyen boasts the longest continuous row of timber houses in Northern Europe. They all have big windows and a homely appeal. I'm reminded of the public schools of my era - wooden, open, accessible. The Cathedral bells toll nine o'clock as we leave Kristiansand. We cycle along a path beside the water with alternating views of encroaching industry and far-off granite islands. Soon enough, we're on a lonely road through a beech forest. It's cloudy and cool and I'm intensely excited to be here. Everything feels different.

The houses are either rough-hewn red-painted vertical-timber dwellings or smooth white-painted horizontal-planked abodes. I like them both. The villages we come across this morning are clustered around narrow inlets. At Langares, two fishing trawlers are moored at the wooden dock, along the narrow bay another thirty speedboats and tinnies are tied up. It's such a small village, I imagine everyone has a boat of some description. The village of Ausvika has a magnificent white timber church surrounded by a grass cemetery. Each of the headstones face south. A woman in a traditional costume of white frilly blouse and long black skirt walks with her children to the Sunday sermon.

After thirty kilometres we stop to eat the last of the honey cake we bought in Denmark. The wind is icy off the water. While there are many small houses along the coast, there are very few farms. Nature rules. It's so different than the past six weeks of cycling through heavily-populated Europe where it seems like every inch of ground is cultivated. Even though we're still close to Kristiansand, it's apparent that while the Norwegians live in nature, they don't necessarily want to tame it. Fishing is obviously a major recreational and income-generating activity along the coast. The only farm we've seen is a small cherry orchard, its trees covered with heavy plastic to ward off the frost.

Near Tregde, we scramble down a rocky embankment to a tiny inlet with a small wooden bridge crossing to a granite island. Our very own island for lunch! The wind dances across the water in gusts, creating intricate patterns on the surface. We sit on an old jetty and eat the stash from breakfast. The islands further west look windswept and washed out, pale grey granite denuded of trees and polished smooth by the harsh seasons. I could sit here for hours. Occasionally a fisherman in a small boat putters past, offering a wave. It's so quiet. From our hide out of the wind, I can see two red houses across the inlet, both with commanding positions on rocky points. Each residence has an identical boathouse down near the water, with the same red paint and white trim. One boathouse has a double door and two front windows while the other replaces the windows with life buoys hanging on the walls. Just in case?

In the late afternoon, we arrive in Mandal, a summer holiday village with a pristine sandy beach just outside of town and the largest wooden church in Norway. It's painted white, with a stocky steeple and is set in the grounds of the cemetery, like so many Scandinavian churches. The old town looks across the Mandal River and is a clutter of white horizontal-board timber houses and shops. Our lodging for the evening is a few kilometres out of town along the river at a campground. The owner, a charming old man with a grey beard and cloth cap happily shows us the Stabburet, a red timber single-room cabin perched on six large stones. It's a Flintstones house! We have to duck to walk inside where it's equally primitive with heavy timber walls and cross beams. It has a washbasin and a small fridge and two single beds. The showers and kitchen are in the main house. He tells us the design is based on a four-hundred year old Norwegian store house, set on stone to raise it above the snow line. How can we resist?

We cook a simple pasta meal in the warm kitchen and when the owner hears I couldn't buy beer in town because of Sunday trading, he returns with two cans left behind by a previous guest. Later in the evening, when Cathie is having a shower and I'm getting close to my

Stone Age self sitting on the front steps, a mother and her toddler walk towards the Stabburet. The toddler is intrigued by the strange house on stones. He drags his mother towards the entrance. I ask if she'd like to show him inside. She smiles and picks up her son and follows me, bowing to get through the doorway. The boy laughs and I'm reminded this cabin most resembles a child's cubby house, so small and cosy. The woman, her husband and son are from Germany and driving around Norway but she admits the cold is getting to them already. She can't believe we're riding north in this weather. In truth, it's not really that cold so I just shrug and tell her we wear lots of clothes and cycling keeps us warm. The boy wants to drag his mother to the next adventure, so they leave wishing me a safe journey. I tell her summer is just around the corner, although I'm not sure she believes me.

I go back to the front step and look over the wide rust coloured Mandal River. I think about our first day of cycling in Norway, characterised by endless hills, windswept inlets and rocky islands along the coast. Around every corner, over every hill, there was a rewarding vista. After so many kilometres of endless Danish farmland, I'm tremendously excited by what lays ahead. I'm not concerned about the mountains or the cool weather. Norway in all its majesty and rugged beauty has already entered my bloodstream. I can't wait until tomorrow.

On a sunny cool morning, we cycle through Mandal and discover a large campground beside the beach on the other side of town. White sand, a pine forest headland and gentle waves tempt me to take a dip. Pity I don't have a wetsuit in my panniers. My sat-nav, Marlene leads us through a golf course with the fairways following the shores of a narrow lake. We soon cross Route E39 heading north-west and enter a steep forest path lined by mossy logs, little streams and numerous birdhouses attached to the tall trees. For the first time this trip, I have to get off Bruce to push him up the steep gravelly path. We pass another long-distance cyclist, a blonde woman in her forties who seems to have overpacked, with panniers front and back. I say a chirpy hello and comment on the steepness of the track. She nods but steadfastly looks ahead. We leave her to the silence. Not every traveller wants to talk.

At Vigeland, we stop for an apple cake and a milky coffee. My eyes are watering from the chill of the downhill or it could be the cost of the coffee. A new section of highway forbids cyclists so we're exiled to a hill climb on the old road lined with yellow flowers, white timber houses and cows with cowbells in the fields. Lovely. There's a small mountain lake at the summit. I wait for Cathie to catch up.

'Every hill we climb, there's a lake on top,' I say.

'Makes it worth the effort,' she smiles.

'Then we race downhill to a fjord,' I add.

'And in between there's usually a waterfall,' she says.

I love Norway.

It snows for half of the year and in spring the snow melts to form these mountain lakes, with the run-off creating waterfalls which fill streams leading all the way to the fjord. And we're privileged to be here at the peak time for snowmelt. We follow a stream rushing beside the road tumbling over huge boulders and cutting through narrow ravines. I stop at a small bridge over the tumult and check my map. Within twenty kilometres of us in a wide circle are four lakes and two fjords. I trace a path ahead for the next few days and quickly lose count of the number of lakes and fjords we'll be passing. The tiredness of the past three thousand kilometres washes off me. I could cycle in this water wonderland forever.

After rejoining the E39, we race downhill to Lenefjorden following the bay hemmed in by a rock wall on one side and shallow mountains on the other. The traffic gives us a wide berth and we cruise for kilometres along the fjord, the sun glistening on the mirror surface. In the town of Rom, an old people's home dozes opposite a brand-new supermarket advertising orthopaedic shoes and salmon. We follow a long slow uphill route beside yet another stream and stop for lunch, sitting on a rock above the rushing water. We can barely hear ourselves talk over the roar.

Midway up another hill, we approach our first Norwegian tunnel. Numerous cycling bloggers have warned us about these passages of doom. They range in length from a brisk fifty metres to a Hades-inducing fifteen kilometres. In many tunnels, cyclists are forbidden. Fortunately, an alternate route is offered, usually up a long winding road over the mountain the tunnel is burrowing beneath. Cyclists get the views but pay for it with nose-bleed inclines.

We attach flashing lights to the front and rear of our bicycles, take a deep breath and plunge into the pit of panic, the shaft of scream, the depths of doom. Actually, the tunnel is very well illuminated and only a few hundred metres long. But when an oncoming truck enters, the noise is deafening. Curiously, although the truck is ahead of us in the opposite lane, the sound appears to be surging behind us. I'm sure we're being tailgated by a impatient truck driver. I risk a quick glance. Nothing. The good thing about a tunnel is no-one can hear your scream. One of us squealed mightily. I won't say who as he embarrasses easily.

Alas, the junior tunnel has an ugly big brother at the top of the hill. Numerous signs warns us that a toll is charged on E39 and that cyclists are forbidden. We stop for a coffee at the 'Pit Stop' café that wouldn't be out of place on Route 66 in the USA. I check the map. Marlene advises we take Route 461.

The detour works a treat as we don't have to pay tolls and the road, while brand spanking new, has very little traffic. We relax into a sunny afternoon. Look, there's a mountain lake. And another. So begins fifteen kilometres of cycling nirvana. We follow a stream which alternates between waterfalls, white-water rapids and gentle pools as it descends. Every few kilometres, we're greeted by another lake. I'm almost tempted to stop and dive into the clear pure water, but I can only imagine how cold it would be. There are a few lonely cabins built on the granite rock surrounding each of the lakes.

We stop beside one large circular lake and park Bruce and Aiwa on a walking bridge over the stream. I remove a small towel from my panniers.

'What's that for?' Cathie asks.

'Maybe I'll go for a swim,' I say.

She smiles and runs back to the panniers to get the camera.

'Just in case,' she says.

From across the lake comes the sound of a house being built on a rocky crag in the lee of the mountains, sheltered from the winds. It's too far away for the builders to see me as I quickly undress.

'Naked time!' Cathie calls.

She removes the lens cap from the camera.

'We will get action shots?' she asks.

I hesitantly step on the mossy rocks. The water is piercingly cold. I'm too scared to dive into the water, so I quickly submerge, bending my knees as a chill shoots up my spine. It's exhilarating. Cathie laughs and snaps away.

'You're braver than I am,' she calls.

'Stupider, you mean,' I say.

It's marvellously invigorating. I hop out and sit on the towel on the warm rock. As George Costanza would say, 'Yes, there was shrinkage.'

I let the sunshine dry my body while we enjoy the view. Rock, water, trees, mountain and an endless sky. It's amazing where two bicycles can take you. The name of the lake is Gluggevatn - Glugge's Lake - an ugly name for a beautiful place. Eventually we make our way back to Bruce and Aiwa and follow the road past even more lakes, all fed by the same wonderous stream. This section of road rates easily in my Top Ten roads of all time, right up there with Passo Dello Stelvio in Italy and the Col de la Croix de Fer in the French Alps. It's much easier to climb than those two monsters yet the scenery is just as rewarding and the feeling of exhilaration just as complete.

It's a pity that Bruce decides at this very moment to get another puncture. I guess I was pushing my luck. I remove the tube as quickly as I can. The stream comes in useful for submerging the tube and locating the puncture. Cathie can't help but take a photo of the spot where I'm repairing the tube. One waterfall and two lakes are in frame. And an upside down Bruce.

I pump as much air as I can manage with the handheld pump into the tyre and we cycle away, nowhere near as deflated as Bruce's rear tube. We pass more lakes, all with cumbersome names - Storefossvatn, Lykkeriholmsvatn and Grunnevatn. After Solasvannet, we reach the top of the mountain and cruise into our lodging for the evening, the rather grand Utsikten Hotel, perched on a hill above the town of Kvinesdal, way down there in the valley. The receptionist says we can leave our bicycles in the basement next to the workman's tools and the dirty linen.

'You see Bruce, this is what happens when you misbehave,' I say.

Our room, in fact the whole hotel, has a mind-bogglingly beautiful view straight down the fjord to the sea. Cathie and I spend the afternoon sitting on a garden seat looking towards the ocean.

'You know, the first fifteen kilometres tomorrow will be all downhill,' I say.

'And after that?' she asks.

'I'll buy you a coffee,' I say, avoiding the issue.

'And cake, to get me up the inevitable mountains,' she smiles.

It's a curious hotel. There seems to be very few guests. The receptionist doubles as a waitress and bartender. We eat in the huge dining room with the same spectacular view. A solitary man sits in the corner typing on his computer and the chef bangs away in the kitchen.

The menu is limited, the food okay but not inspiring and certainly not worth the steep Norwegian prices, but we have little option. Tomorrow it's back to campgrounds.

Don't you love a country that can afford to lodge its roadworkers in a luxury hotel on top of a mountain? We're joined at breakfast by a dozen workers in fluro vests and overalls. They've beaten us to the breakfast steal - each of the workers has packed numerous sandwiches into plastic bags. There is no food remaining on the buffet. I ask the lone waiter if they're be able to replenish. He goes into the kitchen and brings out extra trays of food. We eat muesli, fruit and yoghurt and pack ourselves sandwiches of ham and cheese and salad.

It's a glorious sunny day. The descent into Kvinesdal is refreshingly chilly and we're spat out along a narrow valley road beside the fjord with mountains on either side. This section has three tunnels. We turn our lights on and nervously cycle through them. I'll never get used to the roar of the traffic in the narrow tube. I focus on holding my line and the light in the distance. It's a relief to exit the third tunnel into the fresh air of Fedafjord.

Feda is a lovely little village near the mouth of the fjord. It's also at one end of the longest underwater power cable in the world. The NorNed cable connects the power grids of Norway with The Netherlands through a five hundred and eighty kilometre submarine cable.

While Norway profits hugely from its large offshore oil and gas reserves, it generates most of its electricity through hydroelectric schemes. Many of the mountains and hills we've been cycling through are laced with hydro tunnels and electricity sub-stations. It's a curious anomaly. The country has become rich from a dirty fuel which has allowed it to invest in clean energy. In fact, the government of Norway runs the largest sovereign wealth fund in the world. In 2014, the fund reached 5.11 trillion crowns. Norway's population is a little over five million - the fund holds a million crowns for each citizen. Not that Magnus and Mathilde Norway can access the fund, of course. The government has sought to avoid splurging and is only allowed to spend a little over four percent of the fund each year. This spending is mainly directed towards huge infrastructure projects - tunnels and roads through the Arctic Circle, over and under fjords and through the wilderness.

The downside is it makes Norwegians less inclined to work at menial jobs. A large underclass of foreign workers take up the slack. In fact, one in five Norwegians of working age receive some kind of social insurance.

The underwater cable link with The Netherlands may become even more important in the future. Norway is undertaking extensive research into becoming the power battery pack of Europe. While countries like Denmark and Germany are investing heavily in renewable energy, wind and solar plants as yet don't offer twenty-four hour power. When the wind doesn't blow or during the night, Denmark and Germany must sometimes revert to coal or oil-fired dirty power. Norway is hoping to store the surplus power from wind and solar in the water behind the hydro dams, ready to be used at the opening of a sluice gate. In effect, the wilderness of Norway may house much of the power needs of northern Europe. With the financial backing of the wealth fund, ironically built on dirty fuel, Europe is headed to a clean energy future. Of course, this all begs the question of how Norway can wean itself off the income it receives from its oil and gas fields.

After Feda, we're consigned to the hilly backroads because it's illegal to cycle through the tunnels on the main route. I don't mind. I prefer this shady forest road beside large moss-covered rocks and to be serenaded by birdsong rather than the thunder of eighteen-wheel trucks. Too soon, we have no alternative but to rejoin the E39 where we're welcomed by a three-hundred and sixty metre tunnel. We hold our breath and plunge through, emerging into a long downhill to Flekkefjord, a town of white houses scattered on the hills rising up from the fjord. We find a sunny cafe with a blonde waitress - is there any other waitress in Norway - who speaks perfect English and offers us a delicious custard and cream bolle and a milky coffee. I'm beginning to accept the Norwegians prefer their coffee weak. Flekkefjord has existed as a town since the 16th century, largely through the fishing industry and by mining the plentiful supplies of rock surrounding the town. The Dutch paving stones we bumped over last month could well have been shipped from here. I look up at the surrounding mountains. There's still a lot of rock around.

Our first day of cycling in Norway was dominated by islands and inlets. Yesterday featured rivers and lakes. Today looks like tunnels and mountains. After Flekkefjord we're pitched onto a long switchback climb. These mountains appear as if created by the Gods playing too long with granite plasticine, poking and prodding them into awkward angles, sheer crevices and weathered boulders. The granite peaks rear out of dark clear mountain lakes. The climbing is certainly slow, but immensely enjoyable. There's nothing to do but pedal and marvel at the lakes and mountains. We're passed by an occasional car, so we relax in the sunshine and scenery. Each day in Norway just gets better.

What goes up, must come down and soon enough we're hurtling down a steep incline - look, there's another fjord - into the quaint village of Ana-Sira. We cross a ramshackle bridge over a wild river that looks as if it could sweep away the town if it got angry. We cycle to the wharf with a clear view all the way down the fjord to the ocean. On a wooden pier, we eat ham and cheese sandwiches and debate whether we'd have the courage to go to the sea in the one trawler that's moored at the wharf. *Topsy* the trawler is built of timber and steel and boasts an lurid orange mast and baby-blue cabin. The tide stretches the mooring ropes taut, as if Topsy wants to set sail without a crew. On the sunny deck of a house opposite, a man sets up his video camera, perhaps waiting for the moment Topsy breaks free.

Suitably refreshed, we start climbing again. And again. The switchbacks send my Garmin into overdrive, recording gradients up to 14%. Ouch. Cathie doesn't miss a beat, slowly turning the pedals and heading skywards. After passing the fourth, or was that the fifth mountain lake this afternoon, we cycle beside a granite range with a curious dam-like mound of gravel, perhaps fifty-metres high and one hundred metres across, spanning two peaks. I can't decide whether it's man-made or is the remains of a glacial moraine. I can't see any hydro-scheme, even though it looks very different than the other rock formations, so I reckon it's morainal. The moron says morainal.

At the top of the climb, we meet two German female cyclists. With limited common language, they tell us our campground for the evening is 'scheisse!' We decide to detour to Sogndal in the hope of finding an alternative. With another steep lurch downhill, we reach the famous Jøssingfjord. It was here in 1940, during the early stages of the Second World War that a British destroyer, the HMS Cossack intercepted and boarded a German tanker carrying two hundred and ninety-nine British merchant sailors and prisoners of war. A number of German sailors were killed in the boarding, but all the British prisoners were liberated. The Norwegian navy did not intervene in this skirmish and some historians argue this incident later gave Hitler the pretense he needed to invade neutral Norway. While the raid undoubtedly rescued the merchant sailors and was an early success for the British, it certainly lead to Norway being dragged into the wider conflict.

Jøssingfjord is a narrow inlet ringed by granite mountains. We cycle past a wharf and loading terminal designed for large cargo ships. I look across the fjord and see a car emerging from a tunnel in the sheer rock wall, perhaps three hundred metres above us. Surely our road doesn't go ... oh dear. We've climbed a thousand metres already today and now we have to play mountain goats.

Head down, bottom up and the breath catches in my throat as we hit a 12% gradient which loops around the rock into a death-defying uphill tunnel. Just before entering it, I spy a old road leading left, out on a bitumen balcony overlooking the fjord. Wow! That is some alternative. We lift our bikes over the crash barrier and cycle gingerly along the precipice. It's not the gradient that's causing me to wobble uphill. We're insanely close to the edge of a sheer drop into the fjord. At one point, I stop and look down to the fjord where a large container ship is entering the inlet. From up here, it's looks like a toy. I'm still having trouble accepting we've climbed so steeply, so quickly. The sheer drop makes my head spin.

From here, it's a looping downhill to the quiet village of Sogndal which has a supermarket, a community hall and a pitch of houses, but no hotel. I check my smartphone and find a possibility - a mind-numbingly expensive possibility - a few kilometres away at Sogndalstrand. We head towards the water. The village is a beautiful cluster of white timber houses perched on the rocky bank of a river just before it flows into the ocean. Sogndalstand Kulturhotell is a series of ten houses on the main thoroughfare leading to the wharf that have been converted into accommodation. We enter the old country store, named Gata which acts as the restaurant and hotel lobby. A cheery woman meets us and confirms they have one room available. I try not to faint when she mentions the price. She leads us down the street to an almost identical white timber building. Our room is large and on the ground floor. Across the hall is a conference room perched over the river. She returns after a few minutes and tells us that after cleaning up today's conference she discovered a jug of coffee and plate of cakes we may be interested in? You bet! What a lovely gesture. Maybe the price of the room isn't so bad.

After having a shower, we retrieve two bottles of beer from the fridge and stroll down to the wharf. We look across the small bay to a cluster of houses leading up a rocky hill. A lone fishing boat is moored at the wharf. It's a beautiful village although it's hard to believe that one hundred years ago it boasted twenty stores, four taverns and three bakeries. Salmon and herring provided well for Sogndalstrand, but when the stocks diminished so did the town. Now the only remaining business is this hotel and a regular influx of tourists during summer. The population of eighty people still catch salmon from the river flowing past their doors, although now only for their own dinner plate.

In the evening we eat in the restaurant. An entree of spicy soup followed by a delicious roast veal and potatoes. The line of cars parked in the main street reveal the wealth of the regular diners. BMW, Mercedes, Audi. None of them have the character or have come as far as two charcoal-coloured bicycles resting under a wooden awning.

We fall asleep to the sound of the rushing river. Magical.

It's cool and cloudy in the morning, but Sogndalstrand looks just as beautiful. As does my wife when we tuck into a hearty breakfast. At 7am, I'm surprised by the number of guests awake and scoffing the smoked salmon. We climbed one thousand six hundred metres yesterday and today threatens over a thousand. Our bones our creaking and muscles weary, but we're thrilled to begin every day, knowing Norway promises so much. I could cycle in this country forever.

We retrace our route from yesterday back to Sogndal. Marlene has chosen a quiet narrow road that leads us through fishing villages where the boats and sheds are desperately in need of a fresh coat of paint. The small houses perched on rocks look stoically over the windswept bays. The mountain lakes of yesterday are replaced by grassy sheep meadows and narrow fjords. On a road offering more gravel than bitumen we pass a wooden storeroom built on stones which harks back to our Flintstone lodgings from a few days ago.

'You're very quiet this morning,' Cathie says, as we cruise past a herd of sheep.

'I've been counting fjords and lakes,' I answer.

'And what's the score?'

I check my Garmin.

'In sixteen kilometres we've passed four small fjords and seven lakes,' I say.

'You're kidding!'

'Best cycling country in the world,' I say.

'*Hilliest* cycling country in the world,' Cathie answers.

As if to prove Cathie's point, we cycle up a steep switchback before freewheeling downhill to rejoin the main road. I reach the intersection first and am met by a man on a bicycle. He stops just past the corner and quickly hops off his bike. I say hello and he nervously asks me to stop cycling. I do as he wishes and look up the road from where he's descended. Is this a rather elaborate Norwegian sting operation? Will he make a getaway on the shabby mountain bike?

A posse of teenagers speed down the road on mountain bikes in a whooping joyful burst. They swoop past us. He tells me this is a dangerous corner and his students are still learning. From the speed they were reaching, I'd say they're doing okay. He jumps back on his bike and races to catch up. That's my kind of school lesson.

Cathie and I do our own zooming, at a more adult pace all the way to Egersund where we find a cafe run by a recent Turkish immigrant. We talk to him about his old homeland. He admits to homesickness but seems determined to make a go of it here in the North. Before he makes our coffee, he brings a sealed bag of beans to our table. He opens it with a knife and holds it out for Cathie to smell.

'The aroma takes me home,' he says, simply.

Egersund is a quiet town of white timber houses and is blessed with one of the largest harbours in Norway. It was also the birthplace of perhaps the most macabre musician of recent memory. Øystein Aarseth was born here in 1968 and left to form the black metal band Mayhem. He went under the pseudonym Euronymous, a misspelling of the Greek myth *Eurynomos*, the spirit of rotting corpses who existed in the Netherworld. Don't you just love Black Metal?

In Øystein's short life, he was accused of burning down a church; taking photos of his friend Per 'Dead' Ohlin's corpse after 'Dead' had committed suicide; making necklaces from the bones of 'Dead'; and influencing a entire generation of Oslo's musicians into the charms of Black Metal. He was murdered by fellow muso, Varg 'Count Grishnackh' Vikernes in 1993 at the age of twenty-five. Pictures of Øystein Aarseth show him with ghoulish white make-up and painted black lips. Without make-up, he looks like a teenage kid from the boondocks, with long hair and a wispy beard. Someone who should be riding skateboards and smoking dope down on the waterfront.

We cycle around Egersund. Old ladies wheel shopping trolleys, two men sit at a park bench, one smokes a pipe, the other adjusts the lead on his dog. A mother in jeans and a long overcoat walks past pushing a double pram. As we pass an idling truck, the music I hear from the radio is innocuous sixties pop. I'm pleased to see the wooden church is still standing.

Just outside of town we discover the old Jærbanen railway line, an eight-kilometre section reconstructed for cyclists. The trail is fringed with purple lupins. It loops up and down and at its highest point gives us a sweeping view of Eigerøya Island and Norda Sundet Sound. The government has bought all of the land leading down to the Sound and plans to establish walking trails to the water.

We rejoin a back road but soon enough come upon the Old West Norway Road, a six kilometre gravel track built in 1845 and in use until 1940. The sign advises us of 23% gradients and warns 'you should be prepared for some demanding uphill and downhill slopes.' It also suggests a gentler alternate route. No way!

We wilfully enter the lunar landscape of granite boulders as big as trucks balanced precariously on each other, waiting for the next earth tremor to dislodge and roll on an unsuspecting cyclist. The track is very gravelly, particularly when faced with a 23% gradient. I make it half-way up before my back wheel spins and Bruce starts to wobble. I jump off and push. Cathie is even more daunted by the downhill. On the steepest descent, it feels as if the back wheel could just pitch straight over my head in a painful somersault. My hands go numb from clasping the brakes. It's a barren landscape of wild wind, flowering heather and boulders. I crest one hill and see nothing but boulders and small frosty lakes to the horizon. Despite the difficulty, it's a startlingly beautiful road through a pristine landscape. We stop for lunch and jump from rock to rock before finding the perfect spot out of the wind, our backs against a boulder facing the weak sunshine. There's not a sound except the rustle of wind.

The path finishes at a flower nursery, of all places. Hothouses bloom red, white and pink. On a quiet road, the landscape changes dramatically back to lush green pastures and farms. It's as though we've crossed some unseen border. Small granite rock fences surround each property. We stop in the small village of Brusland for supplies.

My Garmin tells me we've already climbed more than we expected and by the time we cycle up a six kilometre winding farm road, it reads 1600 metres, the same as yesterday. At the summit, we follow a dead-end road through a landscape that reminds me of the moors of northern England - a place of biting winds, wild heather and stark horizons. I can't understand how a hotel can be out here, so isolated from the villages ringing the coast. The owners have no chance of snaring passing traffic.

Late in the afternoon we cycle through a tree-lined corridor to a lake and our hotel, which turns out to be not a hotel at all but a Christian Centre, offering its spare rooms to guests. We enter the reception and in an adjacent room see twenty senior citizens sitting around a table drinking tea. The youngest man, perhaps in his fifties, with a beard and heavy woollen jumper comes to greet us. He's a jovial chap who leads us back outdoors and across the square to the basement of a side building where our room is located. It's rather small. It does have a view of the lake, but I feel as if I've been excommunicated to the worst room. And it's not cheap. He explains that our breakfast will be left in the kitchen upstairs, ready for us at whatever time we prefer. I ask if we can use the kitchen for cooking a meal this evening. He looks pained. It seems as if a Christian conference is taking place and they may need the space. As well as the meeting room two floors above us.

Oh God, please don't let them sing hymns all night.

When he leaves, we walk up to the kitchen and start cooking dinner. We reason we'll cook, eat and be gone before the believers arrive and turn water into wine. Actually, I'm already missing my evening beer. Alcohol is forbidden.

Jesus!

Taking the Lord's name in vain is also forbidden.

We eat a simple pasta meal and look across the lake. It begins to rain. We tidy the kitchen and return to our small room. I sit on a chair and Cathie sits on the bed and we look at each other.

'Bugger it,' I say, 'They sold us a hotel room so there must be an area for guests somewhere.'

'Do you want to join the Christians?' she smiles.

I stand and slip on my jacket.

'Let's go,' I say.

We return to the reception area.

It's very quiet. The tea room is closed.

We're about to venture upstairs when the same man comes out from an office. He seems surprised to see us.

'Do you have a guest's room,' I ask.

He thinks for a few seconds before shaking his head.

'We don't want to sit in our small room,' I say. It's possible I emphasised the word 'small.'

He rubs his beard and, as if deciding we're not dangerous black metal music fans, he tells us to follow him. He leads us upstairs to a huge room with a stone fireplace at one end and wide windows looking out to a moss-covered forest. It's beautiful. He points out the four lounges we can use, offers us a Norwegian newspaper and begins to build a raging fire. We tell him of our journey and where we come from. They've never had Australian guests before. When the fire is blazing, he leaves us but returns a minute later and asks us if we'd like cake. We nod.

He clanks around downstairs for a very long time before returning with a catering trolley loaded with three large cakes, each offering sixteen slices and a stack of pancakes accompanied by bowls of jam and cream. He tells us it's left over from the convention this afternoon. He laughs heartily and tells us to eat as much as we want.

I scoff three slices - two apple, one cherry - and two pancakes. I can't tell you how much Cathie ate or she'll kill me. We sit and watch the fire burn until there are only embers left and then retreat to our heathen dungeon. The Christians upstairs are singing. Our single beds creak. Must be something we ate.

The morning coffee is hot and strong and accompanied by a pre-packed and blessed breakfast overlooking the lake. It is very early on a misty morning, but I still expected company. Perhaps all the old people sang themselves into a torpor last night. We retrieve our bikes and load up. It's a lovely isolated place, four heavy wooden buildings with earthen roofs overlooking a cold mountain lake. It's called the Holmavatn Ungdoms og Misjonssenter, which roughly translates as Holmavatn Youth and Mission Centre. We were the youngest people here last night. Perhaps they should host an evening of black metal headbanging to increase recruitment?

The mist settles on the meadows and everything is hushed. So quiet in fact, that one tiny creak from dear old Bruce sends two cows into such a state that they run helter skelter towards a wire paddock fence. And don't stop. One fence down and two bovines on the loose. Cathie and I stop pedalling and look around. We can't see a farmhouse. There's no choice but to continue on. Except standing in the middle of the road are two very large and cantankerous cows. I inch forward. One of them does her best imitation of Wiley Coyote and skedaddles down the road, briskly followed by her frantic partner. They spot a herd of comrade cows in a distant field and plough straight through another fence to reach them.

As an aside, if you're ever in the need of a fence, don't hire a

Norwegian to build it.

Wiley and her buddy join the herd and start grazing contentedly as if nothing had happened. No-one in the herd suggests they make a dash for freedom through the yawning gap in the fence. They just eat their way to dairy. Lovely docile animals.

In the village of Nærbo, we cycle behind a dozen teenage girls, all tall and thin with long blonde hair. They're cycling in two and threes, laughing and singing and enjoying the day that is already getting brighter. They don't have school bags so I wonder where they're going? We overtake a few of them, a few pass us and we play bicycle hop-scotch for the next five kilometres. We spend most of that time smiling at each other. I'm not sure if we've adopted them or they us? Eventually, I ask a bright-eyed blonde where they're going. In uncertain English, she explains they're on an excursion to the forest. Without a teacher. I'm immeasurably glad to hear this. I like a country that sends their teenagers off on bikes to the forest without supervision.

We wave goodbye as they turn off down a narrow path. A few kilometres further on four teenage girls stop us and ask if we know the way to the forest. I assume it's the same excursion, but these girls don't have bikes. I use my smartphone to locate where we are, but none of us can locate the forest. They smile and continue on their way. Lost and happy. I think of my own country where teenagers are ferried to school, sports and into town by harried parents driving petrol-guzzling four-wheel-drives. Do we want independent free-spirited young people, or spoilt inward-looking numbskulls. Norway has voted and I like the result.

It's a morning of young people. We now pass a conga-line of pre-school children walking in pairs, holding hands, their smiling teachers leading the way. I can't help but smile at how many clothes the children are wearing - jackets, gloves, boots, beanies. What was that about summer?

In the village of Kvernaland, a scatter of modern houses rising from the shores of a lake, we stop for excellent berry cake and average machine coffee. It really is a lovely cake, big enough for us to share, sprinkled in brown sugar and wild berries.

Before we know it we're in Sandnes, a confusion of shops, bus stations and traffic that isn't particularly appealing. Sandnes and Stavanger have expanded to meet each other and the mix is a modern litter of suburbia and industry. Thankfully, the path keeps close to the fjord as we pass a mess of modern buildings. Some are creatively built, but many are designed by people with poor eyesight and envy issues. Is this the future of all modern art - so much of it seems to try too hard and be stridently of the 'look at me look at me' variety. All gloss and no story. Where is the desire for form, function, taste, intelligence and harmony? We are living in Kardashian times, I guess. Sorry, Sandnes - it's me, not you.

Our introduction to Stavanger is the wide Boknafjord, a ring of distant mountains and a marina so crammed with speedboats and cruisers I wonder how they manoeuvre out of their berths. Stavanger is the oil capital of Europe. In 1965, Norway the least-densely populated country in Europe - a land of farmers and fishermen - convinced the supposedly more wily and sophisticated Danes and Britons to sign an offshore oil treaty that gave Norway a huge expanse of the North Sea. Simply put, Denmark and Great Britain did not forsee a time when oil would be extracted from the depths.

Ha!

I'm reminded of an American TV series from my childhood called The Beverley Hillbillies where a bunch of yokels discover oil on their patch of earth and become immeasurably rich. Welcome to wonderland. To celebrate, we sit under a flowering tree beside the marina and eat lunch. I try to count the number of pleasure cruisers. I give up at one hundred and fifty.

At the downtown wharf, a mighty cruise liner is berthed. It's at least ten storeys high and each of the numerous suites has a balcony with tables and chairs. It's a floating palace. On shore, the crowds of people passing are impeccably dressed and coiffured, as if they've just stepped off a cruise ... oh yeah. We clank pass in dusty lycra. Before we admire the oil riches of Stavanger, I have some serious questions to ask a clerk in the tourist office.

'How can we cycle north without catching a long ferry or a bus?'

The short answer is we can't. The sole short ferry service that would allow us to island hop and bicycle has been permanently cancelled. Surely, it can't be because it wasn't paying its way. Who cares. We're in one of the richest countries on earth! Let's channel a little of that highly-polluting oil wealth into a bicycle route north shall we.

Alas, I book two tickets on a long ferry to take us across the fjord tomorrow morning.

Defeated, we attempt to book into our apartment at the very early hour of 1:30pm. The Ukranian woman at the counter cheerfully hands us our keys and draws the location of our room on a map. This service leases apartments in a scatter of buildings around the foreshore. Ours is in a very unusual apartment block. The lower three floors are Soviet brutal, concrete and grey, but some bright spark has balanced a timber and glass fourth floor on top. The windows are four metres high and from the footpath, I can see into each apartment. We lock Bruce and Aiwa in the basement and locate our apartment at the end of a long hallway. I open the door and am overwhelmed by the size of the window. We have a loft bedroom, a small kitchen and a view that looks over the white timber houses of old Stavanger. And how much does this cost? About the same as filling two suburban cars with Norwegian oil. But what a view!

We wander the streets of Stavanger all afternoon, pleased to be out of the saddle. The old church in the town centre is on a slight rise overlooking a small lake ringed by cobblestone streets. Pity they located the bus station opposite. We head back to the waterfront where the Stavanger Major Female Volleyball tournament is in progress. Lots of handsome young women in bikinis are bunting a ball over a net in a very powerful and exuberant manner. It's entertaining, but I have some misgivings about the choice of apparel. Is it because they're playing on sand or to attract an audience of beer-drinking tourists.

'If you've got it flaunt it, I guess,' I say.

'Is that why you wear lycra?' Cathie smiles.

I'm particularly taken with the warm-up methods of certain competitors. A few practice their spikes and lunges, but many are involved in what can only be described as volleyball yoga, contorting their bodies in various shapes that stretch and bend ... and attract a larger audience of males than the actual tournament.

Old Stavanger is a warren of restored white-washed timber buildings on narrow cobblestone lanes leading up from the wharf. It's simply beautiful, like being cast back to 1854 without the serge clothing, dysentery and soot. The two hundred and fifty houses owe their existence to Einar Heden, the city architect who lead a campaign to save the town from being razed and redeveloped. In Einer's honour, I buy a pancake with jam from a group of teenagers who've set up a stall in their back yard. Cathie shakes her head when I suggest two. As we walk away, I offer her a bite. We return and order another. Best value in Stavanger.

We pass a number of hair salons in town, including one full of hipsters with wall-to-wall bushy beards, pomade and rolled up jeans. I enter a few salons and ask how much for a number one head shave. Ouch! I refrain from telling them I could buy forty-two pancakes for the same price. A short distance away from Tourist Central, I enter another establishment. The owner is a refugee from Aceh in Indonesia who came here after the devastating tsunami in 2004. She shaves my head and tells me of her experiences settling into Norway. She finds the people more reserved, but is grateful for the home she has created for her son. She looks wistfully out the window, remembering palm trees, a sandy beach and humidity.

I take my bowling ball head back to our apartment.

In the morning we walk our bikes onto a small ferry, welcomed aboard by a pretty slim-hipped sailor who takes our ticket and shows us where to park the bikes. She spends the rest of the journey talking to the commuters as if they're old friends.

I'm struck by just how many islands there are, often populated by a few windswept houses. For ninety minutes, the ferry plots a route around the fjord. I count off the major islands, Mosterøy, Rennesøy and Finnøy - each with populations of a few thousand hardy souls. But while they may appear to be isolated, each is connected to Stavanger through a series of lengthy road tunnels under the fjord. Norway is so insanely wealthy, it builds multi-million kroner connections to service a few thousand island dwellers. The ferry is just for we cyclists and a few pedestrians.

If there is a boring road in Norway, I've yet to find it. We dock at Nedstrand and celebrate by buying cake at the local store. Coffee is free. I like that. We begin a gentle climb winding our way across a series of islands, connected by bridges. Even this minor road offers us views across fjords to steep sheep meadows and snowy mountains. We cruise downhill entering the pretty village of Skjoldastraumen. Cathie lectures me on always trying to convince her to eat cake. She calls me an enabler.

We walk into the Co-op in the village and I order a single Danish pastry and two coffees. I'm about to bite into the pastry when Cathie says, 'Are we sharing?' Another reason I love my wife.

We follow Route 515 through open fields, past lakes and fjords, up and over gentle hills and barely see another human. In Førre, a lone boy juggles a soccer ball on a full-size imitation grass soccer field. The nets are up, lines permanently marked, he just needs one good friend or a vivid imagination. As I'm watching from the top of the hill, he dribbles the length of the field and near the penalty spot slams the ball into the roof of the net. I feel like cheering.

We stop for lunch near the Førre War Museum which consists of a tank, a water mine, a small cannon and a shed full of memorabilia. A straggle of pensioners leave the museum, climbing aboard a blue and white bus. As it departs, another bus arrives unloading a horde of laughing school children. Perfect timing. We sit at the nearby dock and watch a man paint his wooden-hulled boat. White with nautical blue trim.

From here, it's uphill alongside busy roads on our very own cycle path to Haugesund, second in line to Stavanger in the oil-rich stakes. We find our hotel near the waterfront and they let us check in early. What is it about European hotels - they are always friendly and accommodating - the opposite of what I expect in my home country. We have a room on the top floor with a view looking over the tiny island of Hasseløy, attached to the mainland by a high arched bridge. It's populated by a smattering of white timber houses and a sentry line of pine trees.

Some towns are immediately appealing, others you instinctively look for the exit sign. Haugesund is definitely one of the former with wide streets featuring wooden houses and a town centre that looks old yet well-maintained. The main street is closed to traffic and shopkeepers display their wares along the footpath. We walk past a shop called Palestine overflowing with fresh fruit and vegetables, including mangoes, berries, coconuts, grapes and an exotic array of nuts and spices. There are many immigrant faces among the shoppers.

A few doors along the Totalen Cafe serves excellent rock cake and coffee in a space that was once a ballroom with an ornate ceiling and raised platform where the band played - now the shop counter. Sure enough, a hipster with a long beard, check shirt and a natty hat walks in and orders a coffee. It's that kind of place. In the late afternoon, most of the townsfolk wander down to the docks where a stanza of cafes and restaurants offer outdoor drinking in the sunshine. It's a young handsome population. They eat seafood and drink beer staring across the Smegasund to the island of Risøy where an imposing nearly-completed oil rig rears up, like a creature from a 1950s sci-fi movie. Fishing boats line the pier. Beer barrels or fishing nets. Construction cranes or tourist hotels. Oil rigs or old world cafes. Haugesund walks the tightrope between two worlds with aplomb.

Back at our hotel, the gentleman at the front desk, an old man with a shock of grey hair and sparkling eyes talks to us about the history of Harald the Fairhair - the first King of Norway - honoured just outside of town with a national monument. We list the towns we plan to visit and the old man has a story about each one. I'm tempted to ask if he'd like to join us but I fear he'd leave us behind on the hills. He also tells us about two of the biggest fjords in the world, not far from our destination of Bergen.

Just a few days cycling in fact.

Haugesund is too captivating to spend any time in a hotel room, so we wander the streets after dinner admiring the neo-classical Town Hall - a birthday cake of pink and white decorated with a creeping yellow vine, a row of Doric columns and set back from a park of fountains and flag poles. From classic to contemporary, we walk up the steep incline to the central arch of the bridge linking the city with Risøy. Four young men in wetsuits pilot jet skis down the narrow sound, followed by a single white yacht. The bars are crowded and in one of the warehouses a band starts rehearsing. Scandinavian Heavy Metal, distorted guitars and guttural vocals. What is that all about?

We return to the peaceful promenade and watch the blondes walk by - two by two.

The next morning is cool and cloudy, our default weather for this trip. We begin with a visit to Harald's monument, a large mound surrounded by twenty-nine granite pillars and topped by a seventeen metre high obelisk. It's thought that Harald is buried under the mound, but many pesky historians dispute this. Everyone does agree that the monument commemorates the Battle of Hafrsfjord, thought to have occured in 872, where Harald crushed the army of Rogaland and became the first widely accepted King of Norway. Those who didn't submit to his rule were killed or emigrated to Iceland. Harald died in 933, which by my calculation means he lived to be an exceptionally old man by the standards of those times ... or those pesky historians can't agree on dates yet again. Some suggest the Battle took place in 890. Either way, Harald won and the losers flipped off to Iceland to hunt reindeer and give birth to Bjork's ancestors.

We cross the provincial border from Rogaland into Hordaland and take a sharp left hand turn along the narrow Route 541. The farms are small, running only a few long-haired sheep. While there is an occasional attempt at land clearing, it appears as if the owners have given up, so daunted by the size of the landscape. Everything in Norway is too big, too rocky, too cold, overwhelming in its immensity. Including this steep hill we're cycling up!

'How do you tell the difference between a fjord and a lake,' I say.

'Is this a joke?' Cathie answers.

'No, I've been thinking about it for a week. I reckon there's one easy method,' I say.

'Okay, how?' Cathie asks.

'Look for a fishing boat. If you see one, it's a fjord,' I say.

Cathie thinks about it for a moment.

'You're smarter than you look,' she smiles.

The Norwegians have a long history of fishing and seafaring. Every fjord we've passed, and there's been very many, has had a fishing boat moored in each village. No matter how big or small the village.

The lakes are boat free. I assume this is for a few reasons - the difficulty of access to get the boat in and out of the lake; the lack of abundant fish in each lake; and lakes are for leisure - hiking, swimming, fishing from the bank - while the fjord and ocean is for business and sport.

We crest a rise and see a cruise liner coming into the fjord. I thought we were in the wilderness and here's a boat carrying a thousand people steaming past us. I check the map. We are alongside Hardangerfjord - the second-largest open fjord in the world. It stretches a mind-numbing one hundred and seventy-nine kilometres from the Atlantic Ocean into the frontier of Norway to the small town of Odda. The figures are bewildering - a single branch of the fjord stretches fifty kilometres, it has a maximum depth of eight hundred and sixty metres and is ten kilometres across at its widest point. Big enough to comfortably handle the cruise liner.

We race down hill to a car ferry at Buavågen. We cycle aboard as if it was just waiting for us. The captain blows the horn, the gates are shut and we trundle across the fjord to Langevåg where the cafe is closed. We buy cake from the supermarket. As we're eating it outside on a bench seat, a woman opens the cafe and walks towards us.

'Would you like a coffee,' she asks.

'Yes, please,' we chorus.

'We're not open yet, but I can give you take away,' she smiles.

Lovely.

We are now in the municipality of Bømlo consisting of a mere nine hundred islands, many uninhabited. We pass a cemetery where a man in a brown jumper and khaki trousers is clearing weeds from around a gravestone. When he stands, his back doesn't quite straighten, as if he's still leaning towards the grave. Further on, an old man in black track pants and a white shirt sits on a bench seat, his head tilted back, eyes closed, taking in the weak sunshine. In the garden, his wife bends over to wash the dog. Even though she's quite old, she hardly bends her knees, as supple as a teenager.

We crest another rise and look down on a series of islands connected by three huge suspension bridges leapfrogging across the fjord. This is the famous Triangle Link, connecting Bømlo with Stord at a cost of 1.8 billion kroner. All to link an island with not many people to another island with slightly more people. Thank you Sovereign Wealth Fund. We have our own bike lane on each of the bridges and although buffeted by the wind, it's tremendously exciting looking down at the ink blue water and across the fjord to the snowy mountains. I feel like hooting while cycling off the final bridge.

And then we reach Leirvik. Oh dear.

Our accommodation is booked through AirBnB and is in the basement of a young man's house. It's spartan and none of the photos on the website match the apartment. We sigh and unpack before heading into town for supplies.

Maybe it's a public holiday.

Maybe everyone is at a meeting in the town hall.

Maybe a sports carnival is being held in a nearby town.

Or maybe everyone has left town because it's a dump.

We sit on the pier and look across the fjord to the mountains.

'It's a lovely view,' I say.

'And yet, not even that can save this place,' Cathie says.

We return to the basement and drink a lot of beer.

We wake to a cold windy day and eagerly leave Leirvik. After turning off the highway onto a narrow forest road, we stop to check the map.

'Today is our final day,' Cathie smiles, 'After four thousand kilometres.'

I lean across and kiss her. It's hard to believe we've travelled so far. I'm immensely proud of my beautiful wife who has braved mountains, winds and cold weather for the past two months.

'We'll celebrate with dinner in Bergen,' I say.

'Three days without a bicycle,' Cathie smiles.

'I won't know what to do,' I answer.

It's true. Bruce and Aiwa have been reliable and trusty companions. There is no better way of seeing a country than from the saddle of a bicycle.

We follow a back road north along the west coast of Stord Island before cruising down into the windswept lonely town of Fitjar where a historic battle took place in 961 between the three sons of Eric the Bloodaxe and their uncle King Haakon the Good. I look across the desolate fields and wonder what on earth they were fighting over. We retreat to the port of Sandvikvåg where a beautiful blonde woman sits huddled in a ticket booth. She sells us two tickets for the ferry to Halhjem. She asks where we've cycled from.

'Marseille,' I answer.

'Pardon?' she says.

'In France, on the Meditteranean,' I say.

'On the bicycle' she says, looking rather sceptically at Bruce and Aiwa.

'All the way,' I say.

'You are very strong,' she says.

Let it be known that a beautiful blonde Norwegian called me strong and looked admiringly at my thighs.

'Your wife, she is a hero,' she adds.

Damn!

The ferry is large enough for semi-trailers and cars and two content cyclists. The kiosk serves waffles and coffee. We sit in the warmth and watch the parade of islands float past. The journey is over too quickly for my liking. In Halhjem, we set off again, uphill. Cathie leads. She is a hero.

Although Bergen is still thirty kilometres away, I can't help feeling it's just around the corner. Our final day is nearly over. The villages surrounding Bergen offer good cycle paths, but lots of hills. It starts to rain heavily. Bergen is renowned for hills and rain, so we shrug into wet weather clothes and plough on. After another steep climb, the rain relents, the sun comes out and scores of cyclists arrive to greet us. Well, not exactly. It's a family cycle-day, with everyone except us emblazoned in yellow vests and numbers. I sure wish #2687 would move slightly to the right. He eventually does and we squeeze through and joyfully, merrily, gleefully, cheerfully yet regretfully cruise all the way down to the historic Bergen wharf where crowds of tourists get in the way of our 'end-of-trip' photo. Eventually, a kind Norwegian gentleman takes our photo. We stand behind Bruce and Aiwa - the true heroes of this adventure - and hold hands.

Whereas Marseille looks south to sandy beaches, the Mediterranean and the warm winds of the African continent, Bergen stares north to the Arctic Circle, the Northern Lights and the slowly-melting permafrost of the harsh Norwegian tundra. Bergen is ringed by nine mountains and surely ranks as one of the great port cities of the world alongside Sydney, Vancouver and San Francisco. As we stand at the wharf, I count off the vessels within sight - cruise liners, long-distance ferries, sleek power boats, old-fashioned wooden sailboats, a fleet of sturdy red and white tugboats, fishing vessels of all sizes from simple outboards to those designed to spend a month at sea, steel-hulled tankers and moored at Bryggen, a splendid three-mast barque sailing ship, the Statsraad Lehmkuhl.

A thousand years ago, Bergen existed because of the lucrative dried cod trade shipped from these wharves. Today, while fishing and oil remain important businesses, tourists are the main catch. Cruise liners dump thousands of wealthy travellers every week. Like Cathie and I, their first stop is the historic Hanseatic commercial buildings lining the north side of the main wharf. Listed as a UNESCO World Heritage Site in 1979, the simple wooden buildings are beautiful when viewed from across the narrow channel, their plain red, white or puce colour scheme vibrant when set against the dark northern waters. Up close, the rabbit warren of out-of-kilter beams and wooden struts house tourist-tat shops and expensive cafes and bars. But what can I expect? To survive, they must be used and the only use we accept is to sell things. We wander around for a short time, but our heart isn't in it today. Being so close to this many people wearing Jack Wolfskin outdoor gear and Gucci scarves rankles. Sorry, I'm a bike snob.

We decide to leave the tourist wandering until tomorrow. Tonight, we eat, drink and celebrate.

Before we arrived in Norway, we were told on two separate occasions that food was so expensive, cucumbers were sold by the quarter because a whole piece cost too much. We arrived prepared to eat two-minute noodles and sandwiches every day. Ha! Food is expensive, but unlike Denmark where it was difficult to find a good restaurant, Norway has at least offered hearty meals at acceptable prices when we have wanted to eat out. And if you haven't guessed by now, I'm not particularly interested in cycling thousands of kilometres while living off packaged and tinned foods. I understand the difficulties of budgeting for long journeys, but one of the main reasons we've ridden all these kilometres is to sample the food of each country. We have chosen to eat in simple restaurants that the locals frequent. It's more expensive than baked beans and tinned spaghetti, but I figure we've earned it. With social media and the plethora of review sites, it's much easier to find the cheapest and best places to eat. Bergen is no exception.

For dinner we head to Pingvinen, a cafe/pub serving hearty home-cooked fare. Most dishes cost the same as a typical restaurant in Australia. We sit in the booth and order Fish Pie and a Reindeer Stew. Beer for me, the rare treat of wine for Cathie. We look around the restaurant. We are the oldest people here. Everyone is tall and handsome and judging by the language spoken, there's not a tourist in sight. The food is delicious. Whoever knew reindeer tasted so good? I order a second beer.

'I was looking at the map,' I begin.

Cathie sighs. She recognises my tone of voice.

'Bergen is at the end of the longest open fjord in the world,' I say. 'Remember that old chap at reception in Haugesund telling us we could catch a ferry all the way to the Flam Railway at the end of the fjord?'

Cathie nods. She knows where I'm leading. And she knows it involves bicycles.

'I was looking at the map,' I say.

'You've already said that,' she interrupts.

I take a deep breath.

'We could ride from here to Gudvangen, a World Heritage Site near the end of the Sognefjord. Three days, no longer. And catch a ferry to the Flam Railway, take the train up and down the mountain.' I'm speaking quicker than normal, afraid she'll shake her head and say no.

'I checked. We can catch a ferry from the Flam all the way back to Bergen. Five hours, along the biggest open fjord in the world,' I repeat.

Cathie smiles.

'Buy me another wine and I'll think about it,' she says.

I love my wife.

So there you have it. After cycling thousands of kilometres to reach Norway, we have enjoyed this country so much we want to keep going. We return to the hotel room and consult Google Maps, attempting to make sense of my forward route.

'Three days, I reckon,' I say.

'What are these shaded areas of the road,' Cathie asks, pointing to Route FV7.

'They're ... tunnels,' I stammer.

'They're very long tunnels,' Cathie adds.

'I've checked. Usually there's a road around the tunnel,' I say.

'Usually?'

'Mostly, nearly always,' I add, rather uncertainly.

Cathie studies the map for a long time.

'I'll agree to face the uncertainties of the tunnels if we can catch a train out of Bergen before rejoining the road, to avoid the traffic,' she says.

'And the mountains,' I smile.

I search Google and find the small village of Trengereid, thirty-five kilometres east, is on the main rail link from Bergen. I buy two tickets on the morning train leaving the day after tomorrow.

We spend our rest day wandering the streets of downtown, catching the funicular up to Mount Fløyen into the rain clouds with a misty view down to a city ringed by hills and water. It's hard to believe this narrow cusp of land is Norway's second-largest city. The fjord meanders between islands and headlands to the Atlantic, cold and drear in the morning light. I can cycle down a steep incline without fear, but I cautiously grip Cathie's hand on the funicular descent. I trust Bruce more than heavy steel cables.

We seek shelter in Wayne's Coffee shop - with a name like that it has to be good. It is. We're drawn back to the wharf for lunch. Cathie has read about a restaurant serving local seafood. Don't they all? Well, actually the famed markets lining the wharf tend to offer what's expected by tourists - salmon, shrimp, mussels and ... Spanish paella. It's crowded and overpriced.

In an old warehouse building a few metres north is Starbucks. Walk past this travesty of coffee and turn left. At the rear of the building is Hav Fisk and Skalldyr run by a Scottish chef and a Norwegian fish scientist. We order fish and chips. It's cheap, crisp and tasty and comes with a sprinkle of caviar on top. The chef brings our beer - the cheapest we've found in Norway. He's a handsome bearded young man who tells us the fish we're eating today is sourced from a local sustainable fishery. It's the tastiest fish I've eaten in northern Europe. We talk football and cycling in Scotland. He tells us if we can cycle in the cold and rain of Norway, Scotland is the next stop for us. I wonder if all Scots can cook like this chap?

In the afternoon, we sleep.

Come on, we've cycled a long way.

For dinner, we return to Pingvinen for more reindeer. It's so crowded we have to sit at the bar. We don't mind. Bergen is a lovely town full of lovely people and I'll have another lovely beer, please.

This was meant to be our destination. But Norway is too beautiful not to explore further.

Chapter Nine: Norway - to the fjords

We arrive at the train station early in the morning to find lots of luggage-bound tourists looking for our train. We are the only passengers wheeling bicycles. Eventually, the screen advises us to proceed to platform four. Cue stampede of the Samsonsites.

We wait until everyone is on board before lifting Bruce and Aiwa into the carriage. One minute before our departure, a guard tells us we are on the wrong carriage. This one is reserved for a German tour group who are taking the easy way to Flam. We hop off and race along the platform to the furtherest carriage. The engineman waits while I lug both fully-loaded bikes aboard. The comfortable passengers browse glossy brochures of waterfalls and glaciers. We stand for the fifty minute journey through tunnels and alongside lakes until we arrive at Trengereid. It's no surprise we're the only people alighting at this stop. There is nothing here. Just a siding and a view of a lake. And a very steep hill we have to climb to get to the town, which is a scatter of perhaps thirty houses. It looked much bigger on Google maps. On top of the hill is a cafe and two busy roads, one heading straight through a long tunnel. We drink coffee, eat cake and decide to take the open-air option. The snow lies in drifts alongside the road, water seeps from the rock and we continue to climb. Despite only having a few days rest, I'm feeling rejuvenated to be back on the road.

We cruise downhill into Årland on the shores of what must surely be a lake, not a fjord. But there are fishing boats? I check my smartphone map and trace the body of water all the way from this small inland town out to the Atlantic Ocean. Welcome to the Samnangerfjord. Despite this being a major road, it's relatively free of traffic. We pass lakes and fjords and follow a mountain stream up a long hill until a tunnel looms dark and menacing in front of us. Beside the tunnel, over a narrow tree-lined gorge is the old road. We lift our bikes past the barrier and cycle for a few metres. Blocking our path is a fallen tree. I look down the road. It's strewn with rocks, branches and potholes. We walk Bruce and Aiwa through the debris and listen to the sound of a rushing stream one hundred metres below. It's better than being haunted by trucks in a tunnel.

Back on the main road, the stream becomes a rushing river with boulders the size of cars shorn from the cliffs. They are covered in moss. In the middle of nowhere, we come upon a thirty-metre high waterfall. There isn't a sign to tell us its name. It deserves one.

A few kilometres further along is an even larger waterfall, this one dramatic enough to earn two names - officially it's called Fossen Bratte, but is more commonly known as Bridal Veil Falls. It's been called this for a century, but the name proved tragically ironic when in 1951, a car carrying a newly-wed couple swerved off the road into the river killing both occupants. A memorial plaque is at the bottom of the falls.

More uphill, more tunnels and after one short dark encounter we're spat out into a world of snowdrifts and mountain lakes. Magical. The sun shines brightly and we stop to eat lunch sitting on a log among the drifts. It's a glorious road rambling past ski villages, with earthen roof houses scattered along the slopes. Some cabins have yellow and white flowers growing in the soil on their roofs. Cathie and I keep looking at each other and smiling. We made the correct decision to keep cycling. We follow the road through the snow-covered boulders for another ten kilometres before a rollicking eight kilometre downhill, through - yikes - three tunnels including one impossibly long beast with a corner in the middle. Luckily, this tunnel has lights casting a spooky pale glow over us and a looming shadow of a truck fast approaching my rear wheel - double yikes. The driver kindly waits until we reach fresh air before powering past me.

As a reward for all this, we arrive at the sixth most visited tourist attraction in Norway. Steinsdalsfossen is a forty-six metre high waterfall, the noisiest part of the Fosselva river that tumbles down from Myklavatnet lake. The secret of its allure is visitors can walk up a narrow path wedged against the cliff and stand literally behind the falls, with the cascade thundering just a metre away. How can we resist. We follow the path and soon enough a fifty-six year old child is having his photo taken inside the falls. Everyone on the path is smiling. Nature in all its power and glory does that to we insignificant humans. The sound is deafening. The enjoyment is total.

We cruise into Norheimsund, a small town on the the shores of the Handangerfjord, the second largest open fjord in the world which we cycled past a week ago. There's no sign of the large cruise liner we saw near its mouth. Norheimsund has only one rather expensive but beautiful hotel, a three-storey wooden masterpiece called the Hotel Sandven, built at the end of the 19th century. It has one hundred and two rooms with half in a new tastefully similar construction next door. I prefer the stately old place.

The receptionist tells us our room is not ready yet and we're welcome to help ourselves to coffee while we're waiting. We fill our cups and as there's a tray of cakes next to the coffee, pilfer two slices each. She didn't say the cake *wasn't* free, did she! We take our stash past the high-wing velour chairs, under the crystal chandeliers and out the double doors to sit in a plush lounge beside the fjord. I feel like royalty in lycra.

I'm expecting we'll be given a room in the new section, but for some mysterious reason, the receptionist leads us upstairs to a front room - *front rooms* - with an ornate balcony looking down the fjord to the snowy mountains. Wow! Despite getting a cheap deal, we've been given the best suite in the hotel. It even has a name.

The Geirr Tveitt Suite.

I do some research on Mr Tveitt. Oh dear. He was a renowned composer, born near Norheimsund in 1908. Mr Tveitt was gifted in piano, but tended to align himself with rather extreme doctrines in his long and controversial life. He was an avowed Nationalist and was thought to be sympathetic to Nazis, although there is little evidence for this. After the Second World War, he was largely ignored by the establishment due to his connection - either real or imagined - with the fascists. He was ostracised and sought refuge on the family farm near here. One night in 1970, the house caught fire and many of his manuscripts were destroyed. He became an alcoholic and died in town, embittered and lonely at the age of seventy-two.

But he does have a splendid suite named in his honour. And look, just below his portrait is a rack of lycra drying in the afternoon sunshine.

The forecast for tomorrow is rain. But I'm looking at a perfectly blue cloudless sky. Sunset is at 11pm. Sunrise at 4am. That's a very long day. Surely it won't rain for every minute of every hour? While the sun shines, we stroll along the shore of the fjord, admiring the postcard perfect row of snowy mountains.

'The road tomorrow follows the fjord and those mountains for forty kilometres,' I say.

'Every day gets better,' Cathie says.

We walk to the maritime museum. It's closed, but we step over the rope fence and sit on a deck on the wharf. The exhibits include an old wooden hull trawler, a sailboat, a wooden skiff and a 1939 'agent boat' designed to allow merchants to ply their trade along the fjords, calling on villages with merchandise from Bergen. Dependable and easy to maneuver, these simple craft were a lifeline to the folk living out here. There is also a line of wooden rowboats for sale - beautifully crafted and a steal at six thousand kroner.

It's eight o'clock in the evening. Three children swim in the cool shallows of the fjord while their parents have a picnic on the sand. It's fifteen degrees and I'm wearing a jacket, yet these hardy locals are swimming. I guess it's a case of taking your summer when it arrives. Winter must be very bleak.

We wake to find our stunning view of snow-capped mountains and sparkling fjord has been obscured by heavy cloud and teeming rain. We decide to spend as long as possible at breakfast. This proves surprisingly easy. Breakfast is served in a lovely dining room of chandeliers, wide windows and elegant place settings. A horde of German tourists have woken. They are very well-dressed - ladies in floral frocks and expensive mohair cardigans, men in tailored trousers and freshly-ironed shirts.

I once wore an ironed shirt. It was at my brother's wedding in 2002.

My lime green cycling jersey stands out a treat as I wait my turn at the buffet for eggs, bacon and baked beans. Cathie, wearing a fetching red jersey, is particularly taken with the small pancakes liberally covered in raspberry jam and cream. I sample a bite and rush to snaffle a few before the Germans twig. I'm only doing it so they won't spill jam on their perfect clothing. I finish off my indulgence with a plate of fruit. Who knew they grew bananas in Norway?

For lunch, we slip two ham and cheese sandwiches each and two chocolate croissants into the bag. It is comfort food against all this rain. The waitress tells me that yesterday was their first sunny day in a month. She'd hoped it was the start of summer. She sighs, then looks at my attire and says, 'But it is worse for you.' I try to look rugged and unafraid. Instead, I just look scared.

We load Bruce and Aiwa and roll into the decreasing showers.

'Only two days to go, Bruce,' I say.

He answers by surging up the first of many hills alongside the fjord. I look over the edge. The water is ink blue and menacing. The deepest part of the fjord is just off Norheimsund, a breathless eight hundred and sixty metres straight down. We cycle beside steep cliffs and like yesterday pass rocks bigger than cars. Maybe they clattered off the mountain thousands of years ago, scaring the heck out of dinosaurs and hairy mammoths. Now sheep graze contently among the boulders. The safety rail is pathetically tiny, perhaps thirty centimetres high. Across the fjord is a startlingly vista of endless snowy mountains. If only we could see them. The cloud hugs the fjord's surface and only occasionally offers us a glimpse of snowy majesty. Despite this it's a marvellous road, a balcony strung magically between cliff and fjord.

On this side of the fjord are numerous circular enclosures - salmon and trout farms - each holding a payload of wild fish. Are they still wild if their terrain is no bigger than a suburban swimming pool? Is the accumulation of salmon shit and trout poo expelled from these farms sustainable fishing? Or industrial pollution?

We escape the showers under a little wooden picnic shelter looking across the fjord. On the wall of the shelter are photos of the majestic Folgefonna glacier covering an impressive two hundred square kilometres. It's there, somewhere behind the clouds. After croissants, we pass five substantial waterfalls within a kilometre of each other. I'm staggered by the intensity and amount of water flowing endlessly into the fjord. I keep expecting to see the level rising. Silly I know.

We pass the village of Ålvik, where a ferrochemical plant powered by hydroelectricty is surrounded by waterfalls and a forest. An industrial plant has existed here for one hundred years and now hangs on by recycling waste from aluminium production. It's owned by the Chinese. Maybe the Sovereign Fund should buy the town and turn it into a museum?

The expected climbing hasn't really occured. And there's only been one tunnel. Despite the rain, if we had time I'd ride this road again and again. Fjord, cliffs, snow, mountains, forest, waterfalls ... ferrochemical plant.

We follow a branch of the fjord north to our destination of Granvin with a population of nine hundred people, all huddled around heaters in cosy red or white timber houses. It has a lovely 18th century plain wooden church, a co-op supermarket and one guesthouse. I knock tentatively on the front door. A woman opens the door and I try to explain that we have a booking. She speaks fractured English with a French accent. She tells me to come back when they are open and I can make a booking. I tell her I already have a booking. She says we are too early. I tell her I've cycled here from France. She looks at me like I'm a madman. I ask where she is from. When she answers Toulouse, I tell her we cycled through her beautiful city three years ago. I am doing everything I can imagine to get her to let me in out of the rain. She smiles and tells Cathie and me to come inside. Whew!

She leads us upstairs to our room overlooking the supermarket. A lovely room with an unfortunate view. It's warm and dry. She asks if we'd like to have dinner in the restaurant tonight.

'Is it French cooking?' I say.

She smiles.

'Italian. My husband is Italian,' she answers.

We'll eat Italian in Norway hosted by a French woman. Excellent.

Pasta for dinner, bacon and eggs for breakfast. For our last day on the road, it's rainy and overcast as it has been for much of the past few weeks. But we don't care because Norway is the most beautiful place on earth to ride a bicycle.

There, I've said it.

We retrieve Bruce and Aiwa from their dry spot on the rear verandah and load our panniers for the last time. I don't know whether to laugh or cry. I'm surprised the five safety pins holding my ripped panniers together have held for so long. Skagen was two weeks and a thousand kilometres ago.

On our right are sheer cliffs and clouds, to our left is Granvinsvatnet Lake. The road hugs the lake. There isn't a car in sight. Every twenty metres, water tumbles from the cliffs in a snowmelt stream. At the head of the lake is a cluster of dwellings, the houses are painted white, the barns are red with shingle roofs. Everyone in town has a view down the length of the lake.

Soon after we have to turn right down a lonely road to avoid a lengthy tunnel. Yet again, the detour doesn't disappoint. It's a beautiful back road that winds through green farmland surrounded by granite mountains. Then we hit the switchbacks and climb steeply. Surprise, surprise, there's a stunning waterfall off to our left. After another switchback we come to the viewing area. Skjervsfossen is a waterfall divided in two, the upper section is a pulsating vertical drop of seventy metres, further down the hill is a cascading eighty metre falls. I peer into the spray of the vertical drop and see three workmen in bright orange suits excavating near the pool. Tough, wet job.

We continue up the switchbacks, the cliff walls get steeper and the road leads above the falls with a stupendous view, albeit wreathed in cloud, down the valley. We've only cycled ten kilometres today and already I'm overwhelmed. Norway is serving us a treat for our final ride. Even more so when we rejoin the main road on top of the mountain. It's a fifteen kilometre downhill sweep to the town of Vossevangen.

Ironically, the town is perhaps most famous for the trendy bottled water that is in fact sourced four hundred kilometres from here. Is this another case of Skagen-itis? In a perfect example of marketing trumping sense, the cylindrical bottle of Voss water has become hugely popular worldwide, despite the fact that tests have shown the water is little different from the tap water available near its source. But, it is in a pretty bottle.

But it's not in Voss, okay. What is in town is a lovely cafe serving excellent cake and coffee in a warm homely atmosphere. At Voss we rejoin the main road leading to Gudvangen and onward to Oslo. The national route. However the traffic isn't as bad as we expected and we rumble along, alternating between the bitumen shoulder and a bike path when it's available. Oh look there's another lake. And another. The road cuts through green pastures in a wide valley. Enough room for a posse of winnebagos, heavy trucks and two smiling cyclists. That's the third lake in forty minutes. At the head of Lønavatnet Lake, we stop for lunch on a bench seat.

I remove my waterproof shoe covers. They're soaked, inside and out.

'This is the fourth pair of these I've bought and none have worked,' I say.

Cathie smiles, 'A wise man would have stopped after three pairs.'

'I can tolerate anything but cold wet feet,' I say. I take a hand towel out of my panniers and attempt to sponge dry my socks.

When we hop back on the bikes, Cathie says, 'You've left your shoe covers behind.'

'I know,' I answer, pedalling away.

The road hugs a wild snow melt river as the valley becomes narrower. Marlene advises us to turn left and I look up to see another steep incline. The main road we've been following looks wide and flat.

'There's probably a tunnel ahead,' says Cathie.

'We could risk it?' I suggest.

Cathie shakes her head. 'Let's climb.'

My beautiful wife has mastered the mountains. I obediently follow her up the pass.

In the last hour of cycling on our last day, it's the best decision we've made on this entire trip. On top of the climb is a spectacular view down a narrow valley, steep mountains either side frosted with cascading waterfalls. In the foreground, like a sentry to this narrow pass is a cone shaped mountain. In the distance is a ring of snow-capped giants.

'I feel like I'm in The Hobbit,' Cathie says.

I look at my smartphone map and back to the view. I can't work out where the road leads. It looks like we're surrounded by impenetrable mountains. And then it dawns on me. Somehow, we're going down the mountain to that narrow valley.

'I think we go through that gap,' I say.

Cathie looks at me as if I've lost my senses.

'Really? It looks ...'

'Narrow?'

'Majestic, awe-inspiring, bloody amazing,' she smiles.

We jump back on Bruce and Aiwa and cycle another kilometre until we hit a ridiculously steep descent. Signs in various languages warn of its treachery. So dangerous in fact, that uphill traffic is forbidden. I take a deep breath, grip the brakes tightly and roller-coaster down. Until the first switchback. Even with my hands tight on the brakes it takes me a few metres to stop. I've never experienced an incline like this, not even in the French Alps.

I look back to Cathie. She's stopped. I turn Bruce around and ride back up to her. It takes all my effort and even then I have to zig zag across the road to lessen the gradient.

'I'm going to walk it,' Cathie says.

'But ...'

'It's stupendously beautiful. But I can't look at the view because I'm gripping the brakes like a lunatic,' she says.

I instantly understand. I tell her I'll go ahead and wait where I can. I set off gingerly. My Garmin tells me the gradient hovers between 18% and 25%. That's nose-bleed stuff.

Unwittingly, we have stumbled across Stalheimskleiva, reputedly the steepest road in Northern Europe. It boasts fourteen hairpin bends and claims an average gradient of 14.7%, with many sections well above that. It also features marvellous views of two major waterfalls - to our left is Sivlefossen with a furious drop of one hundred and sixty-five metres, and to our right further back in the valley is Stalheimsfossen offering a fall of one hundred and forty-two metres. As I stop to admire Sivlefossen, two motorbike riders walk up to take photos. I wonder where their bikes are? And then I understand.

They've had to trudge from the bottom of the hill because there is no level ground anywhere to park a motorbike. It would simply tip over. What a road. Eventually I make it to the bottom and cross a bridge over a storming river. I look back up the hill. Signs on either side of the road warn that you cannot drive up this hill. But, cyclists are allowed to cycle up if they wish.

I wish.

When Cathie joins me in the rest area beside the river, I unload the panniers from Bruce.

'I might have a go at climbing it,' I say.

Cathie smiles and reaches into her panniers, offering me the remaining two chocolate bars.

'Take them, just in case,' she says.

All those kilometres ago, when we set off from the Mediterranean my first day was highlighted by a lovely climb up the Col de l'Espigoulier. It seems only fitting I finish the journey with another ascent. I cycle back over the bridge and immediately the road pitches skyward. At the third bend, two photographers smile and give me the thumbs up. My legs already feel like jelly.

When I was a child, I'd climb the steepest road in my suburb by zig-zagging from side to side. I do the same here, back to being ten-years-old. I take the next four bends in a looping contour, side to side until I gather a rhythm. Twenty minutes later I'm on top, my lungs fit to burst, my heart full of joy and wonder. The places you can go on a bicycle. I take a photo of Bruce. He deserves the accolades.

I return to Cathie, waiting patiently beside the river. I offer her the chocolate. We share. We rejoin the main road beside the Nærøydalselvi River. It's a gentle downhill and we spend the last nine kilometres of this journey cruising along looking up at the mountains and the tumbling waterfalls. Extraordinary. My muscles are spent from the climb, but I can't help but smile. Norway is sending us off in fine style. I feel a mix of emotions. Elation for finishing this memorable trip, but it's tinged with sadness. Tomorrow, we will leave this majestic country. Nowhere on earth reminds me so regularly of how insignificant and transitory we humans are on this planet. The power and beauty of nature is front and centre in Norway. We little people are dwarfed beside it.

We trundle into Gudvangen, a small settlement on the tip of the UNESCO World Heritage Nærøyfjord. It's also rated by the National Geographic as the world's number one natural heritage site. Yes, there are lots of buses and snappy-happy tourists. We park Bruce and Aiwa and walk to the water's edge. We've made it. In front of us is Nærøyfjord, a narrow branch of the Sognefjord. The surface of the water is like deep blue glass. The mountains rear up topped by snow, an amphitheatre of granite and tumbling water. For a long time, we sit side by side looking down the fjord, our thoughts on the kilometres and days we've travelled, from the sunshine of the first day leaving the Meditteranean to the joyous wandering through The Netherlands and Germany to the climax of the trip here in Norway. It's easy to plot on Google, just a few distracted clicks of the mouse. But cycling, perhaps more than any other transport immerses us in the landscape so that every person we meet, every hill, every gust of wind, each restaurant and cafe is enjoyed at a human pace. Is earned at a human pace.

Tomorrow, we'll load our bikes onto a ferry to take us through the fjord to Flam where we'll take a train ride up and down the mountain before returning to the dock and catching a ferry the length of Sognefjord back to Bergen. At eight in the evening, we'll cycle off the ferry to Pingvinen for a celebratory dinner and then, with the sun slowly fading we'll cycle to the airport. I'll pack Bruce and Aiwa into cardboard boxes and the following morning, we'll fly to Paris and home to Australia. It promises to be a long day. Or two. Or three.

But tonight, we wash our lycra in the hotel room for the last time and change into plain clothes before walking down to the restaurant cum tourist centre for a dinner of Norwegian meatballs, mushy peas and boiled potatoes, washed down with beer.

In the late evening, we sit outside in the chilly clear air, looking down the fjord.

Our conversation drifts to the usual subjects. Our favourite day - any day in Norway. Our least favourite - the mistral day ages ago in France. The best food - French. The worst - Danish. Best Beer - German. Worst beer - None! Favourite bike paths - The Netherlands, of course. Least favourite - the Champagne region. Friendliest people - everyone.

'If you had a chance to do it again, would you change anything,' I ask.

Cathie thinks for a long time.

'I'd arrange to spend more time cycling here, in Norway,' she says.

I nod. My wife always knows best.
'Should we come back in the future?' I ask.
Cathie smiles.

If you enjoyed **'Cycling North'**
you might like Steven Herrick's other travel books
Available at
http://www.amazon.com/Steven-Herrick/e/B001H9W5YM
for USA readers.
And at
http://www.amazon.co.uk/Steven-Herrick/e/B001H9W5YM
for UK readers.

18419225R00106

Printed in Poland
by Amazon Fulfillment
Poland Sp. z o.o., Wrocław